To
Debra Harris,
our most valued friend.

Fred Stephenson
1/18/2011

MW00898751

TWO 8'S, TWO 3'S, NOTHING WILD

Winning the Game of Life

BY
FRED STEPHENSON

Bloomington, IN Milton Keynes, UK

authorHOUSE

AuthorHouse™
1663 Liberty Drive, Suite 200
Bloomington, IN 47403
www.authorhouse.com
Phone: 1-800-839-8640

AuthorHouse™ UK Ltd.
500 Avebury Boulevard
Central Milton Keynes, MK9 2BE
www.authorhouse.co.uk
Phone: 08001974150

First published by AuthorHouse 11/13/2006

ISBN: 978-1-4259-6998-1 (sc)

Library of Congress Control Number: 2006908983

Printed in the United States of America
Bloomington, Indiana

This book is printed on acid-free paper.

Cover design by David Scotland Stephenson.

ABOUT THE AUTHOR

Fred Stephenson is a 63-year-old recently retired university professor, teacher, Navy veteran, husband, father of 3, grandfather of 4, Christian, and proud American. He has a Ph.D. in Business Administration, authored two previously published books, and is a respected advisor to CEO's, an accomplished leader and manager, a coach, a former head baker, a sought after mentor, and a serious backpacker and adventurer. As this book will verify, Fred is also a humorist, philosopher, and avid story teller. While serving on the faculty of The University of Georgia, he received numerous awards for excellence in teaching including UGA's highest teaching honor, which he was awarded twice. In 2002 he was selected as Elon University's Distinguished Alumnus of the Year.

Fred and his wife Sharon live in Athens, Georgia, where they recently celebrated their 40th wedding anniversary.

Dedicated to our children, grandchildren, great grandchildren, and great-great grandchildren. Some of you have not arrived yet, but all of you are in my thoughts every day. Always know that I love you.

ACKNOWLEDGEMENTS

I am most grateful to the following people who reviewed parts or all of the manuscript, supplied requested information, provided editing and content advice, and most importantly kept me constantly motivated by your encouraging, thoughtful comments: Fred Stephenson, Sr., Eleanor Lovgren, Jeff and Kendra Stephenson, Katie and John Spicer, Ray Stephenson, Kevin Ellis, Joyce Cook, our granddaughters Haley and Sydney, Bonnie Graham, Leslie Graham, Nathan Deasy, Keith Tuttle, Fred and Willa Deane Birchmore, Bob Rader, Sara Seidman, Dick Farrell, Ann Spicer, Jeff and Judy Mason, and Ken "Waypoint" Sowles.

Especially I thank Sharon, the love of my life and the woman responsible for making so many of my wonderful dreams come true. I could not have written this book without your terrific help, our shared memories of 44 years together, your understanding and technical assistance, and your inspiration. There are thousands of decisions that I have made in my life. The best one of them all was to marry you. I love you.

Another person very instrumental to the book's development and publication is our son Dave who designed the cover, wrote the foreword, and gave me outstanding guidance about the book's content and design. What fun it was to work with you doing the book, Dave. Your abilities and accomplishments never cease to amaze me.

I actually began developing ideas for this book in 2001, but serious writing didn't really begin until I was introduced by my sister to Dr. James Graham, a young man of impeccable character and wisdom far beyond his years. Jimmy's encouragement was the driving catalyst that made this book transition from dream to reality. He would ask me to send him chapters as I wrote them, and he would read them, thoughtful critique them, and most importantly urge me to send him more text, and I did this throughout the entire writing process. Jimmy, your belief in this book and in me was instrumental to *Two 8's* publication, and your positive approach to life--one that looks for the best in individuals, constantly tries to help people, and seeks answers to so many of life's challenges--continues to inspire me every day. I can't thank you enough, my friend.

Next, I wish to recognize a most respected businessman and true American patriot, Ross Cook, a passionate reader of the manuscript and strong believer in the need to get my philosophy of life into print. It was my good fortune to have met Ross many years ago through the Terry College's Trucking Profitability Strategies Conference, and Ross, not a day goes by that you don't motivate me to work hard and try to do the right things for the right reasons. Thank you, my friend.

Finally, I could not have written *Two 8's, Two 3's, Nothing Wild* without all the people who for 63 years entered my life and made it such fun and so unforgettable. The hundreds of stories, experiences, adventures, and good times that you will read about in the book are only possible because of these exceptional people whom I was so privileged to know as family, friends, mentors, students, and colleagues. Reliving our times together has brought me great joy. What a pleasure it was to take this long walk down memory lane with so many people I respect and love.

Thanks everyone. I've been blessed by each of you.

Fred Stephenson
Athens, Georgia

FOREWORD

Before I started writing this foreword, I posed the same question to myself that Dr. Stephenson used to ask us in his classroom: "If my life is a poker hand, then what cards am I holding?" Although I'm still young, clearly I know that I have been given a lot of advantages in life. Always I have learned quickly and taken to new things very easily. I was lucky enough to get a quality education with a scholarship paying my college tuition. And most of all I was born into a great, loving family. So, after some serious thought my conclusion is that I am off to a good start. I'm holding an ace and a king of diamonds and the cards are still being dealt.

Two 8's, Two 3's, Nothing Wild is a unique, very intriguing look at life. It is a fun and entertaining read, and amidst Dr. Stephenson's anecdotal storytelling, he presents some great advice. But the book offers far more than entertainment and counseling. I think the best feeling I got from reading *Two 8's* is that it made me realize even more than ever how fortunate I am to be an American. By no means am I an expert on history; however, I know of no place that has ever offered so much freedom, so many resources, so much safety, and so much opportunity to such a wide variety of people. Over time, I have been lucky enough to make numerous friends who are not originally from here. Many of them were forced to flee their homes almost overnight for the sake of safety, and all of them came to the United States because of freedom and opportunity. They, too, have helped me realize that I truly live in a remarkable place in a remarkable time.

Los Angeles is my home, and possibly more so than any other place in America, this city is full of people who truly chase their dreams. After reading this book I stopped to think. "If all of the stories and experiences that occur in *Two 8's* are from the life of just one American, then every one of the 3.7 million people who call LA home may each have an equally interesting story to tell." That to me is the book's main point. Every one of us has a story, and it is not just in LA but all over the country and even the world, and this is why *Two 8's* is so memorable to me. It is a story of a good American. Even more than that, it is a good story of a good guy. It is a reminder that there are a lot of really great people in the world with a lot of things to offer society. Every one of us leads a whole life full of laughs, tears, bad decisions, and lucky breaks. *Two 8's* is a reminder that all those people out there who are in the other lanes on the highways, who are at the other tables in restaurants, and who are just going about their business and being themselves. . . those are the people who make America an exceptional place.

So how is my poker hand turning out? Well, an ace and a king of the same suit are a very good start, and along with some really sound advice from my father, Dr. Stephenson, and his great example of how to play the game of life, I think I have as good a chance as anyone else out there. Will my ace and king turn into a royal flush? Who knows? Maybe it'll just end up as an ace high. Only time will tell. Either way, I'm going to relax and enjoy playing the game.

In conclusion, I think that *Two 8's, Two 3's, Nothing Wild* is a wonderful story. It is an inspiring tale of one man leading one life trying to do the right thing. It is a reminder that sometimes even the people whom you know best probably have done some things that will surprise you and they probably have some advice you could benefit from. This is a book that will make you smile, make you laugh, and make you remember to be thankful for the things that you have. I hope you enjoy it as much as I have.

David Scotland Stephenson

CONTENTS

INTRODUCTION

Two 8's, Two 3's, Nothing Wild is a book that I wrote for my children, grandchildren, great grandchildren, and others to help them win the game of life. It is the true story of a middle-class American, teacher, veteran, husband, father, and grandfather and how he played his far-from-perfect hand to the best of his ability to achieve much happiness and success. It's about the most important lessons that his many lives and experiences taught him. It's my story, and I'd like to share it with you.

Perhaps, though, I should begin with an explanation of the book's title. For 29 years, I was a university teacher of transportation, logistics, and marketing. My first responsibility was to make sure I taught my students the subject matter advertised in the course catalog preparing them for subsequent courses and the rigors of the business world. However, it quickly became clear to me that I shouldn't stop there. What so many of them craved was guidance to help them prepare for life. Consequently, I began searching for ways to help individual students discover their passions, recognize their potential, raise their expectations, and find homes for their unique gifts and skills. In simple words, I just wanted them to have an easier time navigating life's challenges and be happy and successful. Some of them, though, had a lot of doubts about themselves and the future. It's accurate to say they saw their glasses half empty. And I didn't understand that because they had so much going for them, and in America, so many opportunities. What follows is the approach I used to improve their attitudes. It also clarifies the title and central theme of the book.

When the time was right, I would ask students to raise their hands if they believed life was unfair. That always got their attention as well

1

as considerable support, which didn't surprise me, for I agreed with them. Next, I asked them to think of the world as one huge poker game in which every person on the planet is a player. And I said, "At birth, all of us were each dealt a hand. We didn't choose our parents or our genes or our family's wealth and status. So raise your hand if you think you got a royal flush." Only once during the 10+ years when I asked this question of thousands of students did anyone answer affirmatively. "Then," I would follow, "how about a flush? Did you get that?" Usually, a few hands went up. "Did anyone get three aces?" Typically this got more hands in the air. However, when I finally asked, "How many of you got a bad hand?" many hands were raised.

After a pause to let people look around the room, my next statement was, "I've thought about this a lot during my life, and I have concluded that I got two 8's." Always this produced some puzzled looks, smiles and often a remark like, "That's not very good, Dr. Stephenson." Once the class settled down, I would state, "AND two 3's." Again I got more smiles than congratulations. But I quickly added, "And nothing's wild. Now if I could guarantee you this hand in life, would you take it? Would it win far more than it would lose?"

Then I would state, "My hand in life isn't perfect. Nobody's is from what I have observed over the years. I wasn't born into wealth and privilege. My IQ is not as high as I would have liked. I don't have Brad Pitt's good looks. My athletic ability is nothing exceptional. All my life I have been limited by a pathetically poor memory that held me back and far too often left me totally embarrassed. I'm also short and left handed. And a few years ago I discovered what it's like when a doctor says, 'You have cancer.' My hand definitely is not as good as some other people's hands are. But it was the hand I was dealt, and I just made up my mind to play it to the best of my ability. And you know what? It has turned out to be a very good hand. For one thing, against those liabilities I had many blessings, assets like loving parents, being born in America, and a sense of humor that I wouldn't trade for anything. And my guess is, since you are sitting in this class and thousands of others would have given most anything to have been admitted to The University of Georgia in your place, you need to think about this when you get the urge to complain. Just try to make the most of this wonderful opportunity in life that you have. And if that is inadequate proof, after class go to town, walk the streets, and ask yourself how many of the people you see would gladly change places with you right now, no questions asked." And I do think this little exercise had a positive impact on student attitudes in my classes.

The best teacher I ever had was experience, and the number one lesson it taught me is that life is primarily what you make it. My over-riding philosophy, which permeates every chapter and the stories in this book, is that a good life begins with two things: a positive attitude and becoming the CEO of your life--that is, taking responsibility for your life, both of which are within everyone's grasp regardless of the hand you were dealt or currently hold. Thinking of a sports analogy, some teams enter crucial games convinced they are going to win. Others enter games doubting they can win or believing something will go wrong and they will lose. Both prophecies so often tend to come true. Happiness and success begin in our hearts and minds. And by reading this book, you will learn how I lived by these principles and played my hand, not alone but with significant help from many people, to produce a life that has brought me considerable joy and satisfaction.

I need to clarify something up front. *Two 8's, Two 3's, Nothing Wild* is not a self-serving testimonial. It's an honest book that covers my shortcomings, failures, and mistakes as well as my successes. I don't con-sider myself special. My roots and lifestyle are middle-class American. Like millions of other people in the United States, I'm more comfort-able in jeans than a suit and like to be around sincere, down-to-earth people. I like an occasional cold beer, watching football, and taking my shoes off and relaxing. And definitely I'm not the flashy type. What I am is one of those loyal, dependable men who remain faithful to their wives, try to do the right thing and live honorable lives that will make their families proud, take care of their families and responsibilities, pay their taxes honestly, and mean it when we pledge allegiance to the United States of America. Always I have tried to be the same person to everyone and a man you could count on to do what he said he would do. And in today's troubled times I think that is a message not heard often enough and worth repeating and explaining, particularly to our young people. Several of my college students said that I reminded them of their dad, which I took as a high compliment.

On the other hand, this ordinary person has had an extremely interesting and far from ordinary life--actually, many lives. I have sung solos with opera stars, backpacked more than 1,200 miles of the Appalachian Trail, was president of my college student body, spent four years on active duty as a naval officer, lived in the Philippines for two years, traveled quite a bit, published two previous books, and testified before both the U.S. Senate and U.S. House of Representatives. I've been happily married for 40 years and am a father of 3 and grandfather of 4. At different times in my life I scrubbed toilets as a janitor, worked as a bakery clean-up boy, worked heavy construction as a carpenter's helper, was a professional head baker, served as president or chairman of several organizations, was quoted in the *Wall Street Journal* and *Business Week*, founded and ran national professional conferences, taught high school, counseled CEO's, was a tenured university professor, taught more than 10,000 college students, and was a consultant. I also have made countless speeches across America including one in Miami that immediately followed a speech by Sen. Ted Kennedy and earned me a bigger ovation than he received. Each of these and countless other meaningful experiences that will be revealed in the chapters of this book taught me valuable lessons about finding more happiness and success in life and of equal importance, how to deal with the disappointments.

Two 8's

I decided that the best way to share this story was to divide my experiences and tales into ten chapters, each focusing on one of my ten distinctive lives that explains the most valuable lessons that particular life taught me. A quick look at the table of contents makes the topical coverage in several chapters obvious, for example, "Son and Grandson" and "Teacher." Other titles are less evident, like "Tracker," the adventurous tales of my life as a backpacker on the Appalachian Trail, "Pork Chop," an insider's look at military life during my four years of active duty in the U.S. Navy, and "Rotten Baker," the story of my four summers as a baker at Geneva Point Camp in New Hampshire. Some chapters are more humorous than others, like "Husband, Father, and Grandfather," my real-life version of the *Everybody Loves Raymond* sitcom. Others, like "Professor," an eye-opening assessment of modern-day campus realities, "Leader," a common-sense crash course on good leadership principles, and "American," a soul-searching look at what it means to be an American citizen, have a more serious, reflective tone. My goal is to give readers as much topical and emotional variety as possible.   One thing I promise you is that everything in *Two 8's* actually happened. It's the truth. Remember this when you read the story about the night a bear charged me.

Finally, my purposes are not to preach to you, ask you to share my passions and hobbies, expect you to match my values or priorities, demand that you agree with my points of view, or require you to follow my advice. I just want you to enjoy the stories, think about things, and draw your own conclusions, just like I wanted my students to do. I hope *Two 8's, Two 3's, Nothing Wild* will surprise and entertain you, make you laugh out loud, occasionally bring tears to your eyes, clarify many things you might have wondered about, strengthen your faith in yourself and in each other, put more bounce in your step, help fill your glass to overflowing, and encourage you to recognize and more fully appreciate the goodness in people and America. Enjoy.

SON AND GRANDSON

Fenway Park, late 1950s

"Dad. That woman in front of us split her pants! Should we tell her?"

"I think so."

We were watching our favorite team, the Boston Red Sox, and obviously the excited lady jumping up and down in the row directly ahead of us had no clue that she was putting on her own exhibition. Pop decided he needed to inform her before she embarrassed herself further.

"Excuse me madam. You might not want to jump up and down like that because you split your pants."

"No, I didn't!" she fired back.

Isn't it amazing how people who don't know what they are talking about are so sure they do?

Now on dangerous ground, Pop quietly said, "Yes, madam, you did."

"Then what color are my underpants?" she growled.

"Pink."

She stayed parked in her seat for the rest of the ballgame.

Fifty years later, we still laugh at this, just one of the countless humorous, instructive incidents that so filled our times together, those day-to-day unexpected things that make living so unforgettable. Clearly though, I am getting ahead of myself. Perhaps I should start at the beginning.

You Get What You Pay For?

My parents and I first met on April 9, 1943, at Lying-In Hospital in Providence, Rhode Island. Now I wish I could tell you I was a beautiful baby, but other than tipping the scales at nearly 10 pounds, there wasn't anything else impressive about me. Regardless, there was much to be grateful for that day. My parents had a son, and I had a life, and it doesn't get much better than that. They named me Frederick James Stephenson, Jr. honoring my dad, Fred, Sr., as well as his grandfather, Fred Stephenson. Ma said I was worth every pain I caused her, which apparently were many.

It is my observation that there is something very special about giving birth that seals a life-long bond between mothers and their children that fathers, no matter how hard we try, seldom ever duplicate. From the start, it was obvious my mother loved me unconditionally. She told me Pop was so proud that day, a feeling I now fully understand having fathered three children of my own. There are no greater miracles than our children.

Before the exponential surge in doctor, hospital, and insurance costs, there was no rush to send mothers and babies home, so Ma and I luxuriated in our room for 9 days, resting, recovering, and getting better acquainted. The total hospital bill for the two of us was $74. I'm not kidding. It was $15 for the operating room, $5 for the x-rays, and $6 per day for the hospital room. Our share of this was $20. Finish the book and you can decide whether my parents got a bargain or exactly what they paid for. In any case, I got a great deal by becoming the son of Fred and Ruth Stephenson, wonderful parents who spent their lives trying to help and teach me.

Upon leaving the Lying-In, my parents took me home to Cranston, Rhode Island, to my 2-year old sister Eleanor. Soon thereafter, we moved to our new home in Greenville, Rhode Island, 8 miles northwest of Providence. We were the portrait of the American dream: two people in love, two healthy kids, a girl and a boy, our own single-family home, and a nice car in the driveway. Then war changed everything.

A World Turned Inside Out

With the nation desperate to win World War II against the Germans and Japanese, in December 1943, our 37-year-old father was drafted into the Navy, and this, of course, forced dramatic changes in our lives. By week's end, Ma, Eleanor, and I were on a train to Burlington, North Carolina, where we would live with Granny and Papa Horne during our father's military service. Pop had departed for basic training in Sampson, New York, and an uncertain fate. Within a few months, he was on a ship headed to the Pacific.

I can only imagine how tough or scary all of this must have been for my parents, but like so many other Americans, Ma and Pop simply accepted their responsibilities and the big challenges ahead. Hundreds of thousands of sons and daughters made the ultimate sacrifice for our country, a debt that will never be fully repaid. And since there were no promises when or if Pop would return home, my family prayed for the best outcome. When he left us, I was 8 months old. It was two years before we saw him again, but thank God he came home safely.

My Southern Home

Our temporary Southern home was a large two-story wooden house with a traditional big front porch and smaller side porch that my grandparents Sidney and Minnie Horne bought for $1,200. There they raised their 4 children, Harvey, Lillie, our mother Ruth, and Mary. Burlington is located between Greensboro and Durham in the central part of the state known as the Piedmont.

While our father did his part to win World War II, Papa did his part as a good surrogate dad for Eleanor and me. Regrettably, upon Pop's return home with the victorious troops, I am ashamed to say that I made him cry. He asked me to come to him, and I told him he was not my father. I thought Papa was. Always I have felt badly about my rejection of my dad at this crucial time in his life, for he deserved so much better. Among the many sacrifices made by military families, this is one that seldom ever gets media attention, but it is real and painful. Pop determinedly began trying to win me over.

It may sound ridiculous, but I believe I really knew Papa even though he died when I was two. My wife's theory is that I just think

I knew him and am merely recalling the memories others shared with me about my grandfather. What I do know is that daily he put me in the baby carriage and pushed me to town to visit the store, Foster Shoe Company, a retail establishment he owned and ran until his retirement. Papa was a kind, soft-spoken man who always had time for me. The last thing my grandfather did before he died was fasten a small knob on the screen door so I could open it by myself. His last act as a living person was a kind deed for me.

The world lost an exceptional human being that day. During the depression, Papa felt a compelling need to distribute shoes to the poor and just asked them to repay him when times got better. Most did; some didn't. Papa never sought nor expected public recognition for his generosity. His heart directed his deeds. At his funeral the church was so full that many people stood in the street to pay their respects. The Bible says that a good name is to be valued over wealth. Papa taught me why.

Greenville

With our dad home, we returned to Greenville, a small apple-growing village and great place to grow up. Few people accurately visualize Rhode Island. Yes, it is our smallest state occupying a land area about the size of metropolitan Atlanta, about 35 miles wide and 45 miles long; however, it is not overpopulated as many believe and is a beautiful state with a gorgeous bay on the Atlantic Ocean and many fine lakes, wonderful for summer and winter recreation. Surprisingly, the state has many hills, not big ones, but hills nonetheless, and woods and other features that give it much character. Our home for the next 20 years was 3 Danecroft Avenue.

By today's standards, our two-story barn-shaped house was small. It had 5 rooms, about 1,000 square feet of finished living space, a full bath, an unfinished basement, and a separate one car garage. Yet it never felt small to me, for I knew nothing else. Pop and Ma purchased the place brand new for $4,600 and spent the rest of dad's working years struggling to pay off the mortgage. Given our children's current mortgages, they can't grasp the degree of difficulty my parents experienced, and Pop and I are both astonished by the size of their current housing debt. Such is inflation. Our neighborhood was definitely *Leave It to Beaver* country. Most families lived off the father's income, most moms stayed home raising the kids, every house was a two-parent dwelling, every household had one car usually no more than two years old, and everyone looked out for their neighbors' kids as well as their own. Collectively, the adults just tried to keep us on the straight and narrow and healthy. Usually that worked.

What I Learned in Elementary School

From kindergarten through 6th grade, Eleanor and I attended William Winsor School, a small but inviting two-story brick building just beyond the crest of the U. S. route 44 hill that we reached the old fashioned way. We walked. When people ask me what my favorite classes in elementary school were, I tell them the truth: recess and lunch. Daily we got 2 of the former and sometimes an added quick afternoon break and a great hot lunch if we wanted it, which I did. It wasn't the sanitized dietary kind or fast food so often served to our kids today. No, this was real cooking like our mothers made at home such as roast turkey, fresh mashed potatoes with gravy, and all the trimmings, and they let us get seconds, which I seldom, but should have, turned down.

Recess gave us the opportunity to burn off all that pent up energy. And I took full advantage of our large school yard playing baseball, wall ball, where we caromed a rubber ball off the ground and brick wall of the school, and horseshoes, the latter of which I got pretty good at until a kid ran in front of one of my already thrown shoes and got crowned. Fortunately, he wasn't hurt much; unfortunately, that ended horseshoes at William Winsor. When it rained, the teachers just cleared the furniture and let us run around in the school basement. Thank goodness our school staff was smart enough to recognize the importance of giving young children plenty of exercise time.

Elementary school introduced me to bullies, to be exact, a small contingent of troublemakers about 3 grades beyond mine who derived sheer pleasure from tormenting me on my way home. Spontaneously one day I decided that enough was enough and took a swing at the leader. Since he was about a foot taller and 40 pounds heavier than me, it was a pretty stupid thing to do. But I was so tired of his abuse that I took the chance. And it really surprised him. After trading a few punches, guess what happened? He backed off and then tried to be my good buddy, which believe you me was never going to happen. The good news is that he never bothered me again.

Some people, especially some women I've met, can't comprehend why boys and men are inclined to fight. The truth is, ladies, most of us do not go looking for trouble, yet some people have no appreciation for our pacifism. They only understand one thing--a dose of their own medicine. Sometimes people have to fight for what is right. I learned this most important lesson about human nature from my bully. I hope he learned something beneficial from my response.

Ma

I will always be grateful for my mother being home when I returned from school or whatever I had been doing. Her favorite room was the kitchen, and invariably, when I walked up our driveway and looked in the kitchen window, she was looking right back at me. Her presence, hugs, smiles, and homemade cookies made my day, and I always looked forward to seeing her. Ma loved to bake and I loved to eat. What a perfect combination. She was my best friend and most trusted confidant.

What I most appreciated about Ma was her pleasant and positive attitude. When you are around nice, upbeat people like Ma, it rubs off on you. She liked people, loved to laugh, and was so thoughtful, kind, and generous. Ma used to say, "Freddie, I don't know if you will be famous or successful, but there is no excuse for not being nice." Her motto was, "If you can't say something nice, don't say it." The only problem is that sometimes it was hard to understand exactly what she meant because she worked so hard not to upset anyone. Ma, though, was no pushover. She had a stubborn streak. Once she told me that people could ask her to do anything, but they better never order her to do it, or they'll be waiting forever. I operate the same way. My mother was special. She was never too busy to listen to me, ask me how things were going, or help me with my chores like shoveling snow or raking leaves. Ma gave me a great sense of security. However, this doesn't mean she gave me everything I wanted.

Ma had rules and taught us to behave, be courteous, be respectful, and eat everything. Only once do I remember testing the latter when she made Spanish rice that I refused to eat. She made me eat it anyway, and I threw up, which made her feel awful, and then I in turn was ashamed for hurting her feelings. We're both sensitive that way. After that she never pushed the food strategy, and I never turned away what she put on my plate. We had a mutual understanding. Ma deserves much gratitude for teaching me to try new foods, delicacies and specialties that have given me so much pleasure over the years, well, most of them anyway. That grilled marinated python I ate in the Philippines that tasted like rubberized fishy chicken left much to be desired.

Like most marriages, Ma and Pop's wasn't perfect. At times my folks got on each other's nerves, and I do recall some heated arguments and tears, usually over some unexpected need for money we didn't have or our dad's occasional one beer too many. However, my parents kept trying and did work things out. In our home we wasted little and did without some of the luxuries we envied. There wasn't much choice.

Pop and Ma met through our dad's first wife, Arline, who like Ma, worked several summers in Massachusetts at Craigville Inn on Cape Cod. Arline and Ma became close friends, and through this friendship, Pop met my mother. Tragically, Arline died of cancer in 1936. Dad remembered Ma and as time passed, they started dating. When they married in 1939, my mother was 34 and Pop 33, a late start in those days for marriage and having children, but that marriage lasted 55 years until her death at 90.

Pop

Dad grew up in Pascoag, Rhode Island, a blue-collar, textile-mill village located 18 miles from Providence in the northwest corner of the state. Pascoag attracted hard-working immigrants like my grandfather and grandmother, Thomas and Fanny Scotland Stephenson, who came to the United States from England and Scotland, respectively, neither of them with a high school education yet with great resolve to improve their lives.

Pop was the first of the family's eight children, two of whom died as infants. He had three surviving brothers, Bruce, Raymond, and

Wilson, and two sisters, Sibella and Mildred. My grandfather was the boss teamster at the mill in town where Gramma was a weaver. He ran the horse teams that hauled the coal and products for the mill, and she ran the looms that made woolen fabric. Their jobs were very demanding, and hours were long, 60+ hours weekly. Gramma worked from 6 a.m. to 6 p.m. daily and half a day on Saturdays; Granddad worked even longer hours and for $8 per week. As a result, Pop and his siblings were raised by their step-grandmother who had them fed and usually in bed before their parents came home. From the time he was very young, Pop worked at various jobs turning over almost all of his earnings to help support the family.

One of Pop's more intriguing small-boy hobbies was trapping live skunks. That worked great until one sprayed him and extracted his revenge. What a story Pop told me about going to the mill barn and being put in a grain sack by well-intentioned workers and lowered through the scuttle hole into the pit in the hope that the smell down there, which was where they tossed the manure and it smelled like it, would neutralize the skunk stench. When that didn't work, Pop walked into the mill to find his mother, only to be chased out by the weavers. Eventually they buried his clothes and scrubbed him down until he was bearable. That ended skunk trapping for Pop. When I am backpacking, I often think of our dad's story and keep my fingers crossed that the little black and white creatures will just leave me alone.

As mentioned above, Pop and I had a bumpy start. Clearly he deeply loved Eleanor and me, but it took time for my dad and me to grow close. Hindering this was Pop's rather stern demeanor. Although a small man, he had the most intimidating look that let me know in no uncertain terms when I was in trouble.

My parents took a nice guy, tough guy approach to child rearing. Ma assumed the former role while Pop served as the family enforcer, the disciplinarian who spanked me a few times when I needed it. Usually that was not necessary because his look was sufficient to put the fear of God in me. Over time, and much to my relief, he mellowed.

Pop strongly believed in education, an unusual priority for a kid growing up in a mill town, but he gives the credit to Gramma who encouraged him to go to Bryant and Stratton business college where he graduated with a two-year degree, the first college degree in his family's history. In 1927 he accepted a job at the Old Stone Bank where he worked continuously except for his Navy service for 41 years, rising to the rank of branch manager and assistant secretary. In the same year he went to work for the bank, his 47-year-old father died unexpectedly from complications following medical treatment. That was such a shock to his family. Dad said his father was as strong as an ox and to his knowledge had never previously been sick a day in his life. Since Gramma still had 5 children at home including 5-year-old Raymond, Pop did his best to help the family.

Our father was blessed with a fine gift for numbers and an incredible memory that allowed him to recall names and meetings with individuals he met decades before, even if only for brief moments. But he was no politician and wouldn't kiss anyone's fanny to get ahead. At the time of his forced retirement in 1968 at the age of 61, Pop made just over $11,000 per year, a modest middle-class income. What management did displeased him, but he did get the last laugh. As a result of his good health, he has been collecting his pension for 38 years. When Pop was younger, he painted homes for a buck an hour and picked apples to supplement our family's income. Both side jobs required his working many Saturdays and Sundays. However, he never complained, and with the added money he gave us a few of the luxuries we craved like my 3-speed bike. Pop is one of the most unselfish men I've ever known, a man who willingly did without what he personally wanted because of his love for his family.

Play Ball!

Nothing brought Pop and me closer together than our common love of baseball and the Boston Red Sox, our home team that we stuck by no matter what happened. And I was so happy for him when the Red Sox won the 2004 World Series, for no fan could be more loyal. At 98 Pop watched every inning of the 2004 World Series and all the playoff games.

One of the highlights of my life was our annual trip to Fenway Park, just the two of us, to cheer for Ted Williams and our other heroes. How I loved that annual pilgrimage. My guess is that we watched about 20 Red Sox games together at Fenway, and our team lost about two-thirds of them, but Pop and I still had a great time together. Like so many Red Sox fans, we thought WE were the jinx. Especially, we enjoyed taking the train from Providence to Boston, and well I remember the day we walked from South Station to Fenway and back, one long walk for a young boy. I didn't mind, though, for I was doing it with my dad and knew what was in store with the Green Monster. Pop typically got good seats for us, field level behind first base. Back then the price was $2 per seat, and that left money for peanuts, ice cream, and drinks. Now you feel like you need to take a second mortgage on the house to take your family to a game. We were true fans who seldom left their seats for fear we would miss something.

Several other one-on-one activities drew us together and affected my life greatly. Pop loved transportation--any type, and every chance he got he took me to see ships and trains. Another fun thing we did together was go to breakfast nooks and get toast or a muffin. It didn't cost much, but it was quality time when we talked about many things that I was curious about like the mobsters who lived in Federal Hill. Pop could have been the spokesperson for Gorton's; he is such a seafood lover. His favorites are scallops, fried clams, and little necks on the half shell, the Yankee version of raw oysters. Because of him, I still love seafood and take him out for some every chance I get. Pop used to say little necks would put hair on my chest. Maybe I didn't eat enough.

Another of our mutual interests was wild berry picking--grapes, blueberries, and cranberries. He'd say, "Come on. We're going berry picking," and that is all it took. I was ready. One time we were in a swamp in Massachusetts picking high blueberries when we heard the thunder of a big animal running toward us. When he said, "Dive," I did and the animal just missed me. Still don't have a clue what it was. I also remember the day Pop climbed about 12 feet up a small tree to pick grapes hanging from its branches. As he reached the target, the tree began to bend precariously toward the pond below. It was fun watching my family enforcer doing a little sweating on his own. For sure I thought he was going to land in the drink, but he was quicker getting down the tree than I thought humanly possible for a man his age.

Staying Busy

One of my favorite pastimes was sledding on Barnes's Hill, just across route 44 from Danecroft Avenue. Hundreds of times I dragged my sled, a wonderful old Flexible Flyer, 5 feet of oak and glistening steel runners, to the top of that hill for the big trip across the meadow and down to the gully. How I loved to ride that sled, sliding alone or with up to four other kids stacked like pancakes on top of me. It was exhilarating tearing down the slope, face covered in blowing snow. When we needed a greater challenge, we headed down the improvised trail through the hill's back woods. Do you know that when you hit a tree with a kid lying on your back, the steering bar will stop you, and the tree will stop the unlucky person above? I found that out one day. That sled of mine was the fastest sled I ever saw, and I still have it and want my family to take good care of it for future generations of fun.

Eleanor, my small blond-headed sister, participated in many of these activities, and when I made her mad, that girl could bite, pinch, and scratch with the best of them. Eleanor knew how to protect her turf, like in the car where she let my parents and me know exactly where my property line ended. And we used to spend lots of hours riding in cars since Pop liked to take Sunday afternoon rides ending up with ice cream for all, which was fine with us. I used to call her E.A. for Eleanor Ann. Speaking of children's names, let me warn parents to be careful what you name your children. My folks came very close to naming her Ann Scotland Stephenson, a lovely name until you examine the initials.

Before television, which incidentally made its first appearance on my street in the early 1950s, the kids in my neighborhood managed to entertain themselves surprisingly well. One of my favorite things to do before supper was listen to radio western programs like Bobby Benson and the B-Bar-B Riders, Hopalong Cassidy, and The Lone Ranger. Even to this day, few television shows have ever matched the suspense radio created with its dramatic sound effects and my imagination running wild. When I was about 10 we bought a 16-inch black and white floor consol TV that cost an astounding $450 and got three channels, one clear, one snowy, and one full blizzard. That was the days of rabbit ears, an inside the house on top of the set antenna that worked pathetically. The improvements in electronics since then are incredible.

As a young boy, Ma used to read Richard Halliburton's *Book of Marvels* to me. It was my favorite book. Halliburton introduced me to the wonders of Yosemite National Park and the Grand Canyon and thrilled me with his daring trips to places like Machu Picchu in the Andes and the crocodile infested Panama Canal. How I envied him. Between Halliburton's tales and Pop's *National Geographic* magazines that I read regularly and through which I discovered my attraction to naked women, a bug got planted in me to explore as much of the world as possible, and I grew up fascinated with geography and travel. In "Tracker" and other chapters, I'll share some of my trips and adventures with you.

The Crooner

Singing has been such a big part of my life that I almost wrote a separate chapter about my musical life. My first performance before a live audience happened when I was 5, a song named "The Fella with an Umbrella" that Sally Crosby and I, two kids in kindergarten, sang as a duet. Also I remember my first solo about that time when dressed to the hilt in my cowboy outfit, I sang "Don't Fence Me In." Little did I know that this song would become my theme song throughout life. I love freedom. Fortunately, the audience liked what they heard or my formal days as a singer would have ended abruptly. I needed that positive feedback.

Some would call me a classic shower-stall singer because I just love to let it rip for sheer, selfish pleasure. Singing has always been one of my chief sources of self-entertainment. And when I hear music, I just can't stop myself from joining in the tune. It's similar to my love for doughnuts. Every time I see a sign for doughnuts, my car inexplicably jerks hard right. What I quickly learned, nonetheless, was that others liked to hear me sing as much as I did, and the reason is that on the plus side of my poker hand was the gift of an above average voice and what they call perfect pitch.

My suspicions are that this talent and musical interest came primarily from Pop's gene pool. A trained pianist and tenor, Pop sang in church choirs from his 20's until he was 92. Still, at 99, he has a nice tenor voice and continues to sing. As a matter of fact, he calls everyone in the family and all his friends and acquaintances every year to sing happy birthday or happy anniversary, something we all look forward to and find rather amazing. Not many people on this planet can say that they received a personalized message sung by a near centenarian.

Ma loved to listen to music and liked to hear me sing but used to say she couldn't carry a tune in a basket. She also said that she judged how my day went by whether she heard me singing or not when I passed by the kitchen window. If I was singing, she assumed everything was OK, which was a good assessment.

Grace Church Boys Choir

One of the formative points in my life was becoming a member of the Grace Church Boys Choir, one of the top boys choirs in New England. Dad heard that Fred Cronhimer, a most accomplished organist and choir director, was having tryouts and encouraged me to see if I could make the grade, which I did. In the fall of 1952 at the age of 9, I became the newest member of the 34-person choir, and I stayed actively singing in that distinguished group through the spring of 1958.

Good choirs, like most anything else that strives for excellence, require much practice, and ours met on Monday and Wednesday afternoons for boys practice and Friday evening with our men's choir for final preparation for Sunday's services. After school, I would take a commercial bus, mostly alone, from Greenville to Providence and walk across the city to Grace Church. Pop or Mr. Cronhimer, who also lived in Greenville, provided most of my rides home. One sign that times have changed for the worse is that my wife and I would never have sent one of our nine-year-olds to practically any city alone. It is just too unsafe today and not worth the risk.

When I joined the choir, I was paid the minimum of $.25 per rehearsal and was told along with everyone else that I could obtain pay raises that would increase my income to the maximum of $.50 per rehearsal if I did my job well and became an "A" grade chorister. This was my introduction to pay incentives as a motivational device, which incidentally became a strategy that I have strongly believed in throughout my life. Grace Church proved that incentives work. Thus, I did my best and by 1954 had achieved the top pay level following incremental jumps to $.35, $.40, and $.45. When I retired at 15, to the best of my knowledge, I was the highest paid boy chorister in New England, rewarded at the newly created A+ grade. Don't tell me America is not a land of opportunity.

Moving Up

Soon after I joined the choir, Mr. Cronhimer invited me to become one of the choir's two boy soloists, a cherished honor that made me very happy and my parents quite proud. Acceptance meant that I would now need to attend an additional regularly scheduled Saturday morning rehearsal for soloists, so I was up to 5 trips to Providence each week during the school year. I was very lucky to have had a fine mentor, a 12-year-old named Bobby Stamp, who took me under his wing and taught me what to do. In 1952, I sang my first solo in Grace Church at the Christmas Eve Carol Service, but what I enjoyed the most, and what gave me confidence about the future, was singing duets with Bobby, pieces like, "Oh Lord Most Holy." To this day, every time I hear that song I can still hear us singing together.

For those of you unfamiliar with boys choirs, there is a special sweetness and quality of tone in boys' voices that distinguishes the sound from anything else I have ever heard. It was so valued in Europe at one time that top boy sopranos were often castrated to stop their voices from changing. So I guess you can appreciate how grateful my kids and I are that I sang soprano in the 1950s. Bobby and I both had good range and tone that enabled us to get the job done. Yes, we missed a few notes over the years but fortunately not many, and I thank Mr. Cronhimer's fine teaching for that, for he prepared us well.

From that point forward I sang many solos with the Grace Church Boys Choir including pieces performed with visiting New York opera singers. Surprisingly, I never had a real problem with nerves nor ever remember missing a performance in this capacity. It was just what I did at that time, and I felt good doing my thing. Bobby was the choir's chief soloist until his voice began to change. In the fall of 1955, I was given that responsibility as well as the first chair in the soprano section, both of which I retained for the next three years. As lead soprano, it was my job to set the example and come in on time and on pitch whenever sopranos needed to do so.

I have been told by those who attended the church for decades that the Grace Church Boys Choir reached its zenith during the period I was one of its members. It happened because we had a great group of talented kids, very supportive parents, and a wonderful director, all of whom took their responsibilities seriously. Our goal was not to be good; we wanted to be exceptional, and we worked hard to make it happen. This guiding principle stayed with me throughout life. Striving for excellence has been my objective regardless of what I was doing. I never saw much point in doing things halfway.

Back to Earth

The inevitable began in the fall of 1957. For the first time my voice cracked, and when it occurred, it was the beginning of the end of my participation in the Grace Church Boys Choir. Although I was encouraged to stay on and continue singing solos for as long as I could, I was too much of a perfectionist and too proud to risk my reputation on an unpredictable collapse. Singing is not just about having a voice; confidence is a huge part of this activity, and I was losing mine. So I made a clean break at the end of the year, retiring from the choir for good. I didn't want to be remembered as one who stuck around too long. That, too, has been one of my guiding principles ever since. Quit while I am on top. Perhaps some of you may disagree with this philosophy, but it has worked well for me.

As I reflect on what singing has meant to me, I conclude that it was an unforgettable experience that I am so glad I didn't miss. Music gave me outstanding opportunities to test myself and learn, and it introduced me to so many wonderful friends. It was a blessing to have been at magnificent Grace Church in the 1950s, and I am so proud of what the boys and men's choirs accomplished under the direction of Fred Cronhimer. To be a part of such an outstanding group was worth every pound I gained from lack of exercise and every alternative activity I had to forego.

In the years that followed, I continued to sing as a tenor in the Classical High School Choir, the Elon College Alumni Male Quartet and college choir, and several church and civic choirs. Truth be told, though, I peaked during ages 10-13. Never again was my voice as good as it was as a boy. However, if any of you wander by my home at the right time, you might hear some of my short bursts of uninhibited shower singing. And you will know that I am happy.

First Trip to Paradise

To the delight of Sis and me, the day after school got out, typically about June 25th, our whole family locked up our home and moved to our cabin on Echo Lake, also known as the Pascoag Reservoir, where we stayed until Labor Day. Pop had it built before his first marriage and named the place the Camp. It had two bedrooms; a family room with a stone fireplace, sink, and cooking space; and a porch, but it was Heaven on Earth for me because my summers were spent there with unlimited things to do. In the early years there was no indoor bathroom, just a nice one-holer out the back door. Eventually we got running water and that eliminated running to the outside Johnny, much to everyone's delight, especially Ma's.

Echo Lake is a pretty, two-mile long body of water situated just 10 miles northwest of our Greenville home, so conveniently located that Pop was able to drive from the Camp to the bank and back every day. Dad did not own the land because the mill that built the lake would only lease lots like ours in order to maintain control over the water levels. However, Pop had signed a 99-year lease on our lot, one of the choicest on the whole lake because of its beautiful sandy beach, for $10 a year. From the front door of the Camp, I could be in the water in less than 40 feet, which I did thousands of times over the years. We lived in this perfect little cove with its 3 cabins on the beach and protected by a long rocky point, appropriately named "the Point," on our left flank.

New England Lakes Will Spoil Ya'

New England lakes spoiled me with their cool, clear water. But swimming was only one of the favorite past-times I shared with my cousins Phyllis and Bruce and friends Billy, Dickie, Michael, and Joey. Constantly we fished, trolling for bass and yellow perch from our row boats, using hand lines or poles to try to catch bluegills, and sitting propped up with our backs against the big smooth slab of granite at the far end of the Point praying for our bobbers to dive like submarines. Surprisingly, one of the things I enjoyed, except for the mosquito attacks, was digging for worms at the worm patch located in a nearby swamp. It was a gold mine for the crawly things. I can assure you that I caught far more worms than fish, often 10 or more in one shovelful.

Our cabins were inexpensive, barely basic, summer retreats, not mansions like lake homes tend to be today. Ours was painted barn red, a color I have always liked. Although Eleanor and I shared a bedroom, most of the nights I slept on a cot on the porch. And if there is anything more soothing than the pitter-patter of rain on the un-insulated roof of the Camp, I have yet to discover it. Unfortunately, the porch roof tended to leak. One time we came to the Camp after Uncle Raymond had been there, and when we looked up at the red-painted ceiling, it was covered with circles where he had put chalk marks to locate the leaks. It looked like there were hundreds of them. Shortly thereafter, it rained hard again and Pop decided to put X's at his location points. Until we eventually repainted the ceiling, I laid in bed looking up at what appeared to be the world's biggest tick-tack-toe game.

But all things eventually do seem to end, and the day finally arrived when Eleanor and I grew up and left Rhode Island, and Ma and Pop retired to North Carolina, motivating them to sell the Camp. I know it made sense to do so, but it broke my heart. I still have the photos and memories, and I try, when I am in Pascoag visiting our relatives, to drive down Reservoir Road so I can look across the lake to see our still standing cabin, but it is just not the same anymore. Yet while I lived those dreams, they were terrific.

Burlington

Although we remained in close touch with our Southern family through annual trips to Granny's, when I was 10, Aunt Lillie and Granny invited me to spend the summer with them in Burlington. What made it so inviting was that I always loved my Southern home and especially the two of them, and I looked forward to sharing a lot of time with them as well as visiting Uncle Harvey, Uncle Willie, and my grown cousins Bob and John. None of them disappointed me.

Granny and Lillie were contrasting individuals. My grandmother enjoyed peace and quiet, home, and talking with friends and family. Lillie liked to get in the car and go, which we did a lot to buy thick milkshakes, shop, and journey down to her cabin on Badin Lake.

Granny was the principal reason people on Ma's side of the family got college educations. As a teenager in the late 1880s, my grandmother was a trend setter who badly wanted to go to college; however, the custom in those days was that women did not do such a thing, and her dad refused to let her go. It was his opinion that a college education was a waste of time and money for women since they wouldn't need it to assume traditional wife/mothering/household duties. So in 1888, Granny snuck away to college and took a job in the kitchen to pay her way through school, that is, until her father found out and made her quit. It broke her heart but made her determined that every child in her family would be encouraged to get an education, a pledge that not only resulted in all three of her daughters graduating from Elon College but also all of her grandchildren becoming college graduates. Granny once told me, and she really meant it, "Get an education, Freddie. You can lose every cent and every possession you have, but nobody can ever take away your education." That was one of the best pieces of advice anyone ever gave me, and it had a profound impact not just on me but on all of our children, each of whom graduated from The University of Georgia. But somebody had to start the educational process, and in my case Granny made this very wise move as did Gramma on Pop's side of the family.

Granny and I had many great talks. She had lived a long life and had so much experience that she was a walking encyclopedia of information. On one occasion, I asked her if she remembered when Lindbergh flew across the Atlantic. She stunned me when she answered, "Shoot, Freddie, I remember when the Wright Brothers flew." Think about that. An incredible number of things and enormous changes happened in the world from her birth in 1872 through her death at 98 in 1970. I still find it hard to believe that two of my great grandfathers, not great-great grandfathers, from my mother's family fought in the Civil War. That just doesn't sound feasible to me, but it is a fact.

Before eating out became the rage, not only did most everyone in the South eat at home, but also they tended to raise much of their own food. This was true in Granny's case. Her specialty was Southern fried chicken, vegetables, and one of my favorites, home-made chicken liver biscuits. She was a fine cook who seasoned most everything with fatback and a lot of other things that people tell us today will kill you. Well, she lived almost 100 years eating these things nearly every day, and she fed them to me, and did that food taste great. One day Granny said, "Let's go get some chicken." I thought she meant to the store, but we went to the back yard where she grabbed a chicken, wrung its neck, slapped it on a block, and cut off its head. That is the first time I fully understood what "You look like a chicken with its head cut off" really meant. That chicken laid rubber all over the yard until it dropped. What an education I got that day.

Badin Lake

Lillie was my buddy, as good a second mother as a kid could ever want. She'd say, "Let's go to the lake." I didn't need prompting. Sometime around 1950, she and her friend Julia read an ad about lots for sale on a new lake, Badin Lake, south of Asheboro, so they drove the 70 miles down there to investigate. The sales agent was so desperate to sell her a lot that he kept up the pressure until Lillie told him, "I'll tell you what. If you will sell me that lot for what I have in my savings account, I'll buy it." He then asked her how much she had in the bank. She replied, "Seventy-nine dollars." He said, "Sold!" So Lillie bought a lot not on the lake but the next row up and built a cabin on it that she called the Cabin. Julia bought the lot right next to hers and constructed her own place. And it was one of the most important decisions each of these unmarried school teachers ever made. They spent 40 years having fun and sharing good times at Badin Lake. As time passed, Lillie bought two pieces of lakefront property in front of the Cabin for $300 and $450 dollars, giving her direct access to the lake.

Badin Lake was a lot of fun. There was swimming, boating, and fishing with Lillie and my cousin Bob who built his own cabin on the front lots. Lillie and I enjoyed each other's company, and she didn't treat me like a child. Maybe that is why I always affectionately just called her Lillie instead of Aunt Lillie. She was a character but a most generous and loving one.

Foster's

One of my favorite activities that summer was going to Foster Shoe Company. Almost daily, I would walk to town and stay at the store watching all the comings and goings. Uncle Harvey was now the boss, Great Uncle Willie ran the cobbler shop, and Bobby and Johnny worked the sales end. My goal was to help where I could but mainly to share their conversation and company. It never occurred to me that maybe I was a burden to these men because they always treated me so well. Never did I hear Uncle Harvey raise his voice, get angry, or show impatience with me or anyone else. I think that is why I liked him so much, that and his great sense of humor. Ma told me that at her wedding, when the preacher asked, "Who giveth this woman away?" Harvey, who was part of the wedding party, said, "I do and I'm throwing in her sister for good measure." That sounds like something he would do. Papa's brother Uncle Willie was a classic with many great perspectives on the world, such as "golf" that he called "cow-pasture pool" and "Cokes" that he named "belly rot." He ate pinto beans just about every day and lived well into his eighties.

Both my cousins were grown men when I was 10, but they took me to lunch, drive-in movies, and waterskiing on Badin. Bobby was a great woodworker who built boats, cabinets, and anything else he set out to make in his extensive woodworking shop, but what made the greatest impression on me is that he let me help him on numerous occasions, and I enjoyed this greatly. His patient teaching instigated my lifelong interest in woodworking, something I am enjoying so much in retirement.

Reflecting on this Southern summer, what impresses me most is how much respect these adults gave me. Although I sang solos at age 10 before large audiences, in other settings I was quite shy, and my Southern family helped me gain confidence. In particular I appreciated the way they accepted me for who I was and as one of the "guys." And it felt great. Throughout life I have tried to show similar respect toward the youngsters I came in contact with. People tend to act like they are treated.

If You Think Your High School Was Tough . . .

How many A's did you get in high school? I got 3 and am darn proud of every one of them. Smithfield, the town I lived in, didn't have a high school, so I could go anywhere I chose provided the school would accept me and my town would pay the tuition. My choice was Classical High School in Providence, considered at the time one of the three best public high schools in the Northeast in terms of academic standards. The other two were Boston Latin and New York's Bronx School of Science. I chose Classical because I wanted the best high school education I could get and because I was a top student in my middle school who thought he was up to the task. Classical turned out to be one of the most rigorous academic environments I have ever experienced, and that includes graduate school where I earned my Ph.D. Nevertheless, Classical did what I needed. During my first semester of college, I got 5 A's--all A's.

Classical was a college preparatory school that attracted bright, hard-working students from families that understood and greatly valued education and taught that culture to their children. Its graduates typically completed 4 years of math; 4 years of Latin; English, science, and history courses; plus Greek, French, or German, in all, 18 full-year academic credits. There weren't any easy courses that I can remember or easy teachers. We did extensive writing, took an average of four tests each week per course, did considerable homework, and were graded almost daily on in-class participation in every class. On our quizzes as well as on our in-class evaluations, we often got 50's and zeros and dealt with them. I remember one math course in which I got 16 straight 100's followed by a zero. See what that does to your average. Extra credit and second chances were non-existent.

I think about this a lot in today's teaching environment, such as on the day when our son David came home with an interim report card in high school that showed a 126 average in Spanish. Sharon and I asked him what that meant. He responded, "Many kids in our class have bad grades so the teacher keeps giving them extra assignments to raise their grades. So I did them, too, and got the added points." When the final report card arrived, David's grade in Spanish was 106. Jokingly, Sharon asked him why his grade had dropped. He looked his mother right in the eye and said, "Those hundreds keep bringing me down."

Classical has always been my benchmark for judging academic standards. Of the four-hundred students in my class of 1961, only 139 graduated. Most of the remainder transferred to less demanding high schools. At Classical, if you didn't meet the academic standards, your choices were get help from the teacher, get a tutor, or transfer. However, the graduates in my class all attended college, many at America's most prestigious universities like MIT and Ivy League schools. Of the 40 National Merit Scholarship Finalists in Rhode Island that year, eleven of them were my classmates. I couldn't have asked for a finer high school education, and what the hard work, despite only fair grades, taught me is that although I was far from brilliant, I was competitive and bright enough to accept and meet many of life's challenges. My grades didn't reflect what I learned, but I had plenty of self esteem because I knew I earned it.

High school, however, was not a lot of fun for me. When I left Smithfield Memorial Junior High School, I was the president of the student council and voted most likely to succeed, but I didn't live up to those expectations at Classical. The stress level at Classical was high and constant, I discovered the truth about the limits of my intelligence, and my bad memory almost did me in, particularly in foreign language courses where it is such a vital key to success. High school was to me what grad school was later--a serious job requiring long hours of homework. It truly tested me. In fact, I wasn't sure that I was going to graduate until the last week of my senior year. The good news is that I did graduate. High school didn't finish me off. What it did was prepare me for a lot of things I later achieved in life.

The one compelling lesson I took away from Classical that would help parents and their children is to get off the grade, self-esteem kick and put your energies into trying to maximize student learning. Not one grade has ever helped me solve the problems I have had to deal with in life, but I have used knowledge and the skills that I learned in school practically every day.

That's What Friends Are For

My two closest friends in Greenville were George and Sandy, and together we engaged in many activities, none illegal, but just the typical, weird things that boys do. For instance, weekend-long 3-person ping pong tournaments and occasional burping contests. Of the three, George was the tallest, the center on our church basketball team, and a major practical joke artist. I named him Slim. He retaliated calling me Fuzz because of my mild facial hair, which he said looked like peach fuzz. Since Sandy already had a nickname, his alias became The Human Garbage Disposal Unit. That's a story worth hearing, so listen up.

Sandy was a good kid and a lot of fun, but he was extremely tight-fisted with his money. As a result, he had the annoying habit of going to great lengths to encourage his two best buddies to pick up the tab. Every tab. One day Slim and I decided he needed an attitude adjustment. Our warped minds took care of the rest.

Since we both worked in a bakery in Greenville, we decided to fix Sandy a special treat, an éclair, that we knew was Sandy's absolute favorite snack. Our plan was to give him one that night at the high school hockey games we were all going to attend in Providence. This éclair, though, was going to be stuffed with lard instead of custard. Everything we needed was available in the bakery, but making this work required thinking. You see, custard and lard have different textures and colors. They don't look alike. But by adding some food coloring and softening the lard by mixing it, we solved both problems. Then we had to figure how we could get Sandy to eat the darn thing. And we pulled it off brilliantly.

Slim drove and brought the bag of goodies, he the leader and I the willing accomplice. We picked up Sandy and off we went. Within minutes, he asked, "What did you guys bring from the bakery to eat tonight?" Slim answered, "Jelly doughnuts and an éclair, but you can't have any. We are sick of your mooching off us."

"But I love éclairs. They're my favorite."

I then countered, "We know, but you never pay for anything. Don't even think about that éclair. It's not going to happen."

Well this little dialog went on through the drive, through the first complete hockey game, and into the second. The begging and badgering continued non-stop. Then a craving Sandy said, "OK. If you'll give me the éclair, I'll pay you." We told him we didn't believe him. That just made Sandy more determined.

In the third game, I yelled, "Give him the éclair, Slim. He's driving me nuts! He said he'd pay for it. Let him have it so we can enjoy the game."

Slim snapped, "Fine, just give me the money, Sandy. It's yours."

At this point, Sandy boldly declared, "On second thought, maybe I won't pay for it." So more debating followed.

Finally, in the fourth game, I'm talking about four hours after we picked him up, we surrendered and gave him the éclair. Sandy thought he was so smart. You could see the gleam of victory in his eyes. I believe his classic line was, "I knew you guys would give me the éclair. I love éclairs." At which point he shoved the thing in his mouth, bit off half of it, and started to chew." The reaction took about 5 seconds.

Can you imagine how hard it was to keep a straight face in a situation like that? But we did. In a moment, Sandy uttered, "I think there's something wrong with this thing. Did you guys do something?"

"Then give it back. Sandy, you are so cheap!" Slim fired back. "I can't believe you're complaining after you got our only éclair free."

At this point, Sandy swallowed the first half. That was it. We were so doubled over in laughter that tears were pouring out of our eyes. And just when you think you have seen it all, think again, folks. Sandy's next comment was, "If you'll give me the rest of the stuff in the bag, I'll eat the rest of this éclair." We did, and he did. Now don't you think "The Human Garbage Disposal Unit" was appropriate?

Incidentally, Slim was voted the most serious male student by his ninth grade classmates. Obviously, they didn't know him like Sandy and I did. Be careful believing opinion polls. Also, watch what you're eating.

We Are What They Made Us

Whatever we become in life, never should we lose sight of the profound influences that helped us get there, particularly the role our families played in giving us life and sculpturing us, deliberately and sometimes accidentally, with the values, priorities, interests, hobbies, opinions, and activities that define and differentiate us. We are not so much the end results of our own plans but more the outcomes of God-given traits, genetics, circumstances, and teaching. We did not cause our beginning nor do we fully control our destinies. I'm not trying to diminish the impact of the effort we as individuals put forth and the decisions each of us makes, for certainly both play a major role in whatever we become. But it is important, I believe, that we not take too much credit for the good things that happen to us, sometimes even the bad, and remember to express gratitude for all the help, significant in my case, that we receive along the way.

Truly, I was one of the lucky ones, born into a family that believed in me and unselfishly and lovingly did their utmost to help me find success and happiness. My parents and grandparents pointed me in a good direction and then gave me plenty of freedom and encouragement to live my own dreams, not theirs. Many children are not so fortunate.

Papa never had much money, material goods, power or social status, things that contemporary society tends to value so highly, but he was rich beyond imagination in things far greater in importance. He was a good Christian man who lived a life that generated love, appreciation, and respect. Although his work and career were neither exciting nor impressive, his faith in humanity was unwavering, his total loyalty to his family and friends inspiring and admirable, and his legacy great. Through his deeds, character, and positive attitude, Papa set a very high standard for the type of man I needed to become, a goal that gave me much purpose. Of equal significance, he showed me the path through faith to help get me there.

Granny and Papa understood the difference between right and wrong and taught their children that distinction in black and white, not the nebulous gray of relativity that confuses today's young people. Life, my grandparents believed, is very much about choosing the right values and priorities. Papa and Granny exemplified strong marriages, committed families, and honorable lives built from the ground up through honesty, trust, and love, fundamental components of strong relationships and happiness. These traits and their examples guided my thinking and life, directly through my grandparents' lives and indirectly through what they taught my mother who passed their teachings on to Eleanor and me.

Nothing, however, had more direct impact on me than Ma and Pop. If we talk basics, from my personality to my sense of humor and my emotions, I far more closely mirror my mother than my dad. Both of us always liked things to go smoothly, hated confrontation and arguments, and wanted a stress-free home. Two of the most valuable assets Ma passed on to me were her people skills and her positive attitude. She looked for, and expected, the best in people and life, and taught me the same.

The main reason I stayed out of a lot of trouble was because I couldn't bear the thought of hurting my mother. She meant that much to me. On many occasions with temptation knocking on my door, I would hesitate long enough to ask, "If I do this, will it really disappoint my mother?" If the answer was yes, I turned away. I guess you could say Ma was my second conscience. In later years I used to tell my college students this story, adding that now my concerns were more about not wanting to do anything to make Sharon and our children ashamed of me or lose any respect for me, and then I would ask my students in times of crises or indecision to think of the person they least want to hurt and ask this same question before they do something they deeply regret.

Were it not for Pop, the man I once rejected, I do not know where I would be. He introduced me to so many of the things I love in life from baseball to music, transportation that became my career and great interest, berry picking, and my strong interests in lakes, geography, and travel. How revealing it is that so many of his passions became mine. By his teaching and example, Pop taught me to be an honorable man, to try new things, to stand by my marriage vows, to remain humble in my successes, to stick by my word and honor my commitments, to take good care of my wife and children, to be unselfish with my money and time, to encourage and then support my children in their activities, to be understanding when they failed, and to love them no matter what.

Dad taught me to be self-reliant, to earn money and pay my own way, not to think I was entitled to anything except a fair opportunity, and to maintain dignity in the face of disappointment or illness. Hard work, ambition, and doing my best were important objectives he lived by and instilled in me as were his love for his country and his sense of duty to his people. Pop had no tolerance for cheating, lying, irresponsibility, and dishonesty. And he let me know in no uncertain words his distaste for show-offs, phonies, fanny kissers, bullies, hypocrites, elitists, draft dodgers, blowhards, lazy people, the entitlement crowd, and know-it-alls. Neither Pop nor I have ever been too politically correct, which irritates some people no end, and yes, we've paid a price for that. He just taught me to try to do the right thing, and because of this, we have no problem looking at ourselves in the mirror or fears about what people might find in our closets.

In sum, my first life, my childhood, while not utopia, was certainly close enough. There is no way that I can adequately express the breadth of activities and people I was exposed to nor how each one, in their own way, was an important learning experience that helped shape who I am. As I ponder what I took away from these years, I realize how important it is that parents fulfill their responsibilities, not shuck them as an excessive number do today, and take better care of their children, not just because we owe it to them, but to reap the joys and memories that will surely follow. Of all the things I learned from my parents and grandparents, and there are so many, I cherish most that they instilled in me a deep love for family; a strong desire to become not just a husband, father, and grandfather but the best one I could become; a commitment to make sure I take the time, no matter how busy I am with other responsibilities, to share my passions with my children and grandchildren and allow them to share theirs with me; and to love my wife and each and every child as much as I possibly can. It is our jobs, my wife's and mine, to teach our children well.

Life truly isn't fair. The deck is stacked in favor of some, less so for others. However, it is so important that we never lose hope. People can do many things to improve their odds of success and happiness in life, such as by getting a good education, making good decisions, and playing to their passions and strengths. It is equally imperative that parents take measures to level their kids' playing fields to give them the best shot in life, such as by teaching them well and giving them much love and encouragement. Primarily, though, what happens to us in life is our personal responsibility, and we need to be good captains of our ships. But as I said earlier, everyone needs considerable help along the way. Thus, I plan to make sure I will be there to help my children, grandchildren, and others navigate their way along life's challenging path.

ROTTEN BAKER

Nestled in the heart of New Hampshire's lakes country lies Geneva Point Camp, a place indelibly etched in my memories and heart. I was very fortunate to have spent four summers there beginning in 1961 after my senior year of high school and ending in 1964 after my third year of college, working and playing in one of the most incomparable settings I could ever imagine, an environment of great scenic beauty and surrounded by wonderful friends who profoundly influenced my life. These friends gave me a nickname, the Rotten Baker, that even to this day still brings a smile to my face, and I hope, to many of them.

Winni

Geographically, Geneva Point Camp (GPC) was located in Central New Hampshire about 100 miles north of Boston on the state's largest lake, Lake Winnipesaukee, a naturally formed 25-mile long sparkling blue wonder framed on practically all sides by glorious mountains. To the northeast were the cloud crowned Ossipee Mountains, a range featuring Mt. Shaw at 2,975 feet. On the south shore were Belknap Mountain (2,384 feet) and its supporting cast. As noted in the last chapter, I grew up on a pretty lake in Rhode Island, and I also have seen many other bodies of water during my life, but none ever stunned me like Lake Winnipesaukee with its 263 miles of shoreline and more than 250 islands. To this day I still think of it as paradise on Earth, a Mecca that keeps calling me back. In the center of this 10-mile-wide lake and 7 miles out on a peninsula reached by Moultonborough Neck Road sat GPC with its 200-plus acres of lovely old forests, half a mile of lake shore, and views that cameras could never fully capture.

Ironically, I never would have made it to GPC, or as we all affectionately call it, Winni, except for a persistent pastor at my church. At the time, I was the newly elected president of the church Methodist Youth Fellowship (M.Y.F.), and my minister thought I would benefit from attending the United Christian Youth Movement's (U.C.Y.M.) one-week leadership training conference at GPC. He didn't know much about Winni other than that it was operated by the National Council of Churches of Christ in the U.S.A. and that its purposes were to provide fellowship, guidance, and inspiration in Christian living, which I can guarantee you I needed. While I had attended church all my life, I was far from a true believer. But I really didn't want to go to GPC. My reluctance was simple. Why should I pay money to go to a lake when I already had a great lake in Pascoag that was free? Seeing my hesitancy, my pastor said the church would help pay my way, so between that and his arm twisting, I consented.

When it was time for the conference, Ma and Pop drove me to New Hampshire, we said our goodbyes, and I proceeded to check in. It took less than 15 minutes to know that I was going to love this place. The Pascoag Reservoir was very nice, but Lake Winnipesaukee was phenomenal! Winni had a softball field, tennis courts, two sandy beaches, water so clear you could spot lake trout swimming 20 feet below the surface, hundreds of stately whispering pines, miles of inviting trails, and something definitely lacking at the family lake, lots of high school and college girls. That week at Winni changed my perspective on many things, I'll tell you, and I truly hated to leave so soon. U.C.Y.M. and GPC did one heck of a job providing fellowship, guidance, and inspiration. By week's end I felt closer to God than ever before. More importantly, that week at Winni changed me, and I made up my mind right then that I would come back. I just had to. Never had I ever felt better about life nor more love for people. I mean things just suddenly came into focus.

On the next to last day of U.C.Y.M., something significant happened to me. During a short conversation with a member of the camp family, that is, one of the 65 workers who took care of the grounds and facilities, prepared and served all the meals, and did the linens and cleaning of the cabins and Inn, I told him how much I loved Winni and that I planned to return next year to the U.C.Y.M. conference. He then asked me why I was paying to come here when if I worked there, they would pay me and give me room and board. He then suggested I ask for a job. Boy that got my interest in a hurry. I asked him how to apply, and he told me. Consequently, during the fall I wrote the camp manager requesting a job. For months I heard nothing, but then one winter day a letter arrived offering me a position as a dishwasher for $250 for the summer plus room and board. To say the least, I was ecstatic and accepted immediately. Nothing I know of could have made me happier. Life was good and was only going to get better.

What More Could a Guy Ask For?

The day after school got out in 1961, my parents again drove me to Lake Winnipesaukee. Upon arrival, I checked in with the office staff, received my room assignment, and met as many members of the camp family as I could. In my spare time I walked to the beach, sat beneath the tall rustling pines, gazed at the rocky islands and mountains directly in front of me, and thanked God that he had led me back to this wonderful place. For the next 85 days I would have so many opportunities to work and play here, my afternoons and days off to do as I pleased, and 9 guys and *34 girls* working on the staff. What more could a guy who loved sports, the outdoors, and women ask for? And to think they were paying me to be here, too. Unbelievable!

My direct boss, a man named Frank Smyth, the camp chef and head of the kitchen, was a GPC legend who scared the wits out of many in the kitchen crew and most of the waitresses. Quickly the veterans warned all the new workers, especially us six new dishwashers, to do exactly what Frank told us and never ever be late for work, or Frank would make sure we never forgot our mistake. Within a week two guys slept through their alarms, and we all discovered exactly what the veterans meant. The first time I met Frank, a seasoned World War II veteran with black hair, a memorable mustache, and deep blue eyes, he took one look at me and said, "I need you to wash all those pots and pans." Those pots and pans were a huge pile of every metallic object in a kitchen equipped to feed 550 people at one meal. There were dozens of muffin tins, salad bowls, mixing bowls--just about any kind of kitchen pan imaginable. Worse, they were totally covered in vegetable grease, a coating put on each fall to prevent rusting during the winter. But it didn't matter to me. They could have asked me that day to clean every garbage can and toilet in camp, and I would have done it gladly. That's how much I wanted to be there.

I guarantee you that a lot of people today would be offended by what Frank asked me to do, but not this 18-year-old. There was a job to do, and I went to work with a smile on my face. It might be hard for most people to imagine that I had fun that day, but I did. For ten hours I scrubbed those pots and did my best to get them perfectly clean. And while getting dishpan hands, I just kept singing to myself and thinking about this job, this summer, the girls, and all the things I planned to do and what I could learn.

What none of us rookies knew was that Frank and Dave Knauber, the camp baker, had a plan. Frank needed a helper in the cooking area, and Dave needed a baker's assistant, but instead of just giving people these jobs based on our applications, Frank and Dave decided to let us wash dishes and pots for a day and see how we performed. The next day, Frank said, "Fred, we watched you work yesterday, and we like your attitude. Would you like to become the baker's assistant? If you take it, Dave will teach you, and your pay will increase to $290." With the baking knowledge of a man skilled at burning toast but an appreciation of baking from my job as a clean-up guy at George's Bakery in Greenville and watching the enjoyment Ma had in our kitchen at home, I said, "Yes." In 24 hours, I had obtained a promotion and a pay raise, a record few people anywhere have ever broken.

Thus began my apprenticeship as the GPC baker's assistant, and thanks to Dave and Frank's patient and excellent teaching, I learned all I could about baking cakes, pies, éclairs, rolls, cookies, etc. In fact, Dave let me do a lot of the baking so I could see how to do it. Our camp family name for Dave was Spanky because he looked like an adult-sized version of Spanky from the *Little Rascals* kids' movies, that is, short and stout. He, like many people during that summer of 1961, loved to tease people and clown around with everyone, especially Toni, Frank's wife. One day Spanky made her a birthday cake covered in chocolate frosting, pineapple slices, prunes, and lemon writing on the top--all the things Toni hated. One day I asked Spanky, a volunteer fireman back home in Massachusetts, how his fire station did. Without batting an eye, he responded, "Saved 17 basements last year." Dave was so good natured and happy, and he was one of the easiest people to work for I have ever known. Also, he was very generous, allowing me to copy every one of his baking recipes.

During the 1963 summer I got an on-the-job promotion to head baker. When the summer began, our food service company failed to send a baker to camp, so Frank asked me to do the job until one showed up. About two weeks later, she arrived. One week later she was reassigned. Frank, tired of fooling around, appointed me head baker for the rest of the summer, a job I held for the rest of my time at GPC. My last season I was paid $80 a week plus room and board for doing something I enormously enjoyed while still keeping all the great fringe benefits. The 9-to-34 boy-to-girl ratio never really changed. What a country!

Animal House

During my first year at Winni, I lived in the Castle, a building and existence that remind me of the animal house in the movie by the same name. It was a really old basic structure that slept 5 boys. Other workers lived in Stagger Inn and The Other Place, the other two elements of our five-star row of camp family boys' cabins. On the other hand, 29 of the 34 girls lived in a much beloved big old farm house appropriately called the Dump. Naming things like people and buildings, as you can tell, was a tradition at GPC. Even the rooms had names such as Men's Room, Knothole, Inferno I, and Cubbyhole, four of the 9 rooms in the Dump.

Water and food fights were another big part of camp family entertainment. You would be amazed what kind of fun you can have with 48 dozen muffins to throw at each other. Why did we throw them at each other instead of eating them? Simple. I forgot to put the baking powder in them. Do you know what happens when you forget that one little ingredient? Well, when I looked into the oven, I saw 48-dozen miniature volcanoes. They burped and splattered that mix up and around, but they never rose a fraction of an inch. That was not the only mistake I ever made as a baker, but none usually as costly.

The Kitchen

Definitely the best place to work at GPC was the kitchen because that was the center of camp life. It was located in the basement of the Inn, a converted barn that had wide porches with comfortable old rocking chairs and a cupola perched high on the top that not only provided outstanding views of the lake and mountains but also was a great place to have a private conversation with a friend or do a little necking. To everyone in the camp family, the kitchen crew was known fittingly as The Dirty Old Men. Frank was officially The Dirty Old Man, the dirtiest of the dirty, but the rest of us weren't far behind. Our name did not come from being filthy or sex offenders. We just teased people quite often, especially the waitresses, told occasional off color jokes, and collectively pulled off enough pranks to deserve our title. And we wore our name with pride. I considered it an honor to have been a Dirty Old Man. And though we may have been dirty, I guarantee you that there was never a dull moment in the kitchen, for we knew how to make that workplace jump. Our kitchen crew consisted of the chef, 2nd cook, 2 salad boys, baker, baker's assistant, 2 kitchen girls who prepared and served all the beverages, and 4 dishwashers.

Each week GPC served a different conference and space permitting, we accommodated up to 135 guests, that is, people not attending the conference but who wanted to vacation on Lake Winnipesaukee. Maximum seating capacity for the sit-down family-style meals we served was 550 people, or from my perspective 69 pies at 8 pieces per pie and 825 dinner rolls based on our working formulas of 1 dessert and 1.5 rolls per person per meal. This was a big kitchen adequately sized to hold the cook's kitchen, the bakery, cold and dry storage, four big serving counters where we placed our desserts and beverages, room for all the waitresses to collect their food and drinks, the camp family dining area, and the dishwashing space. I liked the kitchen because I was always in the thick of things, and there was never a dull moment.

While I still bake some at home, there has never been a place like our GPC bakery. Everything we needed was in that 12-foot by 16-foot room, and I knew exactly where to find anything I wanted, which is far from the case at home, where I can't seem to find anything. Our food preparation, like rolling pie dough and frosting cakes, was done on a 4-foot by 8-foot table. Just about every baking ingredient came in large quantities from sugar to flour to walnuts or butter. A lot of my time as a baking assistant was spent greasing muffin tins, weighing dry ingredients, and assembling wet ingredients like water and eggs for our mixtures. When Dave and I made anything, it was usually in batches of 50 pounds or more.

My job taught me a lot about leavening agents, different types of flour (cake, pastry, bread, wheat, cornmeal, all purpose), and converting liquid and volume measures to weight. For instance, water weighs 2 pounds per quart. On one occasion, I actually successfully converted Ma's hobnail cookie recipe for two-dozen cookies that she measured in half teaspoons and cups into pounds and quarts and made 2,800 cookies. I don't necessarily recommend doing such, however, because some recipes only work well when made in small batches. Baking to a large degree is applied chemistry; it's about following formulas and knowing the effects of temperature. One of our puff pastry recipes, as in éclairs and cream puffs, would only work with frozen eggs. Fresh eggs or powdered eggs would cause them to rise and crash, something I learned the hard way.

Furry Friends

Two of the cutest creatures I met at camp were Ralph and Ralphina, our pet red squirrels. This happy couple, not a whole lot bigger than chipmunks, lived in the woodpile behind the bakery. In short order, the squirrels and I became friends because they liked the walnuts we fed them. In fact, they became so trustworthy that they would actually come into the bakery and eat walnuts from a pie tin we placed on the blast furnace. The latter was our stove on which we made pie fillings and pudding and frequently burned ourselves and that sometimes drove the working temperature in the room to nearly 130 degrees (really), but when it was turned off, it made a nice platform for the walnut eating. In hindsight, doing this was a big mistake.

One day I left 8 sheet pans of chocolate-frosted cake on the table while I took my afternoon swim. When I returned, I saw tiny little foot prints all the way across the cakes where one or both of the squirrels had taken a walk over to the biggest find in their lives, our 40-pound box of walnuts. Honestly, there was no time to toss the cake and make it again for supper, so I followed those tracks back and forth under a microscope looking for "deposits," which thankfully, weren't there. Then I touched up the frosting, cut up the cakes, put the pieces on the serving plates, and decided that there are some good times just to remain silent. This was clearly one of them.

After dinner, one of my favorite waitresses came into the bakery and gave me a most sincere compliment (which was unusual), "Fred, I have always admired the neat way you frost and decorate the cakes, with the swirls and drawn lines across the frosting, but you really outdid yourself this time. How did you put those little holes in the frosting?" I told her it was a trade secret. Somehow I couldn't find it in me to tell her that what she had looked at with such admiration were tiny claw marks left by my favorite pets at GPC. Nevertheless, apparently the cake tasted really good. Every piece got eaten that night, and the camp nurse had no visitors.

Learning from the Best

No boss I ever had in my life taught me more than Frank Smyth, a high school graduate and self-educated man who knew far more about things I consider important than most of the college graduates I ever met. When Frank was young growing up in a poor Irish family in Massachusetts, his job was to go to the library with his siblings each week and bring home as many books as they could carry for the family, which he told me was usually about 35. Frank then read all of his books and as many of the others as he could squeeze in. In the process, he got quite an education and developed a tremendous love for reading. At camp, Frank commonly read paperback novels cover to cover in a day. He could read that fast. This got me really motivated to read, something I previously did quite reluctantly, and for the rest of my life I have loved reading books. But what Frank taught me that I value most was a whole lot about baking, life, and managing people, for he was a great mentor both in and out of the kitchen.

One thing so obvious to me was how much pride Frank took in everything served. During one of our many conversations, he told me always to make the best food I could and not ever risk our reputations by serving anything bad. His opinion was that it takes a long time to earn a reputation, and it is foolish to risk losing what you worked so hard to get, plus, he believed that our customers deserved to be treated well. One of Frank's favorite sayings was that people eat with their eyes, not their taste-buds, and if something doesn't look great, they won't eat it. He also thought that people ought to do their jobs right, not close to right.

During the first week on the job as baker's assistant when I was dishing pie onto the dessert plates on one of our counters, Frank told me to improve two things: first, try to cut every piece the same size because no one likes being slighted and second, if I could put pie crookedly on plates, I could and should put them on there evenly. After that, I did both, and our desserts looked like a prize winning precision drill team. And the effect did convey greater eye appeal and told others I took pride in my work. I must tell you, though, that kitchen work requires much planning, speed, agility, skill, knowledge, and fast thinking, and while you may want things done precisely by the book, that is not always possible or practical.

Like any kitchen, at GPC things happened, mostly innocently and without posing significant risks to customers, like stripping bacon with bare hands. Remember, this was 30 years before our nation became so passionate about what goes on in kitchens. But I still have no problem with what we did because Frank's philosophy was stay clean, work hard, and enjoy life, which we did. And what we did I suspect is exactly what most families still do today in their own kitchens. How many of you wear gloves when you cook at home? Frank had a lot of sayings. One I especially used to like was, "When it's brown it's cooking; when it's black it's done." That was his way of saying, "Pay attention!" Bakers quickly learn to tell if goods are done by how brown they are turning, sometimes by looking at the top (pie crusts) while at other times checking the bottoms (biscuits). The point is that Frank's advice made a lot of sense to me so I followed it and took great pride in my baking.

It meant a great deal to me when people praised us for the desserts and rolls we made. I fairly quickly began to think of myself more as an artist than as a baker or tradesman. And indeed we did serve great food and baked goods at GPC. The best evidence I can give you is that the typical GPC waitress gained 10 pounds each summer--roughly 1 pound every 8 days. And Frank was a master at motivating me. One way I got faster was to set personal speed goals for tasks like making pies, and I'd continuously strive to break a new record. Well, I got pretty fast relatively soon and one day averaged making a pie in 2 minutes: rolling the bottom, adding the filling, rolling the top and putting it on the pie plate, and so forth. I felt especially good until Frank told me a top baker could do that in 90 seconds. It took a while but one day I did 35 pies in 45 minutes. Good one, Frank.

Mincemeat, Everyone?

Other people I worked with at Winni also taught me many things, the boss's wife, for example. First, though, let me ask you a question. Do you like mincemeat pie? I bet you that most readers immediately said "No" even though they have no clue what it even tastes like because they've never even tried it. Most don't even know what it is. But it sounds nasty. Well, I understood what mincemeat was, and while I personally liked it, I also was positive that a lot of people wouldn't touch it with a ten-foot pole. Why? Perception. What's in mincemeat are chopped apples, raisins, spices, suet, and sometimes meat. It's an acquired taste. So why, since everyone received the same dessert at GPC, would Connie, the camp manager's wife, put it on the menu? I had no idea.

The first time I saw mincemeat pie on our weekly planning menu I went to Frank with my concerns. Should I still make one piece of pie for each customer or make less, given that I just knew we would have a lot of leftovers? Frank told me we better be safe than sorry, so make a piece for everyone, all 375 people. So I did and wound up with 125 extra pieces, 5 of which I ate, but most of which the next morning went into the garbage can. What a dismal, unpopular failure that menu item turned out to be. But do you know what? We had mincemeat pies once a week for the next several weeks, and every time I wound up throwing a huge number of pieces away.

After the first error, Detective Fred went to work to learn why the boss's wife wasn't acting normally. Guess what I learned? The mincemeat came already prepared in a lovely wooden container, a well-crafted pine bucket just perfect for storing magazines or sewing items. When I first saw the container, I asked if I could give it to my mother. "Sure," the Dirty Old Men said. It turns out the boss's wife wanted that container, and since she didn't get it, we had mincemeat every week until her girlfriends and she got one. This was a valuable lesson in marketing and human behavior that I never forgot. Much gets sold not because people want it, but because of the package. And people do strange things to get something they want.

Where'd the Name Come From?

The Rotten Baker legend began with Toni Smyth, a woman I used to tease and joke with regularly. I can still remember her saying, "Fred, you're rotten, rotten, rotten!" Perhaps so, but I was trained by the master, Slim, and I picked up a lot from the Dirty Old Man himself, none other than her husband Frank. Anyway, the next thing I knew, everyone in camp was calling me Fred the Rotten Baker and it stuck. Actually, I liked it. No doubt I earned that name through trickery and worse.

This is a true story as is everything else in this book. One day I was making lemon meringue pies, about 40 of them, for dessert. The steps were these: roll, spread, and bake the pie shells; make the lemon filling and scoop it into the baked shells; whip the meringue and spread it on the lemon filling; and bake the pies until the meringue looked golden brown. I got about halfway through stage 2 one morning, when Frank looked at the 15 pies I had already filled and said, "Fred, isn't that filling too pale?" I had been pretty groggy that morning, and sure enough, as I re-examined the contents more closely under my single 100-watt bakery light-bulb, he was most definitely right. But I knew I couldn't take the lemon filling back out of the shells without pulling the crust right with it, as sticky as that stuff was. So I asked Frank, "How about if I just put the remaining filling on the mixer and beat in a little yellow cake coloring?" "OK. Try that," he replied. And I did so, except the yellow cake-coloring bottle slipped out of my hand spilling far more color in the mixing bowl than I ever intended to use. Aware, though, that the coloring had no effect on the pie's taste, which I knew from experience was delicious, I made an executive decision just to mix it up, fill the rest of the pies, and take my chances, which is exactly what I did.

My problems began about 4 p.m. when we started cutting up the pies and putting them on the serving dishes. The contrast between the pale ones and their neon brethren was startling. And when things really got tense was when we ended the last row of the former and began a row of gaudy ones right next to them on the counter. You almost needed sun glasses the brightness was so overpowering.

About this time, one of my favorite waitresses popped her head into the bakery and confidently declared, "We got you this time, you Rotten Baker. I don't know what you did, but you really screwed up the lemon meringue pies."

Calmly I replied, "What are you talking about?"

"The color!"

My response: "Have you ever made a lemon meringue pie?"

"No, I haven't."

"And I bet your mother never told you the difference between California and Florida lemons, either. Right?"

"I didn't know there was any difference between California and Florida lemons."

"Well, there are a lot of things you still need to learn about baking. The pale pies are ones I made with Florida lemons, and the bright ones came from California lemons."

She bought that and apparently sold it to the other waitresses who in turn must have convinced our conferees and guests because I didn't get any more complaints and had no leftover pie that day.

In life, sometimes you just have to think fast.

Pineapple Upside-down Cake

Now, if that story amused you, I think the next is better. One day I asked Bob Ripley, "Rip," one of GPC's biggest practical jokesters, to come into the bakery. I needed his help. When he got there I told him that I was going to pull a practical joke on another family member named Pete, who was known to have pulled a few himself, and I needed his assistance.

"Great! What are you planning?"

I told him I was going to put shaving cream on Pete's pineapple upside-down cake the next time we had it on the menu, and I needed him to sit next to Pete and make sure he got it.

Rip got really excited at this and said to count him in. He also said he couldn't wait. Both of us knew that Pete loved pineapple upside-down cake.

It took some time until the cake appeared on the menu. In the interval, Rip came by the bakery with increasing frequency to share his impatience to do the dirty deed. He was more enthusiastic about this than I was. When the big day finally came, I carefully colored the shaving cream (coming out of the can, it is bright white whereas the whipped cream that I made from scratch had a beige tint to it), put the end result in a pastry bag, squeezed out a generous portion, and topped it off with a cherry. It looked just like the real McCoy. Next I enlisted the help of a trusted, dependable waitress to make sure she absolutely knew which of those 200-plus pieces on the counter was the shaving-cream delight so that it didn't accidentally get passed to a customer and get me in trouble. And I prepped Rip once again on his duties.

When dessert time came, the waitress passed the cake to Rip who set it down right in front of Pete, who then loudly exclaimed for all to hear, "I love pineapple upside-down cake." Then he took a big bite of cake and topping and started chewing. Immediately two things happened. Pete recognized that he had been had by the Rotten Baker, and Rip jumped out of his chair, pointed at Pete, and yelled, "We got you! We got you! Pete's cake has shaving cream on it!" And he kept laughing and carrying on. Never had I seen Rip more elated. Unfortunately for Rip, he didn't know that I had also fixed his pineapple upside down-cake with shaving cream, and after his laughter subsided and he sat down, the unsuspecting camp manager took a big bite of his shaving cream. And as he chewed, he did his absolute best not to let on what was happening. In the meantime his face got redder and redder.

At that moment, I tapped him on the shoulder and asked, "Rip, how's the cake?" And I will always remember his response as he tried to hide his mistake.

"Fred, if it takes me a lifetime, I'll get even with you!"

For about a week he gave it his best shot, but he never succeeded. You see, it is very difficult to get even with the guy who is feeding you. For about two weeks thereafter, just about every member in the camp family did a complete security check of everything they ate that I made. They'd pick it up, turn it all around, sniff it, open it, take the smallest taste possible, and only when they were absolutely sure it was OK would they eat it.

So this is why they called me the Rotten Baker, and I think it was perfect. Frank told me to have fun, and I truly did.

Camp Family

Rarely was I ever bored at GPC, and here's why. First I stayed busy working five and a half days, roughly 56 hours, a week, starting my days at 6 a.m. and ending after dinner at about 7:30. Thus, I remained in the kitchen working and having fun with the Dirty Old Men and waitresses from early morning until about 1:30, and then I returned at 4 p.m. to handle dinner duties. Always my afternoons were free, and I took full advantage of them to enjoy my three favorite pastimes: softball, swimming at the beach, and being with girls. During my first summer I spent many afternoons taking walks with my girlfriend Alison where we talked and made out. If body language means anything, Toni and Danny seemed sure that we were doing far more than kissing and hugging, but we never did. Just a lot of talking, hugging, and kissing were all that took place, your basic 1960s first-base necking, a growth experience no one in life should ever miss. Once I commenced dating Sharon, my future wife and fellow student at Elon College, I no longer dated at camp. But I spent many peaceful afternoons with my friends just talking, socializing, and sharing each other's dreams, concerns, and company, which I really enjoyed. GPC taught me how truly wonderful and unique women are, and I appreciate so much how openly my "girl friends" and I were able to discuss most anything on our minds. It was more like close sisters and brother.

Males seem to come in two main varieties: those who date multiple women simultaneously, what Ma used to call "playing the field," and sequential daters who date one female at a time. Both tactics have their merits, but I was one of the latter types. When I tried doing the former, I just felt dishonest, disloyal, and uncomfortable. Both categories of men, however, have a common characteristic: They think about women and hidden pleasures 24-7, especially from the ages of 15 to say, 100. I figured out later in life when I became a dad that the reason fathers are much more protective of their daughters than their sons is that they were teenage boys once. They know just how strong testosterone is. You don't even need to be awake for it to work.

Favorite Places

Speaking of making out, GPC had a legendary place called Pine Hedge for doing just that before camp curfew at 10:30. Pine Hedge was a stately line of tall pines positioned most conveniently just west of the Dump. Every night beginning at about 9:30, camp family couples went there to get their final embraces on the soft needles under the pines and until Mrs. Grinnell, the housemother at the Dump, blew her annoying whistle calling the girls home. While this cozy spot got pretty crowded at times, few cared because other things were on their minds. There was one exception. One of my buddies for some unknown reason ceased bringing his girlfriend to Pine Hedge. When I questioned him about their absence, he gave me a wink and said, "We found a much better place--more privacy, close to the Dump, and nice soft foliage. It's behind the propane tank." My thought was, "Good for them." About one week later both of them showed up for work covered in poison ivy, which, as you probably guessed, came from their secret hideaway. You see, neither of them ever went there except after dark. Remember this lesson boys and girls.

Another popular place at Winni was the Rock, a big slab of granite forming the right boundary of the main beach and that was the designated "Camp Family only" area. It was our gathering place for sunbathing, swimming, socializing, and opposite-sex people watching, as in young bods in swim suits. Remember, this was a church camp, so this was one of our rare opportunities to check each other out. GPC had the luxury, and I mean this in all sincerity, of no television, no newspapers, and few magazines. I also remember only one radio. This was also a time in history far before electronic games, computers, cell phones, boom boxes, MP3 players, and so forth that many of today's kids can't live without. When no such distractions exist, people actually spend their time being with others and deepening their relationships. So what else did we do to have fun?

Skinny Dipping

"Let's go skinny dipping!" I guarantee you that if someone ever makes that statement in front of a bunch of teenage and college boys, immediately it will get everyone's attention, just like it did that sweltering night at the Castle. What I know is that I had previously never done it but for some unknown reason was truly tempted. And I guarantee you I wasn't alone in my thinking, for to the person everyone seemed highly motivated to do the deed. One thing then led to another and finally, all of us decided, "Let's go!" The clincher came when one of the guys said he had heard a rumor that some of the girls might also be going skinny dipping. That did it. But how exactly could we pull this off? Never was it our intention to swim naked at the main beach. That was just too risky. However, there was a dirt road right in front of the Castle that led straight to an isolated spot on the lake.

A plan rapidly developed to make our way clandestinely to a small pier at the road's end where we would take the plunge and finally cool off. The next big consideration was whether we should wear our clothes to the water's edge and strip there or just get naked in the Castle and take our chances. The group concluded that it would take too much time undressing and redressing at the lake; thus, we'd just leave our clothes in the cabin and jog to the water, which is exactly what we did. And that plan was executed perfectly until someone yelled, "I think I see car lights!" Sure enough, someone was picking a most inopportune moment to drive straight toward us. Well, ladies and gentlemen, I don't think I have ever seen prettier swan dives in my life than the six of us naked jaybirds diving head first, both to the left and right, into the bushes adjacent to the road. And brother was it close. We just made it to cover before the car was right on us.

After it passed, we had a discussion to figure our next move. Nobody suggested retreating to the Castle. No, we would not go home defeated. This was one mission that we intended to see through to the bitter end. So seeing no more lights, we started sprinting down the road, right off the pier, and straight into Lake Winnipesaukee, which felt superb. And our spirits stayed sky high until it quickly dawned on us that somehow we had to get back to the cabins dressed in nothing but our shiny white birthday suits. Well, we scouted the area in all directions and collectively took off flying up the old road, successfully, I might add, and much to our collective great relief.

I have reached several conclusions about skinny dipping. Would I do it again under the same circumstances? Absolutely. I can see a lot of moms saying, "Dr. Fred, what are you teaching my kids?" Was it risky? You bet. Was it fun? Oh, yeah! Did anyone get hurt? Let me put it this way. Men, it is not a good idea to dive face down naked into bushes. Will I ever forget that adventure? No way. Any disappointments? That was a bum rumor about girls skinny dipping that night. But all in all, no harm was done by our skinny dipping adventure. It was one of those so called rights of passage from boyhood to adulthood, a part of growing up, another piece of the puzzle that was no longer missing. And it was definitely memorable.

Where There's Music

One pastime that most of us thoroughly enjoyed, as lame as this may sound today, was singing, and we did it everywhere--during work, on our trips to town, and especially at our weekly Sunday evening sing-alongs led by our Skipper, the 1961 Camp Manager, Charles Sewall. Skipper played a mean guitar and knew all the great camp songs like "Gee, Ma, I Wanna Go Home," "The Inferno Song," and "Home in the Dump." There was something very therapeutic about uninhibited singing that made friends of strangers and brought people together both physically and emotionally. Gus Gustafson, Rick Welch, and I got so much into this and folk music, which was so popular in the early 1960s, that we wrote our own songs about camp life, mostly sung to Kingston Trio music. Some of our masterpieces were titled "The Dirty Old Men," "Baking Soda," "The Grubber's Legend," "The Legend of Succulent Rolls," and my favorite, "The Story of Robert Ripley," which reminded everyone why they should always check their pineapple upside-down cake before eating it. We formed our own folk trio in 1964, named The Dirty Old Men, (Did you really expect something else?) that sang often and with great gusto at camp. Singing, you see, was embedded in our camp culture. It was a simple, expedient way to express our happiness.

Movie Night

One of the things most eagerly anticipated was movie night in Meredith, a town about 15 miles from camp. I think we just needed to get a return-to-civilization fix. So one evening each week, anyone who wanted to go would cram into the station wagon, adults' cars, and GPC blue truck and head for town. Always, I tried to ride in the back of the truck because of the good times that I knew were waiting. Our Dutch-boy-blue straight truck had an open bed with three boards running horizontally across each side, and for our seating pleasure, the maintenance guys covered the floor with mattresses on which up to 15 people sat gazing at the stars. All the way going to and returning from town we sang camp songs and cracked jokes and snuggled together to keep warm. Up and down the many hills and around the many curves along Moultonborough Neck Road we went.

Our destination, the Key Theater, was located on the second floor of a retail store and was the tiniest movie house I have ever visited. Typically, we had the place almost exclusively to ourselves. When the movies ended, we took our traditional trip to Chase's to fill up on burgers, ice cream, and their specialty, hot fried bread that tasted great but sank in our tummies like lead. Then the journey home began, and to me it was the most memorable because of the hugging and kissing under the blankets. I had my love to keep me warm, and in later summers a whole lot of female friends who snuggled as close to me as they could. Thank you ladies. You were very understanding. What a shame that none of this is likely to be repeated in America ever again. Between our becoming almost paranoid about safety and understandably fearful of multi-million-dollar liability lawsuits, there is no way any camp that plans to stay in existence could risk letting workers ride in the back of a truck. I would never want any of my kids or yours to get hurt, but boy are they missing some wonderful growing-up experiences.

Typical Day at the Office

In 1964, my assistant baker Chuck Sewall and I lived in our own cabin, Bakersville, about 1,000 feet from the bakery. It was tiny, had one bunk bed, and a sink and toilet. There was no heat, and while it reached the 80's in August at Winni, in the morning it got down to the 30's. So Chuck and I had a routine to save us from freezing. We would get the night watchman to turn on the bakery ovens about 4 a.m. Then we would hang our clothes on the bedpost, in the morning slip right into them without stepping on the cold floor with our bare feet, and sprint to the bakery where we immediately threw open all the oven doors and warmed up. Our work day started at 6, and this usually meant we needed to bake muffins or cornbread for breakfast, the ingredients and pans for which we got ready the previous evening. Breakfast came early so we had no time to spare.

After breakfast, we immediately began preparing our desserts for lunch and dinner, and I really enjoyed making cakes, brownies, gingerbread, frostings, and other delights so much that I seriously considered going to culinary school and choosing a career in hotel and restaurant management. The biggest drawback, and it stopped me in my tracks, was the bad hours people work in this field. It would have meant missing a lot of time with my future hoped-for family, something I did not want to do.

Now you might believe that the temptations from working in a bakery would make us eat sweets constantly because of the direct access we had to so many tasty things, but quickly I got very tired of smelling and tasting sugar. In fact, I made so much whipped cream that I would have to get others to taste it to make sure it had the proper sweetness. It all began to taste sickening to me. I just couldn't stomach continuous doses of that rich topping. Incidentally, neither Chuck nor I ever gained weight at Winni. Maybe that's the secret to losing weight: work in a bakery. The keys to good baking, however, are knowledge, proven recipes, fine ingredients, and much, much caution. Like carpenters say, measure it twice and cut it once. As previously discussed with my volcanic muffins, you better not leave anything essential out or put either too little or even too much of certain ingredients in the mixing bowl or you'll definitely pay a price.

We worked fast and diligently during our mornings rarely taking more than a 15-minute break. This was necessary because we had 350-500 conferees, guests, and camp family members waiting for our goodies. Just before lunch we always prepared our dough for our hot dinner rolls. Yeast and bread flour are the key ingredients in great rolls, and the combination taught me some interesting facts. For instance, bread dough can rise so much if you don't punch it that it will crawl right out of the mixing bowl. Also, the yeast causes dough to heat up so you can somewhat control how fast the dough rises by using colder water.

After stuffing ourselves with Frank's great cooking, it was off to the beach or elsewhere on the grounds. Usually Frank did us a favor and punched the dough during the afternoon, but when we returned at 4 p.m., our big job was making our dinner rolls, and there is nothing I remember more pleasant about baking than the wonderful aroma of freshly baked bread, something that made every day delightful.

Like Spanky before me, I taught Chuck everything I could, shared all my recipes with him, and let him take the lead in making a number of our products. And I am proud to say that Chuck succeeded me as GPC baker. But while I was at Winni, my goal was to master all I could about baking, become an excellent baker, and make as many customers and friends as totally satisfied as possible. My other objective was to do as many little things as I could to make life more pleasant for everyone, such as making an extra pie for our head maintenance man Big John and his wife. Other than that, I just tried to enjoy each day to the fullest. And I think that was a key to my love affair with Winni. Throughout my life, whether I was cleaning up somebody's yard, washing the floors in the Greenville bakery, doing my janitorial duties at my church, or working heavy construction in the blazing summer heat in North Carolina, I always found a way to motivate myself to do a good job and enjoy the effort. I really like Big John's philosophy of life when he said, "I take things as they come, and I am happy. I have work that I love. What more can you ask from life?" That made a lot of sense to me.

Baldy

During my life, I have hiked dozens of mountains; however, my all-time favorite remains Mt. Baldy, a rocky round granite bald on the side of one of the mountains in the Ossipee range that caught my gaze and admiration daily while at GPC. Baldy had a lure that drew me back for a climb and picnic lunch on its summit every summer, and the way this was all possible was my day off.

The first time I climbed Baldy was in 1961, when Stan Marsden and I rowed across the two-mile width of Moultonborough Bay to Melvin Village, one of Lake Winnipesaukee's several small lakeside communities, and then walked the three miles to the base of the mountain where we just hiked through the woods until we reached our goal. Baldy gave us the greatest unobstructed views of Lake Winnipesaukee we could ever imagine. While enjoying lunch from our 1,000-foot perch above the sparkling water, we could scan the entire lake taking in its substantial length and wide breadth, and for the first time really gain a perspective of the extent of its numerous, marvelous islands. There before our eyes we saw the full expanse of Geneva Point Camp, clearly visible some four miles away. My most memorable trip to Baldy was this first hike, for not only did we really grasp the magnificent gifts of this beautiful lake and its majestic surrounding mountains, but also we delighted in signaling our friends at GPC and receiving back their mirror flashes recognizing our achievement. It will take an incredible mountain to ever surpass my love for Baldy, and if you ever get a chance to hike to its top, don't miss it.

Winni Spirit

A long time ago I learned two very important lessons. First, although we can physically revisit places that meant so much to us in times gone by, they are never quite the same because the people and places have changed, as have we. Second, it is asking a lot of people to try to get them fully to understand and appreciate the wonderful events and places in our past, for they just didn't live those dreams by our side. Still, I must try my best to gain your understanding about Winni because there are some powerful lessons that can be drawn from my days at GPC that have helped me enormously throughout life and that I know can help others if I can successfully communicate these lessons. The place was truly special, not just in my mind and heart but also in the minds and hearts of the vast majority of camp family members who worked there over the years. This I know absolutely because many of them from my 1961-1964 summers have shared their love for Winni with me in their spoken and written communications.

GPC overwhelmed us with the natural beauty of that captivating lake, the glacier-rounded green mountains, rustling tall pines, the cries of loons far out on the bay, and gorgeous sunrises and sunsets that we so often watched across the lake and above the mountain peaks. This was truly one of God's and nature's masterpieces. But it was something else that meant more to us than the setting and that was the wonderful people we met and worked with on a daily basis. Winni had this grand, unique culture developed by those before us and continued by those that followed, and never have I been in any other organization that matched the positive attitude nor sustained the desirable atmosphere that encompassed my camp family, the conferees, and our guests, something that everyone simply called the Winni Spirit.

The Winni Spirit was not the kitchen or the Castle or Dump but the relationships established between friends. It was how everyone treated each other and approached their work and life. Its central themes were cooperation, friendliness, courtesy, decency, being nice, un-hesitatingly taking over a friend's job when they were sick, sharing generously, feeling as happy at someone else's good fortune as the direct recipient was, and being sad right along with them when they got bad news. The Winni Spirit appeared as individuals voluntarily joining in every single activity whether it was spontaneous singing, a worship service, a group discussion or softball. It was giving and receiving love. In all of my existence I have never been surrounded by so many people practicing the Ten Commandments, following the Golden Rule, and obeying organizational rules, the latter not because we had to but because we trusted our leaders and their judgment that these rules were necessary and would make the camp experience better for all. If I bring this back to basics, the Winni Spirit was loving, respecting, and appreciating each other and accepting people for what they were, not what others wanted them to be.

I especially like the words I read by an anonymous writer in the 1964 issue of "The Wash," our camp newsletter, which said, "The Winni Spirit was a wonderful feeling that our fellowship together gave us. We were a close-knit family that worked, played, and lived together in harmony, putting others' needs first and remembering always to keep smiles on our faces. Regardless of the weather, the sun always seemed to be shining in this place filled with kindness and laughter." As I read this again recently, I could imagine many of this book's readers thinking this sounds impossible or that I am indeed making this up or grossly overstating GPC's strengths, but it was true because I lived it. For us, Winni was a summer's journey to find life's meaning, a beautiful experience of personal growth, understanding, faith, and hope. That is what happens, I think, when individuals live in a culture that is focused on finding the good in life and in people. But I can understand anyone's doubts because what I lived there seems rare in our society today.

Would I trade anything for every one of my four summers at Winni? Absolutely not. Was everything perfect? Of course not. Not everyone bought into the culture. Some individuals believed the rules were silly and made to be broken. On one occasion I remember a worker being fired and sent home. But these were rare exceptions. However, these and other troubling signs, like less thoughtfulness, a growing coarseness in the language, some insincerity, an increase in drinking, and more complaining, began to test and weaken the Winni Spirit. Some of this had to do with leadership errors and hiring mistakes, but I suspect what was occurring was more a reflection of a nation and people starting to feel the effects of the great social upheaval that began to change America in the 1960s. Essentially, though, the Winni Spirit remained intact for all my years in New Hampshire.

All I know is that I was extremely blessed to have had the opportunity to have lived in about as pure a society as I could have ever hoped for, one that brought me considerable joy and significantly shaped my values, goals, and outlook on life. I only wish more people could have been there with me to share what I was a part of. Forever I will be indebted to my GPC camp family friends for what they taught me and for the wonderful times we shared together. I love you.

What Winni Can Teach Us

I decided to end this chapter with a partial list of the many valuable lessons I learned at Geneva Point Camp that I know can help others who have never been there to find more happiness and success in life. Please take the following to heart.

What is really important in life is how you live it and help others.

Surround yourself with good friends and try to be a better friend to them than you want them to be to you.

Happiness begins at home. Nothing will improve relations faster than having a good attitude and looking for the best in people.

And when happiness is your goal, take jobs where you support the workplace culture or at the least give that culture and the people who lead it every chance to win you over.

Get to work on time and be somebody people can count on.

Get out of that rut. Consider what I would have lost if I had turned down my pastor's request that I go to the conference at Geneva Point Camp. Being willing to try new things is so important in life.

In any job you do, stay positive and work hard. You never know who may be watching you or what you will gain as a result.

When you reach positions of responsibility, be an encouraging generous teacher as well as a good mentor to the people beneath you. Don't fear them. Try your absolute best to help them succeed.

Laugh loudly, laugh frequently, and never take yourself too seriously. People get in trouble when they begin to believe the press clippings.

Nobody is perfect, and nobody in their right mind expects any human being never to make a mistake.

Welcome new challenges and be optimistic about the results. Few things are more important in life than believing in yourself and having people that you respect show confidence in you.

Show love, appreciation, and respect for others and in return you will receive each one back in abundance.

Strive to exceed expectations and constantly raise your standards.

Make a hobby out of a job. Have more fun at work.

Be more accepting of people who are different from you.

Try to learn something good from everyone and every experience.

Limit your complaining.

Make sure you spend a lot of time with people of the opposite sex.

And as Ma used to say, be nice.

I challenge everyone to develop your own Winni Spirit. Paul Taylor, a good friend of mine once said, "Fred, we may not be the president of the company, but we are the presidents of our own lives." I know that within each of us is the power to change who we are, what we think, how we act, how we treat others, what we say and in what tone of voice, and what our priorities ought to be. What it takes is purpose, faith, the right attitude, and determination. I like to think about how much better the world would be if each of us would just become more caring, thoughtful, loving, grateful, considerate, honorable, friendly, and understanding.

ADDENDUM

Who's Who Selections Voted on the Rotten Bak-er by the Geneva Point Camp Family

1961
sleepiest

1962
best natured
most likely to succeed (second)
most athletic (second)
most ambitious (second)
best all around (second)

1963
best natured
friendliest
best worker
done most for Winni
best all around
president of the camp family

1964
best natured
friendliest
best worker
most respected
best all around

PORK CHOP

Newport Naval Base, Rhode Island

"Get in line. Stand at attention! Straighten those backs! What are you looking at, mister?" The shouting by the MPI's (drill instructors) began immediately after we stepped off the bus and continued unabated all day. I don't care how much friendly advice you receive before you join the military, basic training is a cultural shock. The descent from big men on campus to low men on the totem pole was precipitous.

"Welcome to the United States Naval Officer Candidate School (OCS). Remember, you are all volunteers." It was time to take a deep breath and get used to military life. OCS, the place where staff officers and upperclassmen dedicated every waking moment to the challenging task of making men out of recent college grads, was now my home and job for the next four months. During World War II, Pop's generation called OCS graduates "ninety-day wonders." And if the first day was any indication that we were going to earn more respect than that, it wasn't apparent.

While there are three chief routes to becoming a naval officer--the United States Naval Academy, university ROTC programs, and OCS--the single largest source during the 1960s, producing more than 50% of all junior officers was OCS. Most of my classmates came to Newport to become line officers, the men who command and run ships and lead the fighting. My goal, however, was different, for I was there to qualify for admission to the Navy Supply Corps School, a six-month crash course for staff officers who run the business functions of the Navy.

First, though, I had to graduate from OCS and get commissioned as an ensign, and that definitely wasn't going to be easy.

Day One

Weather-wise, September 24, 1966, was a nice Saturday but a bad day otherwise. I had made the decision to enlist in the Navy and was accepted to Officer Candidate School. Was I nervous? Anxious might be a better description. When people are barking at you and you have no clue about what's coming next but assume the worst, that's justified. Actually, we didn't have much time to dwell on it. In quick order the MPI's assembled us into military ranks and off we went on one of the toughest walks I had ever taken, a non-stop march across the base to Nimitz Hall, the massive 940-man dormitory where I would sleep ever too briefly each night during my OCS vacation. You'd be amazed how heavy a suitcase becomes when you carry it non-stop for a half mile like we did that day. Brother, did I wish I had traveled light. My arms felt like they were going to fall off. Here I was, one guy, a part of one of the biggest classes in OCS history, beginning the journey to fulfill a strategic need in the growing war effort in Vietnam.

The command put me in H Company, in the military alphabet, "Hotel" Company, one of 16 companies at OCS. Our section, H-703, consisting of 32 men, was one of Hotel Company's four sections. We were 1st quarter officer candidates, the rookies who joined the three other Hotel classes that had already been here for one, two, and three months, respectively. We looked up to these upper classmen for advice and instruction, mainly with admiration because they were still here, but sometimes with contempt. It all depended on how they treated us. By the time Class 703 graduated on February 3, 1967, the Navy had 533 newly commissioned ensigns.

What I remember most vividly from day one was that for the first time in my life I was in control of virtually nothing but my attitude. From the moment we crossed through the base's guarded gate until the second the lights went out in my Nimitz Hall room, my job was to listen and follow orders, answer the questions I got asked, begin in-processing, pick up my clothing and gear, and meet my designated roommate, Rick Stephens, who fortunately turned out to be a great guy from Terre Haute, Indiana. And we marched and we marched and we marched from building to building to mess hall to Nimitz, all over that base. If you need a refresher, rent the movie *Stripes*. We weren't quite as dysfunctional as those clowns, but I am sure just as humorous in the eyes of some of those charged with shaping us into a disciplined fighting machine. Dad had told me, "Son, just keep your mouth shut and do what they say." That was good advice, Pop, and that is exactly what I did. H-703 was truly a smorgasbord, young men from 18 states and in every description imaginable. Our only common denominator was that we wanted to become good naval officers, and for sure we didn't want to get tossed out of OCS for any reason. And you know, where there's a will, there's a way. Over the next four months we found it.

Ten Seconds

"I WANT THAT ONE!"

This sounds like something Uncle Sam said in one of his recruiting pitches, but in this case the spokesman was none other than one of the base barbers desperately wanting to get his hands and clippers on our longest-haired candidate, and I'm talking down to the shoulder blades. Mr. Barber, with his deep, guttural voice and Yankee accent, sounded more like a hit man, and after what he did to our buddy, that likeness was not too far off the mark. He scalped him! We were next.

Do you remember the two recruits in the first *Police Academy* movie who had their hair cut down to the roots, the two stool pigeons who looked like skin-heads? Well, we all resembled those two at the end of this 20-minute ordeal. I swear my haircut start to finish took 10-seconds. Actually, the whole episode was pretty funny, especially watching the serial barber put another notch in his clippers. You've got to admire a man who loves his job that much. If my recollection is right, that was our only laugh for the day. Still, in that tension-filled atmosphere, any humor was much appreciated.

I can't be certain if it was day one or the next that we first met Chief Knowles, Master Chief Boatswain's (pronounced *bow-sin*) Mate Knowles, to be precise. However, long before he came into view we could hear him yelling, "All right, you #&+##%@ instant insects, blaa, blaa, blaa." That was his affectionate term for OCS want-to-be ensigns.

Bo's'ns are known throughout the Navy for their colorful language, as in "you swear like a bo's'n mate," but this was all new to us sheltered civilians. Remember, it was the sixties. But when we finally saw him, were we surprised to see how small he was. All I could think of was Popeye the Sailor Man. Rick was absolutely fit to be tied by Chief Knowles's verbal onslaughts. One day Rick said to me, his face as red as a beet, "Who does that guy think he is? I have a bachelor's degree from Purdue where I studied under some of the top marketing profs in the country. I have an MBA from Indiana University, a great school. And this guy has the nerve to call us #&+##%@ instant insects every time we are within 100 yards of him!" Well, the chief did, and we took it because that is what was necessary to survive the first month at OCS. About all we could do, and it did help, was vent to each other in abundance. You really didn't think we complained to higher authorities or had a one-on-one chat with the chief, did you?

The First Two Months

One good way to describe OCS is two months of hell followed by two months of endurance. Let me run through a typical day for you. At 5:30 we were jolted out of bed by the bell sounding reveille and required to hurry to the hall outside our rooms where in our Navy-issued boxers we participated in PT, i.e., physical torture. Sorry, I meant to say "training." This was done on our as-hard-as-concrete cold linoleum floor, a surface with so much friction that it wore a blister the size of a half dollar on my fanny from doing sit-ups. Our leader was an aspiring kid built like a rock who thrived on muscle toning far more than the rest of us did. Anyway, after about 30 minutes of push-ups, jumping jacks, sit-ups, and other pleasurable conditioning exercises, we hit the head (the bathroom), got shaved, tried to take a one minute shower, returned to our rooms to make our beds and clean up, and prepared for inspection--of us and our rooms.

Oh, yeah, I forgot to tell you about how many hours we spent polishing, spit-shining, tucking, and refining our uniforms so that we might look presentable to the inspecting officers, guys with eyes like hawks. Nor did I state that Rick and I got so frustrated with the lack of blue gigs (good marks) and our accumulating collection of red gigs (demerits) that one day we scrubbed the deck (cleaned our room's floor) with toothbrushes and made our beds so tight a quarter would flip over when dropped on the covers from three feet above. As a matter of fact, we quickly learned that if we very carefully slid into bed, we could get through the night without hardly disturbing the bed covers, which we did with great skill once we got the hang of it. It helped that we were so dead to the world we hardly moved a muscle once we shut our eyes.

By the way, some enterprising classmate figured out that red gigs were rewarded for 63 specified official offenses at OCS, and Rick and I unofficially were living proof that there were only 3 ways to earn blue ones. Anyway, all of this remarkable effort on our part to spit-shine our deck, while deeply conveying our 110% commitment to naval excellence, produced very few bonus points. Ah, well, such is life. Nevertheless, it did teach me something significant and that is that some people just look great in a uniform and some don't no matter how diligently they work to satisfy inspectors. There's one picture in our family archives of me in dress blues that more closely resembles a penguin than a naval officer.

About 7:00 a.m. we took off marching as a unit to breakfast, a 30-minute lesson in speed eating. Then it was off to classes, usually 50-minute sessions on military, tactical, organizational, and technological subjects--554 hours in all packed into four months. Also, we spent two hours a day either in close order drill, swimming, physical torture (Darn, I did it again.), or similar activities. Between classes we marched hither and yon. My favorite activity, however, was getting vaccine shots, 26 I think it was before we graduated, that were jammed with regularity into our arms during interim stops on our way to class or to and from meals. Since the Navy did not know where we were going or what strange diseases might be awaiting us, they just gave us the whole nine yards of shots to prepare us for virtually any contingency. I got so used to getting shots and stayed so tired that soon they didn't even faze me.

Love Is a Great Motivator

Do not forget that this was a school with tests designed to measure our progress or lack thereof. Grades were very important both because there was a lot of competitive pride in our section and we fully comprehended that academic achievement would greatly influence our future naval assignments; furthermore, if we failed our coursework, we could be tossed out on our cans. Of more importance to me, however, was that grades determined if I could get an additional few hours of liberty on Wednesday evenings, a privilege awarded after the third week provided a candidate's overall grade-point average was high enough. Why this was so paramount to me is that I wanted and needed to see Sharon, my bride who accompanied me to Newport but who lived alone off the base. The regular liberty granted from 11:00 a.m. Saturday through 7 p.m. Sunday simply wasn't adequate. Thus, I was determined to make the academic grade to see my bride more frequently. We really missed each other, and I felt badly that she was there alone.

The problem was that the 3 hours of study time provided us from 7 – 10 p.m. nightly were simply not enough for the amount I felt was needed. That first week, though, we were offered an option to study an additional hour from 10:30 – 11:30, so I jumped at the chance. By the third night, however, it was obvious that I just could not keep doing this without falling asleep in class. I was exhausted. Thus, I decided right then to sink or swim with the regular study hours, and this forced me into the art of prioritizing. With only 24 hours in the day, something had to go so another thing could stay. In a nutshell, out of this I became more efficient--a most important lesson that helped me for the rest of my life, and thank God it worked. I made the grade cut much to Sharon's and my joy.

Life Beyond the Gate

Sharon and I very much enjoyed Newport, a beautiful port city with a rich naval and architectural history. Our apartment was located about 1,000 feet from the Atlantic Ocean and near the Cliff Walk, a world-famous, scenic four-mile trail right on the edge of the rocky Rhode Island shore between the pounding surf and the front yards of many of America's most fabulous summer mansions. Around the turn of the twentieth century, from the late 1800s through the 1920s, Newport was the summer playground of America's wealthiest families, the Vanderbilts, Asters, Belmonts, and others, who built extravagant and beautiful "cottages," several, like the Breakers and Marble House, of marble and gold. One time I determined that the latter two, each of which cost millions to build, would today in inflated dollars each have a construction price of several hundred million dollars. This should give you an idea of the quality of homes still found in Newport. In all, there were about 100 such cottages along the Cliff Walk, Ocean Drive, a beautiful road that follows the coast around the southern tip of Newport, and on the rolling landscape nearby. The good news is that several of these intriguing homes have been preserved and are open to the public, and I highly recommend that you spend time in Newport and see them. Sharon and I loved reliving this part of the gilded age of American history.

It was rare that we left Newport during our OCS days. We didn't have much time to travel with our limited liberty hours, and the penalty for not getting back on time and being restricted to the base was too extreme. While at OCS, the rule was that we had to wear our uniforms in public. This was a pain at times, but I can assure you that through doing so I began to feel more like a naval officer and developed a much deeper sense of pride from being identified as a man serving his country. I imagine that was the point.

"Let's Rig for Movies"

Guess who H-703 got as our teacher in seamanship? None other than Chief Knowles. On that first day of class he swaggered into the room and in that gruff, attention grabbing voice of his informed us that he was going to show us movies in class and by #%&, if he ever caught any of us sleeping, he would personally kick the chairs right out from under our butts. "Don't even think about it, you #&+##%@ instant insects!"

Well, very soon we decided that we had to get some sleep regardless of what the chief threatened to do. This wasn't mutiny. We simply couldn't stay awake. So a plan was launched to take our chances and catch some shuteye, and it went like this. When Chief Knowles said, "All right, you #&+##%@ instant insects, let's rig for movies!" and then he switched on the projector, turned off the lights, and left the room, in a flash, one of us would post guard, give the all clear, and around the room you would hear, "Good night, Rick. Good night, Fred." And so forth. At OCS, we mastered the art of catching a nap any legitimate occasion that was available, and I learned to fall asleep in 1 minute flat. Likewise, we could wake up instantly when anyone sounded the alarm, "He's coming!" which happened many times.

We college boys thought we were so smart, convincing ourselves that we were pulling one over on BMCM Knowles. To the contrary, when I got to know him better, I became sure he knew exactly what we were doing. My guess is that he spent a lot of time in the other room chuckling over our erroneous cockiness. Actually, the chief turned out to be one of my favorite people at OCS, and my respect for him runs deep. This was a man who had put his life on the line many times during his naval career and who had lived through several harrowing near death escapes such as when his ship was sunk in combat. That screaming and threatening was just part of his repertoire to let us know that we had a great deal to learn. Chief Knowles was just doing his job. And you don't make E-9, master chief in the Navy, unless you are outstanding. This is the highest enlisted rank you can earn, and I was always honored when a master chief worked for me. They were the true technical experts in the Navy, not the officers.

Finishing School

Clearing the two-month hurdle was monumental for most of us. While the rigors of OCS remained, our self doubts began to dissipate. We could sense that we not only were going to graduate but also do just fine as naval officers. After 2 months at OCS, a period when we became fully entrenched in the Navy culture and mastered the ropes on getting through our long days and academic classes, there was a pronounced change in my buddies and me. It helped that we similarly noted changes in the demeanor of our officers and chiefs toward us, a transition that showed us more respect and conveyed their growing faith in our potential to make the grade in the fleet. It felt very good.

Pass in Review

Every Saturday morning, the entire regiment of 4 battalions and 16 companies, nearly 2,000 officer candidates in total, staged an impressive marching drill called Pass in Review (PIR). This was part of our military training in discipline and precision and a competition to win the colors as best company that week. Although I wish I could rave about Hotel's PIR record, for most of my time at OCS, Hotel was terrible, repeatedly finishing near the bottom of the heap because somebody or several candidates always messed up. Because this was embarrassing and the ridicule we took from other companies unacceptable, we made a vow to get better. So we worked at it during the weekday drills, and one week we stunned everybody in Newport by going from 16th the prior week, dead last, to 1st, winning the competition. You would have thought we won the war by ourselves. All we really were trying to do was get into the top four companies. Nobody was happier than our company chief, GMCM (Master Chief Gunner's Mate) H. E. McQueen, a great guy we really liked.

You should have been there to see his reaction. "I can't believe it; I can't believe it." Over and over he kept mumbling this. He was dumbfounded and celebrated with us. Honestly, we were happier for him than for ourselves. He was our leader, and we wanted him to look good. I wish I could tell you that our success forever changed Hotel Company. The very next week, we finished 15th, the catcalls returned, and if I recollect correctly, we never cracked the top ranks again. Still, we did it once, and it felt great. No doubt it's better to win once than never.

With the end of OCS in sight, people in the section started to get a little slaphappy. As a result, we started doing things unimaginable during our first month in boot camp, I mean, OCS. One night we instantaneously forgot who we were and started sailing our covers (hats) up and down the hall like Frisbees. Who knows what started it or why. We were just letting off steam and howling like skinny dippers in mixed company. But the greatest OCS story I ever heard is this one.

"All Secure, Sir!"

Each night one of our section members had the duty to haul the collected trash for 16 rooms out of Nimitz Hall to the Dempsey Dumpster, and it had to be done in the 30-minute slot between 10:00 and 10:30 p.m. Nobody liked this job because it left the pack mule no time to clean up for bed, plus the bearer had to hustle to get back before curfew because it was about a quarter-mile round trip. The dumpster, a semi-trailer-like trash box, was in the parking lot way behind Nimitz.

One night I noticed a buddy taking his time and encouraged him to speed it up or he wasn't going to finish in time. He said, "Screw it." He told me he was tired of running his fanny off every time someone said "Jump." So he took his time, and I knew he would never make it on schedule.

The next morning, I asked him what happened, and he told me this tale. True to his plan, he walked, not ran, to the Dempsey Dumpster where he proceeded to climb the 10 steps to the platform from which we threw the trash in the trailer. As he neared the top, he thought he heard a distant noise and when he looked back, he was startled to see a man in uniform turning the corner of Nimitz Hall and heading toward him. So he said he did the first thing that came to his mind. He opened the dumpster lid, jumped in, lowered the lid, and prayed. Shortly, he heard footsteps coming across the tarred parking lot and slowly up the dumpster steps. "Thump, thuMP, THUMP" they came. Then the dumpster lid began to open.

"What did you do?" I asked.

"I snapped to attention, gave a salute, and said, 'The Dempsey Dumpster is all secure, sir!'"

At which point he heard. "Very well." And the lid was slowly lowered, and the officer left.

Isn't it nice to know that even staff officers have a sense of humor? My friend got back late to his room but not a single word or repercussion ever resulted from his dumpster incident. Officers like this one are the men I most appreciated in the Navy.

The Gouge (the Word)

In retrospect, OCS was a lot of things to a lot of people. Our commanding officer, Capt. Lemmon, once told us, "After you've been through OCS, you can leave the Navy, but the Navy will never leave you." This I found to be true. Officer Candidate School was designed to teach civilians the system, its regulations, and its requirements, and while we both respected and feared this system, it brought to us discipline and a new sense of alliance, a tacit bond between the men in our section and company. And while I have made light of some of my OCS memories, let me assure you that OCS was a serious business that the staff and candidates approached with determination, for in short order the decisions OCS graduates would make had the potential to save or kill people, especially the enlisted personnel we would lead. Such are the accepted responsibilities of naval officers soundly instilled in us at Newport.

OCS was all about attitude, learning to take orders before we gave them, and getting in excellent physical shape. In some ways it was like going to college; the significant difference was in how determined officer candidates were to learn the material. OCS taught me a deeper understanding of military history and culture and how good it felt to become a member of my new military family. The place only admitted bright, competent men with leadership potential and transformed them into a brotherhood of teammates dedicated to serving our country with honor and distinction. Wearing that uniform and my ensign bar made me feel a part of something very special, and I have never lost that good sensation. Capt. Lemmon was right. Although I spent just four years on active duty, the Navy is still a big part of me.

Navy Supply Corps School

Right after graduation, Sharon and I packed our things and drove to Athens, Georgia, home of the Navy Supply Corps School (NSCS). This pretty, small Southern city seemed like a most strange place for a Navy base, seeing as how it is about 225 miles from the ocean. Illogical or not, the Classic City had been the site for the Navy's business school since 1954, and every Navy supply officer since 1954 has graduated from there. I cannot imagine a Navy school held in higher esteem by its graduates. NSCS was the finest 6-months of business school I ever experienced.

Along with 31 other newly commissioned ensigns and warrant officers, I was assigned to Echo Company (1967). To the person, we were very focused on learning the curriculum as well as possible because we knew we would need all the knowledge we could absorb to handle the demanding jobs on the horizon. More than 80% of supply officers leaving NSCS traditionally went to sea, often as the only supply officer responsible for every business endeavor on a destroyer. Most of the others would go to larger ships like aircraft carriers where they might specialize in disbursing and pay 5,000 people or have 300 people working for them in food service. But since no one knew what assignments would follow, NSCS prepared everyone identically for essentially "the worst case scenario," being the only supply officer on a small ship with total supply responsibilities.

Navy supply officers are called Pork Chops. I know it sounds strange, but the nickname comes from the corps' insignia, an oak leaf cluster, that does indeed look a lot like a pork chop. And we like being called Pork Chops because we are proud of the Corps' rich 200-year tradition of service to the fleet. There's an old saying that an army moves on its stomach. So does the Navy. Pork Chops not only feed the fleet but also pay and clothe sailors, launder their uniforms, cut their hair, and keep ships supplied with whatever is needed to keep them armed, running, and fueled. Most people understand how crucial our job is to military operations.

Definitely Not OCS

NSCS was quite different from OCS, for now we were officers and treated with the respect and courtesy accompanying the rank. Although we still faced inspections, the yelling and harassment were over. And, thank God I was again free to live at home with Sharon. What supply school closely resembled was graduate school except we were treated with far more dignity in the Navy. And while we were still primarily students at NSCS, now we were full-fledged members of the Navy family. And always we were welcomed at the Officers Club.

NCSC had a rigorous curriculum that was taught by highly experienced fleet supply officers and chiefs. Classes provided current, practical, fleet-tested information. In addition, the courses and daily lessons were meticulously planned and integrated like no others I ever saw on university campuses.

The day we hit Athens, every student automatically became Ensign W. B. Ellis, the supply officer on the USS Duarte (DD-901), and every assigned task made us do something that ENS Ellis had to do on his destroyer and to/with/for the people in the crew.   For example, one class might have us compute MM2 (machinist's mate) Hodge's pay and then make payroll.   In another Hodges would be in the supply office requisitioning parts to repair a motor.   In a third we would be supervising him on KP (kitchen patrol) duty. NSCS was like one vast 6-month-long totally connected relevant case analysis. It was as if we were actually at sea doing ENS W. B. Ellis's job leading his enlisted men and solving problems that we would soon face. NSCS's motto is "Ready for Sea," and the instructors made sure we were as ready as they could possibly make us.

When people ask me what I did at supply school, I tell them I went to class from 8 a.m. until late afternoon each day, carried a ton of thick manuals everywhere I went, constantly updated those manuals with errata, studied several hours in the evenings, and spent as much of the remaining time with Sharon trying to continue our OCS-interrupted honeymoon year. If you ask the bachelors in my class the same question, I believe they would answer that they squeezed in more socializing and sports. In fact, they still get a big smile on their faces when you mention the NSCS Officers Club and University of Georgia coeds in the same breath. You see, when we attended NSCS, Clarke County where Athens is located was a dry county. The only two places one could buy a drink at a bar were the VFW and the O'Club, and the latter and its handsome ensigns were a magnet for cute coeds, which UGA had in abundance and still does. More than a few ensigns met their wives in Athens, another reason why they love the place so much.

Ready for SEAP

Mainly what we studied were disbursing, personnel administration, supply management, food service/retail, and computers. Again, grades were important because our future billets (job assignments) were highly correlated to our overall grade-point averages. The latter were computed by averaging all our course grades and printing a weekly public list in descending order and to hundredths of a decimal point. Believe me when I say that list got everyone's attention. The gouge was that 95% of my class was going to sea. Had I been single, hitting the high seas would have been terrific, but since I married Sharon before I joined the

Navy, I figured that she would see a whole lot more of me if I got one of those rare shore billets. The odds of that happening were low but not impossible. Some people, however, just struggled to pass the courses, and for them NSCS created SEAP.

SEAP stood for the "Student Educational Assistance Program," a mostly involuntary tutoring lab for students in academic trouble. It worked well, but in no time "Ready for SEAP" emerged as the supply school's more humorous second motto. Interestingly, one of the finest leaders the Navy Supply Corps ever had told me he spent a lot of time in SEAP, which proves once again that natural intelligence and high grades are overrated as keys to leadership results.

The good news is that I not only managed to avoid SEAP but did well academically achieving an overall grade-point average (GPA) of something like 89.51%, very good by any measure because NSCS wasn't easy. The bad news was that my company broke the all time NSCS record for GPA. What are the odds of being a member of the brightest supply school class ever? Therefore, I wound up ranked at about the 50th percentile. That convinced me I was going to sea, so I requested a submarine tender because such vessels tend to stay in port more than others. So you can guess how surprised I was when my orders directed me to report to foreign shore duty at the Navy Supply Depot, Subic Bay, Philippines and that it was an accompanied tour. That meant Sharon would be joining me at Subic not long after I arrived. We were so happy.

Final NSCS Thoughts

Soon after Echo Company graduated on August 10, 1967, my bride and I left Athens and NSCS for what we thought would be the last time. I had no intention of making the Navy a career. All I wanted to do was serve my time on active duty, enjoy the experience, and do the best job I could. At the time, I knew several important things. For six months, I had moved in lock step with some of the most motivated men I could ever imagine knowing, people who without question I believed were going to be very successful whether in military or civilian life. We were good friends who helped each other in class and enjoyed each other's company. Additionally, I learned a lot about teaching business students, something then that I had no way of realizing would help me considerably when I eventually became a business professor. Next, I felt well prepared and reasonably confident that I could handle my first supply job. Another conclusion was that I didn't need to know everything about supply. There would be others, particularly skilled enlisted men, to help and teach me. And last, Athens was a very nice town. Sharon and I liked it there. With these thoughts and nearly one full year of schooling behind me, it was time to get to work. I had no idea what I was going to do at Subic, but I was eager to find out.

Welcome to the Philippines

From 10,000 feet, the land below the breaking clouds looked peaceful and green, a scene of countless rice paddies cut by occasional rivers and dotted with small villages. This was Luzon, one of the Philippine archipelago's 7,107 islands bordered by the Pacific Ocean to the east and South China Sea on the west. When our chartered jet touched down at Clark Air Force Base, Charlie Truett, my Echo Company classmate, and I were greeted by LT Majors, who had driven the 60 miles from Subic Bay Naval Base to pick us up. For a moment I was stumped. I thought he said lieutenant major, a rank that I had never heard of. Then I got it. When Charlie and I introduced ourselves, LT Majors said, "We knew Charlie was coming but not you." How reassuring.

The next morning CAPT Everett, Commanding Officer of the Naval Supply Depot (NSD), asked his department heads who needed me. Max VanValkenberg, Department Head of the Freight Terminal Department, said he did. Thus I was assigned under Max, a fortuitous bit of luck for me as later pages in this book will verify.

I came to the Philippines about as ignorant of NSD as one could imagine; nevertheless, I immediately began grasping the significance not only of NSD but of Subic Bay Naval Base, both of which were the largest of their kind in the Far East. Lying less than 1,000 miles east of Vietnam, my new home was the Navy's biggest offshore support base for the U.S. Navy fighting the war. At times the harbor was filled with 30 or more warships seeking supplies, fuel, repairs, and R & R (rest and recreation). Subic was an incredibly busy, exciting place.

Max appointed me Household Goods Division Director. This meant I would be the officer in charge of handling the furniture, appliances, cars, and personal property of more than 10,000 military and civilian workers and managing an office of approximately 20 employees. It also meant that I had a job for which I had not had one hour of NSCS training. What helped me succeed were my skilled, patient, and highly professional employees.

The first thing I learned is how much people love their personal property. Next to family, nothing meant more. Especially this is true of heirlooms and family photographs because so many of them are irreplaceable and are direct links to special memories. My problem was that I could manage a shipment of 10,000 pounds of furniture, get it to Subic 12,000 miles from its origin not only on time but also early, and if one beloved wine glass was broken, the shipment was a failure in my customer's eyes. Another lesson learned was that I was going to catch the blame for things over which my office had no control, such as damage caused by a packer in New Jersey. All of this taught me to treat the items we did pack and ship with special care, and we did this very well most of the time, but much to my chagrin, not always.

"Has My Car Arrived Yet?"

I guess I had been on the job about 2 months when an enlisted man began calling me regularly inquiring when his car was going to arrive in Subic. He was an E5[1] enlisted man with far more years in the Navy than me, whom I will call ET2 (electronics mate) Smith.* As I always did when such shipment status requests were made, I would check the records and provide the most accurate estimate of the due date. Unfortunately, for unexplained reasons Smith's car was far behind schedule, and it was obvious that he was getting more frustrated by the day.

---

[1] There are nine enlisted ranks. E1 is the lowest and E9 is the highest enlisted rank. An ET2 is an E5, the mid level of the enlisted ranks. There were 3 levels of chiefs. An ETC is an E7 chief; an ETCS is an E8 senior chief; and an ETCM is an E9 master chief. The rank between an ET2 and ETC is ET1. The letters preceding the rank identified the enlisted person's rating, that is, his or her specialized skill area.

* If you see this symbol, the name is fictitious.

One Monday I got to work early, grabbed a mug of coffee, flopped in my chair, and put my feet on the desk. I was in such a good mood because things had been going so well. Then the phone rang, and the conversation went like this.

"Ensign Stephenson, this is Enrique* at the freight terminal. You need to come over here right away."

"Why, Enrique?"

"Just come over here soon and meet me at my office. I'll tell you then."

I hate calls like that because they seldom mean anything good is following. At any rate, I jumped in my vehicle and headed for the docks. Enrique was my household goods receiving clerk, and his office was at the far end of the warehouse on the pier.

Upon arrival at the ocean freight terminal, I parked the truck and began the long walk to my destination. Half way there I noticed a large object about three feet high covered by a tarp. I debated going over to inspect it, but feeling an urgency to keep going, I passed it by. A few minutes later, I reached Enrique's office.

"Hi, boss. Sorry to bother you."

"OK, Enrique, what's the problem?"

"On your way here, did you see a blue tarp covering an object on the pier?"

"Yes."

"Well there's a car under it. We dropped it from the sling while offloading it from the ship. It flipped over and fell 40 feet onto the pier, flattening it like a pancake. You need to call the owner."

I'm thinking, "Me? Did I do this? You want me to call the owner?" But I just said, "Let's go look at it and see whose it is."

Well, much to my dismay, that car was none other than ET2 Smith's. Now what? You can not imagine how much I dreaded making that call.

So I returned to my office, my great day now a wreck, living Murphy's Law ("*Whatever can go wrong will.*"), convinced that Schultz's law was right ("*Murphy was an optimist.*"), and knowing that this day I must make that call. Let me digress briefly. I was an officer. Smith was an enlisted man. Why was I worried about Smith's reaction? My answer to you is that protocol is not exactly what most civilians believe. A lot can be said forcefully to an officer, particularly to an ensign, without crossing the line that results in retribution. In my opinion, Smith was simply a man, and no doubt he was going to be really upset and deservedly so for our mistake. So I did what any unsure novice would do. I practiced over and over what I was going to say to him until I had the message right and the guts to make the call. It went as follows.

"Is this ET2 Smith?"

"Yes, it is. Is this ENS Stephenson?"

"Yes."

"I thought I recognized your voice. Did my car come in?"

"Yes."

"You don't sound too good. Is it OK? It's not totaled, is it?"

"Unfortunately, yes. We had an accident."

At this point I was waiting for the inevitable uncontrollable burst of outrage from Smith, but what he next said blew my mind.

"Great! It was a piece of junk anyway. I'd rather collect the insurance."

From that day forward I never quite got as nervous about calling anyone. People are so unpredictable.

That Log's Moving

Jobs on overseas bases are unique adventures filled with the unexpected. One day we unloaded a man's household goods just in from the states and found 13 refrigerators inside. What the heck was he or his stateside household goods agent thinking? The answer was that he was a Filipino working for the government and returning to his native land for retirement, and he thought he would ship, illegally I would add, a bunch of appliances back to his native country to make some bucks selling them on the black market. On other occasions, we would open shipments from the states and find coffee grounds still in the pots where packers had taken everything as is and shoved it in boxes. A lot of weird things happened in the Household Goods Department.

Another story I love was one told to me by my chief household goods inspector. Very early one foggy morning he was driving to a home near the base hospital on a road that passed through dense tropical foliage, jungle, actually, when at a bend he noticed a log across the 2-lane street. What made it really unusual was that the log had a big bump in it. Since he couldn't drive over it, he stopped his vehicle. Suddenly, the log started to move. That was no log but a huge python that eventually was caught. It was 26-feet long, and the bump was a 50-pound pig it had swallowed. And it was living on the base near residential quarters. Did I tell you that the Philippines has many snakes, including by one estimate, hundreds of varieties of poisonous snakes including cobras which we occasionally found around base homes?

Speaking of snakes, I noticed that very few Americans went into the rough to retrieve errant golf balls. But now listen to what transpired in our back yard. One day I came home to find the neighborhood in hyper mode. It turns out that someone spotted a python's head right behind our home on base, I mean less than 100 feet from our back door. Immediately a call was placed to the base snake-catching squad to come get it, but the team was not successful. So leave it to a Texan to solve the problem.

What Sharon told me was that our neighbor, a fellow officer who lived directly opposite us on Grouper Street, said, "I'll get it." And he went into his home for his lariat. I'm not kidding. And when the snake lifted his head, he dropped that rope around its neck like the steers he used to catch back home. It took four men to pull that 16-foot snake out of the vegetation, and I have to tell you it was a beautiful reptile. It also had three dog and cat collars in it, which explained where the missing neighborhood pets had gone. The Texan staged a Grouper Street python barbeque where we all got to taste this renowned Philippine delicacy. In chapter 1, I told you my reaction. But we were young and willing to try most anything. At least I was.

FTD

I only stayed in household goods for 5 months. No, they didn't fire me. The captain wanted me to relieve Jeff Mason as NSD Disbursing Officer. Why, I questioned, did they want to take me away from a job that I had just figured out? But that is the Navy Supply Corps' way. Senior officers display great faith in the ability of the Corps' officers to handle multiple tasks and quickly grasp the essentials of new jobs. This in turn is a great confidence builder, plus it kept us highly motivated because there was no time to get bored. However, before I take us to the Disbursing Office, I need to comment on a part of my prior job that really turned me on, and that was night duty officer at the pier.

Periodically, each supply officer in the Freight Terminal Department stood night duty at the ocean terminal. This was our central receiving point for ships bringing in general cargo and containers for Subic as well as Clark Air Force Base and other U.S. Philippine installations. I must admit that the idea of working all day and then all night for 24-hours straight was not appealing. That is, until I found I could crawl all over those ships from the bridge to deep inside the holds and often eat fine meals with the officers in the wardrooms. This duty introduced me to Sea-Land, an American company started by Malcolm McLean, a man who did not invent containerized shipping but proved that it worked and at a profit. Some of the first ships Sea-Land ever put in service came to NSD Subic while I was there.

International shipping totally fascinated me, and in these vessels and their 35-foot-long boxes we shipped everything we could including cars. Max deserves a lot of credit for the success of containerization world wide. He grasped its potential, encouraged its use, and defended its continuance against higher-ups who questioned its benefits. Today, containerization is the way virtually all general cargo moves between major ports internationally, and I was a part of its birth.

Three Greatest Days at Subic

Hail and farewell parties were a tradition at NSD, a chance for departing officers and U.S. Civil Service employees to say their good-byes and the occasion to welcome newcomers to Subic Bay. It was a good time for all. The tradition was that departing officers had to take the floor and say a few words. Usually they made serious, reflective comments about how much they loved the place and would miss their friends, but not always. One of our lieutenants dropped this gem on our unsuspecting captain and us when he said, "There are three great days at Subic. The day your household goods arrive. The day your wife arrives. And most importantly, the day you get your orders to leave." You had to be there waiting for your furniture to finally show up, waiting for your spouse, and longing to see your loved ones in the states to fully appreciate the hilarity those words produced, even as exaggerated as they really were, for I do miss those times and people at Subic.

It took quite a few weeks before Sharon joined me in Luzon, but I can assure you I was thrilled when her plane touched down at Clark AFB. Our immediate task was getting settled into our apartment in Olongapo, the town adjacent to the base. Since we were far down the waiting list, we knew it would be many months before we received our on-base quarters.

On the High Seas

Right after Sharon arrived, NSD sent me on two weeks of temporary duty to the USS Intrepid, an aircraft carrier at Yankee Station in the South China Sea.[2] A carrier is something to behold anytime but particularly so during wartime operations. Although one of the Navy's oldest carriers, the Intrepid was still a big, highly effective warship. For two weeks I watched the intensity and professionalism of 3,700 men performing very dangerous jobs, working day and night flight operations, and routinely handling 16-hour days. Nothing impressed me more than the 18 and 19-year-old sailors doing their crucial jobs on the flight deck arming aircraft and launching and retrieving jets where even the slightest lapse in concentration could have killed people and lost multi-million-dollar machines. After seeing how responsible and capable these young men were, I found it very hard later in life to buy the excuses I heard from college kids rationalizing their poor behavior or failures on being young. Navy personnel on aircraft flight decks do incredible feats not once but hundreds of times during a cruise. And most of them haven't reached the age of 20 when they are doing this.

During my days at sea, I thoroughly explored the ship and met and talked with many officers and enlisted people. The most instructive were the pilots, men who flew the combat missions into Vietnam, people who opened my eyes to the difficulty of their tasks and their frustrations with bureaucrats. One explained that U.S. military pilots were required to fly certain vectors to reach targets. By this I mean

---

[2] If you are ever in New York City, the Intrepid is located at a pier there and is open to the public.

civilian officials in Washington set policies that ordered combat pilots to take certain routes, which everybody knew including our enemies who lined their SAM missiles and anti-aircraft weapons along them to shoot down U.S. planes. He told me it was like fighting a war with his hands tied behind his back, and his argument made great sense to me. That ridiculous policy cost American lives.

Another told me the story of a Russian ship sitting at a pier in a harbor in North Vietnam that Washington said under no circumstances was to be targeted. This was an American policy set by politicians trying not to offend the Soviet Union. However, the ship was nothing more than a decoy, a screen for a SAM site on the pier. One day a SAM launched from that site shot down this pilot's friend. He told me he saw the whole thing. "And I didn't care what country that ship was from. When my friend's plane went down, I blasted the hell out of that SAM site." I was proud of him and would have done the same thing.

We didn't win that war in Vietnam, but I remain convinced that we could have if Americans hadn't caved in internally and politicians had demonstrated more common sense. What most troubles me, however, is the disgraceful way many of our citizens treated returning veterans who were just doing their duty. I hoped that America never again would send its sons and daughters to war without giving them every means to win and return them home safely and with gratitude. Two weeks at sea were sufficient to intensify my respect for our combat forces and motivate me to do everything I could at NSD to support their efforts.

Life in Olongapo

Our off-base apartment in Olongapo was something to behold. For starters, when we got it the place was stripped clean. Even the light bulbs were missing. So I screwed in a bulb and to my amazement it got brighter and brighter and then popped. I just assumed it was a faulty bulb and screwed in another. Pop! I got the same result. Only then did I realize we had 220-volt current, which is typical in the Philippines but was foreign to me. Next I learned from our blown out stereo that the current also fluctuated. It surged and destroyed the speakers. Now, try to imagine what happened every evening when the nightclubs opened along the Olongapo strip. Our lights dimmed and stayed dimmed. "Adjust, Fred," I kept telling myself. This wasn't home.

The Philippines is a year round hot place. Subic, which is located a few degrees north of the Equator, has two main seasons, not fall or spring, but rainy season and dry season. The former runs from June to October and provides most of the 160 inches of annual rainfall. March to May is the dry season, a period of virtually no rain and plenty of dust. Most people, as a result, preferred November to February. I forgot to mention that our apartment had no air conditioning.

So how hot did it get? Hot enough to turn straight foot-long candles into 180-degree arcs. That was how hot it got in one day alone. It happened in our living room. Then there was our water system. No, we were not on a municipal water system but instead derived our water from a private tank in the back yard that was perched high enough to let gravity do its job. Our shower was even more intriguing. We had hot water, but to get it, we turned a water valve and pressed a switch that sent a trickle through a small electric coil that heated the water during its downward descent. Most of the time this worked OK, that is, until the workers moved into our back yard.

One day without warning a truck with four men drove into our back yard. Our landlord sent them. For six months, they lived right outside our bedroom window and never left. Their mission was to build another apartment on the lot, which they did almost non-stop. Every concrete brick was made individually in a box. Each board was hand-planed from rough-sawed lumber and cut to length and width on the spot. But the worst thing was when I was totally lathered in soap in our shower and the water stopped. The culprit was the crew tapping our tank water for the bricks. If you want to duplicate the sensation, on the hottest day of the year, soap yourself all over and go outside for 30 minutes. But this was just life in Olongapo.

Did I tell you about the pig? Necessity required that we sleep with the windows open and the fans on to make it through the night. This in turn had culturally enlightening dividends such as from hearing some very strange noises, like a significant series of crashes that woke us up just about every morning during the dry season. When I couldn't take it any more, I laid in wait for the party causing the problem. And one morning I caught her doing the deed. It was this humongous Philippine sow, a 400-pound pot-bellied pig that was walking down our street, back and forth from one side to the other, knocking over everybody's trash barrel so her ten little piglets could eat. Ever experience that in your U.S. community? I left the pig alone. There was no way I was going to confront a 400-pound protective mother.

Kalayaan

We will never forget the day we first saw our on-base residence at 3A Grouper Street, the right half of a lovely duplex set high on the side of a hill in the jungle in the Kalayaan officer housing area. Now we finally had many of the amenities of stateside living, 110-volt electricity, base water, a nice grassy yard, and much improved safety. Plus we had good friends who frequently gathered at one another's homes for parties and at the Cubi Point beach or one of the officers' clubs for enjoyable times together. If you have ever wondered how people lived before television, this was another good example. Many happy hours were spent just enjoying each other's company. And there is nothing quite like a quiet afternoon on a South Seas island beach. I really miss that experience.

However, when you are so far away from home, it takes no time at all to develop a craving for the things Americans so regularly take for granted, such as fresh milk. It took me two years to satisfy that need. And I longed for specialties like desserts. One day I had this powerful urge for ice cream and saw banana splits advertised on the base restaurant menu. So I ordered one. What was delivered was ice cream on two canned peach halves with various sauces on top. Now, I'm sorry, but this is not a banana split.

"The banana. Where is it?" I asked the waiter.

"We don't have any."

Look, we lived in one of the banana capitals of the world. Indeed, a banana tree full of the ripe fruit greeted me next to the restaurant's front door as I had entered. And I took the waiter for a walk to show it to him. Still, I only got the peaches.

This was a great lesson in cultural differences. Banana splits were foreign to my waiter's diet just like marinated barbecued python was abnormal to mine. Keep that in mind when you travel.

The Stud

Many officers' wives got pregnant in the Philippines including Sharon who was expecting our first baby. Late in her pregnancy, she whispered, "I think my water broke." That definitely got my attention. But she was only in her eighth month, and this was not a gusher. That made us wonder if it was a false alarm. However, for cautionary reasons, she gathered her belongings, and we drove the six miles to the base hospital. There, Sharon insisted I leave her suitcase in the car because she was convinced she was not staying. Then I walked her to the reception area where we met a Filipino nurse who told her that indeed she needed to check into the hospital. Sharon then told me to get her things from the car, but to my astonishment, in that brief time, someone had stolen her suitcase. So I returned to the hospital, reported the theft, and asked Sharon what to do next. All she said was "Go get my things from home and bring them here."

I didn't have a clue what "things" meant and told her.

"Then go get Judy. She'll know what I need."

Thus, I drove to our friend's place, picked her up, went to Grouper Street, grabbed some clothes, and headed back to the hospital. Once there, Judy and I walked into the building where we ran into the very same nurse.

Her look was priceless. You see, Judy was quite pregnant herself, and this nurse just assumed I had made her so. It was clear to both Judy and me that the nurse thought I was quite some stud. I could tell she admired me. Judy and I often joked that we should have gone home right then to get Nina, another friend who was about 8-months pregnant as well. It would have been worth it to see the nurse's expression. That was the only time in my life anyone ever considered me studly.

On a more serious note, Sharon presented me with the most beautiful brown-haired daughter, Kathryn Elizabeth Stephenson, that I have ever seen (yes, I am biased) and joy beyond description. My number one dream, to become a father, had become reality, and I just couldn't stop thinking about this wonderful blessing we had been given.

Disbursing

You will never know how glad I was that I took six months of disbursing classes at NSCS when I got my orders to take over the NSD Disbursing Officer (DO) duties. This was a huge operation paying 20,000 military, U.S. Civil Service, and Philippine national personnel, managing three offices on three bases (the others were Cubi Point Naval Air Station and San Miguel), paying all the invoices for debts incurred by the Navy, and serving as the funding officer for the Seventh Fleet. By the latter, I mean supplying all the ships coming into Subic with cash for their payrolls.

It was a big responsibility managing 50 individuals including 7 chiefs and a civilian supervisor and millions of dollars in cash, and I do mean millions. At one time I had more than $12-million in cash in my safes. And if any of that was ever taken and if I, as Disbursing Officer, had not done everything I could to have prevented it, I could have been subject to repayment charges or even jail time. This is the difference between responsibility and accountability, and I was accountable and uneasy. Disbursing taught me that money tempts honest people to do dishonest deeds. Not everyone is honest, including some disbursing officers, and we were told that there were more former Navy disbursing officers in Portsmouth Naval Prison than any other type of officers. I wasn't worried about my honesty, but the rest of my concerns were legitimate, given that I was robbed twice while the DO.

It took me one month to count all the money and checks, put my name on the dotted line assuming full accountability, and relieve Jeff Mason (Judy's husband), the prior disbursing officer and the person who became my best friend at Subic. He influenced that friendship substantially the first day on the job, for I was $10,000 short and couldn't find it. In a cold sweat, I knocked on Jeff's door and told him I needed help. Calmly he responded that we'd check it out after dinner and a beer. On his face was not one sign of concern. However, unlike yours truly, he had a master's degree in accounting from the University of Chicago, and I didn't even have a business degree. So he took his time, and I stayed tense, but eventually we meandered over to the disbursing office where in one minute, he pronounced, "There it is. You transposed these two numbers. Actually, you were $10,000 over." Now that is how you spell "RELIEF" and "STUPID" simultaneously, but it did warn me that if I was going to stay out of jail and avoid having a heart attack, I better calm down. When I took over disbursing, I was 24.

Scrooge McDuck Lives

There are so many good stories I could tell you about my 15 months as DO, but I'm forced to be choosy. Consequently, I'll tell you two of the better ones. The reason I feel OK discussing the first one is that the base no longer exists. So here goes.

As noted, my job was to provide the cash needed by the fleet, an amount that in the 1960s tallied about $10,000,000 a month. Therefore, I needed a monthly re-supply, and the way I received it was by aircraft, specifically a C-130 cargo plane that flew into Cubi Point. Money is heavy, so heavy in fact that one time this cargo plane had to return to the terminal because it was overloaded. All it had on it was cash and about 10 security people. I'm not talking a small plane here, but a four-engine big one. You're probably thinking bills; however, most of the weight was in change. Bags of change--quarters, dimes, nickels, and pennies--are heavy.

On one occasion after the plane touched down with my three tons of cash, I got a call from base security that we had a problem. During offloading, the forklift operator smashed open the crate holding the cash. He wanted instructions.

Well, I knew I couldn't leave it on the tarmac, and I was already on the way to Cubi with my escort pick-up truck in the lead, a semi-trailer flatbed next, another escort pick-up following, and in the company of my Marine disbursing clerk. He and I concluded that we would just have the money piled on the flatbed, he would ride on top of the pile with his 45-caliber pistol in clear view, and I would ride shotgun in the second pick-up, and that was what we did. And you can not believe the expressions we saw along the 5-mile stretch back to Subic. That Marine was not afraid of anything, but what he looked like atop a five-foot mountain of sacks of money and more than $6,000,000 was Scrooge McDuck, Donald's billionaire uncle.

Our first stop was the base bank where we offloaded all the change. I stayed with the truck. It seemed like the parade of employees hauling the cash took forever. What really fascinated me, however, was that the civilians just couldn't take their eyes off those bags of money. They were mesmerized by a bag of pennies worth $50, and I was sitting alone on a box that contained nearly a million dollars in twenties. They just didn't know that. Perception, perception, perception. By the way, do you know that a million in $20-dollar bills weighs 96 pounds? It's true. I picked it up once just so I knew what it felt like to be a millionaire, even if it wasn't mine. My annual salary at the time was $7,100 a year.

"Send the Worst One We've Got"

One day I received a set of orders directing the disbursing office to send one of our junior military disbursing clerks on 3 months of temporary duty to Singapore. Immediately I called my chief to the office to discuss this directive.

"What should we do, chief?"

"Send the worst man we have because we are not going to ever see him again. I bet you they will extend his orders, and he will stay there forever."

While I understood his logic, I had a hard time agreeing with it. We had many deserving young enlisted men working for us, guys who theoretically were eligible for nice R & R trips to Hong Kong and other attractive locations, yet in reality they seldom ever got to go. The reason was that there were limited aircraft seats available, and assignments were based primarily on time in the Philippines. As a result, most seats went to U.S. civil servants who had been at Subic for years, people who already had taken multiple trips. That didn't seem fair. Furthermore, I believed that rewarding the worst workers was bad policy. In Singapore, our DK was going to live in a three-bedroom home with all the amenities and work in civvies (civilian clothes), a far cry from barracks life.

Although it is not the greatest idea to override your top chief and definitely not after you asked his opinion, sometimes you gotta do what you gotta do. That is why you are the leader and boss. So I told him my thinking and asked him to watch all the junior enlisted men for a while and then tell me who the best worker was. A month later he entered my office and said, "It's DK3 Rodgers."*

"Good. Call everyone together because I am going to tell Rodgers the good news and everybody how we selected him."

If I interpreted the chief's facial expressions, skin color, and body language, any previous doubts that he worked for an idiot were gone. It is not the first time someone drew that conclusion. As for Rodgers, he looked like he had won a $300-million lottery, and I was very happy for him.

Thus, off he went to Singapore. And two months after he left NSD, his orders were extended for 3 more months and again, a few months later for a year. True to the chief's word, we never saw Rodgers again. Furthermore, every time a copy of the revised TAD orders came to the office, there was a most obvious, unspoken "I told you so!" expression emanating from the chief's unhappy face. And it was justified, because he and others had to pick up Rodgers' work in his absence for many months until his replacement arrived.

But my decision was not foolish. Everyone in that office worked incredibly hard for the rest of my days as DO, hoping for the next great set of TAD orders, which unfortunately never came. Not once in my entire life before or after did I ever intentionally reward the undeserving. It only encourages more of the same behavior or worse. However, when you do your job for me, you can take it to the bank that I will try to honor and reward you.

Far East Adventures

Sharon and I took a number of short trips to places in the Philippines like Baggio, a mountain retreat in northern Luzon, and to nearby Manila, Bataan, and Corregidor. We enjoyed seeing the countryside and loved our adventures like shooting the rapids in a dugout canoe to view majestic Pagsanjan Falls. Another great memory was our banca boat trips to the Caponi Islands for swimming and shell collecting. As our time at the base and savings increased, we also took trips to Hong Kong and Japan. The latter was where I was introduced to Japanese hot baths, high in the mountains of Honshu.

Upon checking in at our hotel, we were told that interested guests could use the natural hot baths up the road a piece free of charge. My modest wife, at the thought of being naked with other women in a public bath, said she would pass. I, the experienced skinny dipper, said,

"When in Rome, do as the Romans do." Besides, I was probably only going to get this opportunity once.

After dinner, I put on the robe and sandals provided in the room and walked up the hill to the bath building. In I went. Immediately, though, I discovered a problem. There were women's and men's sides but no directions in English, no attendants to ask, and no other people of either sex going through one entrance or the other. So I sat there until I saw a man choose the correct door. Then I followed him in. In the first room I found lockers located in the center and sinks all around the walls. The actual hot pools were in an adjacent room. I gathered that the idea was to clean up in the sink before getting into the pool. Thus, I got naked and walked to the sink--about 2 seconds before a Japanese woman walked into the locker room to talk with her husband, the other guy keeping me company! I kid you not, if I could have jumped into that locker, it would have happened. I'm no exhibitionist, and I was definitely more modest than those two obviously were. Instead, I quickly slipped back into my robe and waited for her to leave, which she eventually did.

At that point, I said to heck with the sink. If I was going to take a hot bath, I was going now. Sound familiar? So I disrobed again, dashed to the next room, and slid my body into that water up to my neck, and that is the moment I thought I was dying. It was the hottest water I have ever experienced. But I got used to it, and after a few minutes, I became so relaxed and weak-kneed that I thought I might pass out. But I couldn't! Somehow, like at Winni, I had to get back to the locker and find my robe before somebody's girl friend came calling. Oh, did I tell you that a woman came into the pool area to chat with another man in there? It's true, and all that did was raise my anxieties even higher. This place was crawling with fully clothed females. I told you life is unfair.

When I shuffled in my sandals back to our hotel room, I replayed my adventure to Sharon who laughed her head off.

Are People Really Different?

The years have taught me that people of different cultures are similar in fundamental ways. Just like us, they worry about their children, desire to find meaningful work, and love freedom. But my experiences abroad revealed many significant cultural differences as well, such as in what people eat and their traditions, norms, beliefs, and even practices. I learned not to assume too much about anything, particularly that people think like we do. They also don't behave as we do. Another of my Japanese experiences illustrates this latter point. While I was using a urinal, a cleaning woman suddenly appeared and began scrubbing the one next to mine. To her, this was perfectly normal behavior. To me, it was embarrassing.

One of my findings is that Americans are not the only people with cultural biases. During this trip to Japan, Sharon and I were called ugly Americans, the only time we ever felt the sting of that degrading and often irresponsible put down. The setting was a vast theater where we were seated, behaving ourselves, and enjoying a live Japanese stage performance. Suddenly, a row started between the couple sitting right next to us and a man and woman just behind them. Something the woman in our row did offended the woman behind, and the latter spoke to the first woman about it. Angered by the complaint, the first female put her program behind her head to block the woman's view. Reacting quickly, the woman behind grabbed the glasses of the person in front and snapped them in two. Then both couples began arguing with each other in English. It was really irritating and upsetting.

Then we heard a voice behind say in broken English, "Ugly American." Then another person repeated it and another, as Japanese patrons reacted to the inconsiderate, obnoxious behavior of the people near us.

Here's the mistake. While both couples spoke English, they were definitely not Americans. Lots of people around the world speak English, for goodness sake, but Americans don't have the accents these four people did. I don't know what countries they were from, but it wasn't the United States. However, it was assumed that the low-lifes had to be Americans because the Japanese who said "ugly Americans" wanted to believe it was so. The only two Americans present were just trying to enjoy the arts in peace.

I think the whole world needs to take a deep breath and understand that what appears so absolutely obvious is often still incorrect. In the meantime, if we must criticize each other, we have a responsibility to get the right people. I don't know about you, but I am getting tired of the anti-American bias. Sharon and I first saw it in Japan, and now it's almost epidemic. Most of it is unjust.

Thereafter

NSD did not end my active duty days. I requested and was granted an extension of duty and was reassigned to Quonset Point Naval Air Station in Rhode Island where for the final 13 months before going back to civilian life in 1970 I served as the base disbursing officer. That job, too, carried with it a lot of responsibility and satisfaction.

Serving in the military was truly a most rewarding experience. Though I didn't accomplish anything heroic or hugely significant, I am proud that I wore the uniform of a naval officer and helped my country. Like the more than 20 other people in Sharon's and my family who served in the military from the Civil War right through the current war on terror, we never shucked this duty. I'm proud of all of them but particularly my dad and his brothers who simultaneously fought in combat during World War II, Pop in the Navy in the Pacific, Raymond as a radioman working with the Signal Corps in the Army in several significant island battles in the Pacific, Bruce as a member of Patton's Army at the Battle of the Bulge, and Wilson who died in combat in France. We weren't warriors. Not one of us wanted to fight. It wasn't a passion. It was simply a responsibility that we honorably fulfilled.

The Navy remains a big part of me. I won't forget the outstanding and ever so competent individuals I worked under, beside, and over every point along the way. Since my release from active duty, I have heard many foolish, ignorant, even insulting comments about military people such as the remark by one of my faculty members in graduate school. He asked me if I had any management experience, and I replied, "Yes, in the Navy," and he fired back, "That doesn't count. I mean civilian experience." And I thought to myself how biased and wrong so many people who have not served must be, for I knew what I had just done and how demanding my jobs were.

In graduate school I got the distinct impression that many professors assumed the military ran by simply ordering those under us around. To the contrary, it is hard for me to recall even one instance following OCS when I was commanded to do something. Usually I was consulted and asked, and this is also the way I led my enlisted and civilian personnel, just as I know our son-in-law, CAPT John Spicer, SC, USN, motivates his people. I am not saying that there aren't exceptions, but the perception that most of us couldn't lead without pulling rank is ludicrous. Moreover, you don't become an officer by being average, and you don't get promoted or get to stay for a career if you don't consistently perform at high levels of achievement. And I can tell you from being the assistant NSD duty officer on January 23, 1968, on the evening of the day the USS Pueblo was illegally seized by the North Koreans, that the U.S. military can act quickly. Our crew re-supplied a squadron of nine ships that day with fuel, weapons, and other needs and sent them after the North Koreans, not in the normal 3 days but in 5 hours.

Mainly, however, I just wish people would appreciate more what military families contribute and distinguish between the civilians in Washington who set policy and the troops who have a legal obligation to carry out their directives. The military does not declare war but acts on the orders of this nation's elected and appointed officials. It furthermore concerns me, and it ought to concern all of us, that a decreasing percentage of our top elected officials in Congress have any actual military experience. Perhaps if more of their children put on the uniform they would see things more clearly.

On a more personal note, I will never be able to express my full gratitude for my Navy life. Definitely the Navy accelerated my maturity, clarified my priorities, and strengthened my leadership and management skills. The Supply Corps got me thinking like a businessman. In the Freight Terminal Department, I got my first work experience in transportation and logistics, a field I find so fascinating. Through the G.I. Bill, I received scholarship money that provided Sharon and me the incentive to further my education. The Navy gave me many good opportunities to test and prove myself. It exposed Sharon and me to distant lands, exciting adventures, and unique cultures and people. It gave us Katie, our wonderful daughter who was born in the Philippines, and Jeff and Judy Mason, two of the best friends we have ever had. It made us feel like valued members of so many new families such as the Supply Corps and Subic and Quonset Point communities.

Any regrets? Sure, there are always regrets. If I did it over, I would make a much stronger effort to get to know the Filipinos who worked for me better. They were good, honest, and generous people. I also really wish I had experienced a full sea tour because I know I missed a great adventure and envy the camaraderie that my son-in-law shares with me in his tales of shipboard life. It's likewise really disappointing that when I became a professor I failed to motivate more of my college students to join the officer ranks and at the least just investigate this option before closing their minds, for they missed great experiences as a result. Finally, it's a shame more Americans do not live overseas for at least a year. Anywhere is fine with me, for I know it would deepen their love and respect for this great nation, make them more appreciative of its bountiful blessings that they daily take for granted, and certainly enrich their understanding and acceptance of others.

Friends, life is about opportunities. First you have to see them. Second you need to seize them when you get the chance, for who is to say you will get another chance. Thank God I took my opportunity to become a naval officer. It was an honor to have served our country and my fellow citizens.

TEACHER

For nearly half of my life, 31 years to be exact, I was a teacher, a proud one I would add. Never was there any doubt in my mind about the importance of teaching and education to my students' and this nation's futures. However, teaching was not one of my childhood career dreams. It just sort of happened. I also wasn't a born teacher. Whatever I accomplished as a teacher was more the result of a strong desire to learn, improve, and excel. It was the product, I believe, of commitment and hard work. But the most important thing I can share with you is that I made a great career choice, one that well matched my interests and skills with work that brought me considerable satisfaction and joy. And for these things, I am most grateful.

My boyhood dream was to become, like my hero Ted Williams, a professional baseball player. Ted was the greatest hitter of all time. In my teens I wanted to become a naval officer. So how did my path lead to teaching?

Listen to Your Mother

I'm now convinced it started with my mother, my closest boyhood mentor and a person who taught elementary school for quite a few years before marrying Pop and leaving the public schools to raise Eleanor and me. When we were young, Ma used to tell us stories about her former teaching days, and from the joyful expressions on her face and our conversations, it was clear to Eleanor and me that Ma really enjoyed teaching and was proud to have been a teacher. We also determined that she strongly believed that teaching was an honorable, vital profession.

Surprisingly, though, she offered the opinion that she was not a very good teacher. One of her former pupils convinced me otherwise.

As previously mentioned, I'm a crossbreed, the son of a Yankee father and a Southern mother. Following their marriage, Ma left her North Carolinian home for Rhode Island where Pop lived and worked. But on an annual basis, sometimes more frequently, we packed the car to the hilt and journeyed south to Burlington, North Carolina, to see our Southern relatives.

The first time I remember meeting one of Ma's former students was when I was 7 or 8 years old. I was doing two of my favorite things, swinging in Granny's back-porch hammock sipping a Coke, when a man knocked on the screen door asking for Miss Horne. Miss Horne was my mom. His reason for visiting, I quickly discovered, was to pay his respects to a teacher he loved. Granny explained later that due to a learning disability, this man really struggled to pass his school work. Worse, students and teachers alike ridiculed him for his inability to learn. Ma, his fourth grade teacher, did something incredibly important that changed his life. She showed him that she cared for him and believed in him, and this in turn helped him believe in himself. Because he never forgot her love and help, every time he heard Miss Horne was in town, he came to Granny's door to thank her. That was as powerful a statement of the importance of good teaching as I have ever witnessed.

Interestingly, this man went on to a very successful career, for while he didn't grasp book information easily, when it came to fixing electrical things, few could match him. That, too, taught me something I never forgot. Most everyone has the ability to excel at something. Maybe it's not the traditional things that our society puts on that pedestal like getting good grades, being a celebrity, having a big job title, or making tons of money, but our nation would cease to exist without high achievers in every profession.

A central tenet of good teaching is trying to help students find and develop the unique gifts from within, for there is nothing we can give them as teachers more important than hope and self-confidence. I always thought this was my main responsibility as a teacher. Ma used to say that everyone has the capacity to learn, some just not so quickly as others. And that rule can be applied in reverse as well. Someone who is slow to learn the things we grasp easily quite often leaves us in a cloud of dust when it comes to learning certain other things, maybe mechanics or computers or playing a musical instrument. My wish is that all of us should just try harder to encourage each other to develop our unique gifts and knock off being so judgmental when others don't do what we do well. The results would be amazing.

Thanks to my mom, Aunt Lil, and Eleanor, three dedicated elementary school teachers, let's just say I was culturally biased toward teaching. Several of my teachers who taught me well and obviously enjoyed being teachers also contributed to this interest.

Down but Not Out

When I enrolled at Elon College (now, Elon University), the truth is that I didn't know what I ought to major in or what I wanted to do following graduation, and it bothered me because I thought most everyone else had these things figured out. In hindsight, I got stressed out for nothing. Practically everyone there had the same problem. It's just that I didn't know that. How I came to this conclusion is from talking with hundreds of my own college students as a professor, at least 90% of whom were essentially clueless as freshmen about their majors and careers. Even the ones who boldly stated they were sure of the answers often changed majors before graduation or careers later in life. Much of the certainty about majors and careers I observed at Elon was just good bluffing. It was acting, good acting, but still just show.

In my confusion, I decided for two main reasons to become a math major. Pop and others told me there were great opportunities in the field, and math was my best subject, the area that produced my highest grades in high school. So it seemed logical to choose math. When I further determined that I could complete the education courses leading to a teaching certificate without extending my stay in college beyond four years, I also chose to do that. My thinking was that if I ever wanted to teach in the public schools, then this would make it possible; if not, what did it cost me? Incidentally, throughout life I have tried to keep other options open, just in case, and this strategy saved me more than once. It just makes good sense to have a Plan Y handy. And math has helped me in numerous ways throughout life.

Subsequently, I practice-taught math at Graham High School in North Carolina, got certified to teach, finished my AB degree at Elon, and went directly to North Carolina State University during the summer of 1965 to earn my masters in math. My intention, after grad school, was to get a job in industry, doing exactly what I wasn't sure. Unfortunately, the strategy blew up in my face. I did very poorly and received a C and D in my first two math courses. Even worse than the grades was the depression I felt knowing how many people I had let down. Rarely in my life had I ever failed at anything, and when my N. C. State debacle happened, frankly, it shocked me. I didn't understand failure or how to handle it.

My courses were theoretical algebra and advanced calculus, both of which depended heavily on conceptual thinking and remembering everything you learned in prior days so you had a fighting chance at solving the next piece of the puzzle. And when your memory is awful, as was my case, this is most difficult. Adding to my misery was the fact that I really did work hard every day, often to midnight, trying to solve the problems and proofs. It was just so discouraging that I debated long and hard about whether to persist or call it quits.

Many things define Americans, but several big ones are that we like to compete, love to win, and have little tolerance for quitters. You've no doubt heard the saying, "When the going gets tough, the tough get going." Sometimes, though, I truly believe life is trying to send us a helpful message. In my case, I needed to determine whether I believed I had the ability to pass the N. C. State program. Truthfully, I wasn't sure. I knew I would work hard, but I had already been working hard with bad results. Look, I'll admit it. I am not the smartest guy on the block. My intelligence is above average, but just slightly so. Not much comes easily and never has. But I figured out as a young man that I could still get there if I just worked harder than most people. Always, I was willing to study more hours than most of my peers. This time, however, that didn't work. I additionally asked myself two other important questions. If I could pass, could I excel at math? A long time ago I realized I didn't want to be mediocre at anything. Second, what was holding me back from achieving success?

My conclusion was that I faced poor odds in accomplishing great success in math, primarily because I didn't love math enough. Unlike my N. C. State professor whose hobby was trying to solve math problems that no one in the world had solved, it dawned on me that in my entire life I had never solved a math problem that hadn't been assigned by a teacher. That was a very telling moment. I truly believe that if people want to do exceptionally well at anything, first they need great passion, and I didn't have it in math. Consequently, I made a very difficult but good decision to drop out of the graduate program and try to find that passion elsewhere. I just needed to keep looking and trying.

Western Alamance High School

That evening I called Aunt Lil and asked her to inquire about openings in the Alamance County, North Carolina, schools for a high school math teacher, me. The next morning she informed me that there was a job open at Western Alamance High School near Burlington, and I told her I wanted it. Sight unseen, no application submitted, no interviews, just trust in my word and Lil's that I was certified and qualified, the deal was closed. Bingo. I was a public school teacher hired for an annual salary of $4,100, and was I pleased to get it. But I want you to know that it took me a long time, from 1965 to 1973, to stop feeling awful and apologizing for my humiliating performance at N. C. State. Time, some other successes on my part, and understanding hearts fortunately helped me pass the point where I felt the need to explain that blot on my resume any longer. Indeed, the sun does come up tomorrow. Besides, that major setback turned out to be a huge break for me.

People have said that we learn more from our failures than from our successes, and you won't get any argument out of me on this one. I know it for a fact. Failure, as I used to tell my students, within reason, is healthy. Setbacks are reality checks. They give you empathy for other people's troubles, prepare you for the tough challenges ahead, and definitely help you more fully appreciate eventual successes. Without question, many of my students benefited from my academic troubles in school, because I knew what it was like to work hard and still have trouble learning.

I like to think of disappointments and failures as speed bumps on the interstates of life and as a form of necessary mental and emotional conditioning. They bother you, they slow you down, they make you unhappy, but they should make you a better person if you learn from them. The thing we must guard against is letting setbacks ruin the present or future or stifle our passions. A good analogy is the great pitcher who just served up a home-run ball. It happened, he regrets it, but he keeps winning because he has the ability to put it behind him and focus on the next pitch. That is what we have to do in life. We must move on. And don't give up too early on things you absolutely love. Don't overreact. Failure and disappointments happen in life. Accept them, make the needed adjustments, and get up and keep moving forward. Stay positive.

In the fall of 1965, Western Alamance was a rural county high school with an enrollment of about 600 students in grades 9-12. The math department consisted of four teachers: two senior instructors and two first year teachers. Unlike me, though, the other rookie at least looked his age. I was so young-looking that a teacher once stopped me in the hall and asked me what I was doing out of class.

Just so today's teachers can see how times have changed, I visited with the principal just one time before classes started. He explained the few basic ground rules, assigned my classroom, gave me my teaching assignment, and informed me that his secretary was there to teach me how to obtain books and run a ditto machine. The latter was a hand-cranked cylindrical device that made both the copies and the teachers purple. As an added bonus, the ink stunk. This may come as a shock to today's teachers and students, but we had no phones or calculators in our room or any copy machines, fax machines, TV's, air conditioning, or computers in the building. Amazingly, we still got the job done.

The principal told me to develop a daily lesson plan for each course, which I did faithfully, and only one time can I remember another member of the staff reviewing one of my lesson plans. Lesson plans at Western Alamance had one purpose, to help me do my job, not hold me accountable, protect an administrator's fanny, or give my substitute teacher a fighting chance. Besides, substitutes were rarely needed anyway because teachers seldom missed class. Compare this to the current situation. It's revealing.

"Seniority counts" was one of the first lessons I learned as a high school teacher. My assignment was to teach four classes of general math, one class of first year algebra, and a study hall. Since our two senior math teachers had been at Western Alamance since the school first opened, they took all the higher level math classes and a disproportionate number of the more serious high school math students, which was fine my first year. I was naïve and in no position to argue.

My favorite class was algebra. Study hall, mainly because I spent much of my time trying to calm down exuberant teenagers, took the honors as least enjoyable. The general math course was designed for students who really weren't ready for algebra. In too many cases, though, it became the home for bright students who easily could have done algebra had they put their minds and energy into it.

Walking the Fence

As is typically the case with first-year teachers, my teaching techniques were somewhat shaky; my attitude, nevertheless, was good, and I was definitely motivated to win the hearts and minds of my students and teach them well. Rapidly I learned how difficult it was to walk that fence between class manager and friend. What I knew, and still believe, is that learning increases when students respect and trust their teachers. You want an open, inviting classroom environment, for when this is attained, students pay more attention and want to learn. However, if teachers get too close to their pupils, as in "Mr. Stephenson, my good buddy," children tend to have a hard time changing gears when instructors need them to settle down and get to work. The problem is not much different in the military where I learned that good reasons exist for maintaining a degree of separation between officers and enlisted. It's just common sense. The art is in finding that happy medium that establishes that you like students and care for them, but where they instinctively know that there is only one leader in the classroom--you. Thus, I had to learn to stay on that fence.

To my students that year and their parents, please accept my apologies for any mistakes I made. None were intentional, but I made some and still regret them. Once I sent a young man to the office for misbehaving in class. Did he deserve to go to the office? Most definitely, but it never occurred to me the principal would suspend him for 3 days, which in those days was a shameful punishment. What I should have done was ask the principal right then to reduce the penalty; however, I didn't do this because I didn't want to make the principal look bad in front of the parent. Fortunately, most errors were less consequential than this one. Usually they happened during my efforts to try to make the class more fun and appealing to my students. I was just trying to create more energy and enthusiasm for learning.

Well, I got my wish in the enthusiasm department, but not quite enough with the energy and learning parts. I wanted my pupils to approach their studies more seriously. They wanted to have fun. And I don't fault them on that goal. It was mine, too. But it is hard to teach and learn if students distract others and interfere with the process. And they did like to cut up in class. But these boys and girls to the person were nice, respectful people. I credit this largely to their upbringing, to societal norms in North Carolina during the 1960s, and mostly to parents who taught their sons and daughters to respect their teachers and each other. And compared to what many teachers deal with today in the public schools, my students were saints. I can't remember a high school student whom I taught at Western Alamance who ever did anything truly disrespectful, harmful, or hateful in my presence. They were just good kids transitioning from youth to adulthood. In a way, so was I.

Dealing with the Doldrums

Thanks to trial by fire, as the year progressed, so did my teaching. At the same time, though, boredom started setting in, not in my students but in me. The main problem was that teaching general math four times daily got old. To offset this, I invented ways to help me enjoy it more. Suppose for instance that I was teaching long division and needed to show students how to divide 12,956 by 41. I would go to the board, write down 12,956, draw the division box, write the divisor (41), and then step back toward the class, pause, act like I was really thinking about it, kind of frame the problem with my hands (body language is good), and say, "I know. It's 316." Then I would go to the board, take them step by step through the long division process, and *voila*, the answer was indeed 316.

Based on their body language, more than a few were really impressed by my ability to do long division in my head. And I let them think it. The trick was that by the time I had done this problem during lesson planning and then repeated it in the two previous classes, I had the answer memorized. Did I feel guilty fooling the kids? Not really. Students were skilled counter-attackers. Once one of them asked my fiancée, "Why are you marrying him? He is not that good looking. He drives an old Buick. And he has no money." Sharon still married me. You can evaluate her judgment better after you finish the book.

Back to the boredom issue, people need to understand that if an instructor teaches the same lesson repetitively, particularly covering content below the instructor's level of expertise or interest, it does get monotonous, and when teachers get bored, so do students. It's like yawning. Once one person does it, it's all over. This is why I have such fond memories of Barry Hodge, a teacher friend who had a room just down the hall. Barry had a great sense of humor and loved to laugh as much as I did. Together we drummed up ways to make teaching more fun. Bat Man, for example.

For many of you younger readers, this will mean little, but when we were teaching school in the 1960s, the rage on TV was the Bat Man show. At my suggestion, the teachers at Western Alamance produced a Bat Man skit for our high school. Another teacher and I wrote the script, the actors were teachers, but Barry was Bat Man and I was his sidekick, Robin. We had no choice. Barry was about 5 inches taller than I was, and the TV Robin was a small, young looking guy, which fit me perfectly.

Picture this, a gymnasium packed with students, the lights go out, suddenly Bat Man music blares throughout the gym. A spot light illuminates a large bat circling the gym. Dramatically this light catches two figures in tights and capes flying across the room on gym ropes. Well, that was Barry and I, and the place went wild. Instantly, two teaching legends were born. The down side is that from that day forward a lot of students jokingly called us Fat Man and Bobbin, something that definitely did not help separation. The skit was, however, one of the most fun-filled and memorable things I have ever done in my life.

It was a different time then, a much less challenging period than teachers face in schools today. Was it free of problems? No. I remember observing the envy on the faces of some of our poor rural students as they watched the country-club students arrive in their new cars and designer clothes. That was hard to take when you lived in a home without running water and with an outhouse in the backyard. Despite the poverty, the kids, to their credit, kept their sense of humor. One said to me one day, "Hey, Mr. Stephenson, we have running water at our house. My mom gives me a bucket, and I run out back and get it." But they did struggle.

Especially, I recall the day when one of my students was caught cutting an Izod alligator emblem off another kid's shirt. When asked why, he said he was going to sew it on his clothes to feel better. Obviously, acceptance and self esteem were very important then, too. Mostly, though, I remember the nine high school freshmen girls who got married that year, and even as young as I was at the time (22), I couldn't help thinking about what opportunities in life their decisions most likely had eliminated.

Why would kids marry at 15 and 16? The scenario, as the girls typically explained it, went like this. The textile mills offered their boyfriends a night job, enticing them with the opportunity to buy a car, a big deal to these poor boys in the 1960s. The pitch was to work at night so that they could continue to go to school during the day. Then came the second pitch, after they had worked a few months. If they could get their girl friends to do the same, they would have two incomes. Marriage wasn't far behind followed by both quitting school because they were just too tired to work and study, plus they seldom saw each other. The mills weren't the only motivator. Some of these kids just wanted to escape tough situations at home. Actually, young marriages were fairly common in the South at this time. Regardless, marriages of high school freshmen were foreign to me. People just didn't get married voluntarily at 15 or 16 in Rhode Island. But it happened in 1965 in Alamance County, North Carolina, usually with unhappy results. And I couldn't stop it. I tried.

We Want YOU!

It was about this time when I received a letter from Rhode Island draft board inviting me to take the tests to enter military service. As instructed, I complied and passed both the physical and written exams. Now if I told you I relished serving in the Army in Vietnam, I'd be lying;

however, life and my dad taught me the difference between what one wants to do and what one needs to do. Well I remember the day when I said to the draft-board official, "Sir, it was my impression that if I was teaching school, I would be deferred." He kindly put his arm around me like a big old daddy and in a quiet tone replied, "Son, I know you're doing a lot of good for those boys and girls in North Carolina. But, this is Rhode Island, and you are doing nothing to help our children." When I next asked him what he suggested I do, he said, "Enlist or the Rhode Island draft board is going to draft you." That seemed clear enough. On my dad's recommendation, I decided, if they wanted me, to enlist in the Navy. And they did, so I did. You have already read the rest of the story in "Pork Chop."

Overall, my teaching experience at Western Alamance had been pretty good, for people appreciated me there and treated me well. Still, the reality was that I was not sufficiently stimulated by what I was doing. The passion for math had just not made its presence known, and by the day I was growing more annoyed by some of the kids' immaturity problems and lack of motivation to learn up to their abilities. Their failure to shoot high and study hard, though, was not entirely their fault.

I remember one case where I got through to a fine young man of humble means who became motivated to think seriously about college. I talked with him one day, and he was so happy and excited. The next he seemed down and defeated. Looking me right in the eyes, he told me that his momma said I was filling him with garbage. There would be no college, and she wanted me to stop. That really hurt. Both of us. Despite efforts to bring him back, his fire just never reignited. Sometimes I felt that certain parents didn't want their kids to grow for fear they might turn away from them. At other times, I think they were just being realistic and trying to minimize the costs of broken dreams. But I can assure you that a child's education and dreams are the responsibility of far more people than the child and his teacher.

Once again, I knew it was time to move on. When I informed my principal that I had enlisted and wouldn't be coming back, he said, "I can get you out of it." Honestly, I didn't want to get out of it. My heart was not adequately in high school math teaching, at least as I did it that year, and another earlier postponed dream of mine, the one about becoming a naval officer, was about to be realized. As previously explained, that was one of the best turns I ever took on the road of life.

The Second Time Around

What, then, pulled me back into teaching? It began with my resignation from the Navy in 1970 to attend graduate school in business at the University of Minnesota. Sharon and I enjoyed the Navy, but we just wanted more control over our lives, which is something we didn't really have with the Navy's ability to cut orders whenever it wanted. My goal was to earn a masters degree in transportation and logistics and get a job working in railroad management. What more precisely turned me back toward teaching, however, was one of my professors, Dr. Fred Beier, who during the second year of my masters program asked if I had interest in continuing on for my doctorate. My response was that I didn't know. I then told him that the only reason I would even consider the Ph.D. program was to teach, and the first time around hadn't overly excited me.

Fred then asked if it would help me change my mind if I was given an opportunity to teach a Principles of Transportation class. Since this seemed like it would answer the question and Sharon agreed with me, I took it.

Great teaching takes a lot of things but none, I have found, is more important than having passion, and not one type but four types of passion: passion for learning, passion for students, passion for teaching, and passion for your field. This topic is covered more thoroughly in our book *Extraordinary Teachers: the Essence of Excellent Teaching*, but I had never really experienced that fourth form of passion until I began teaching my first college course. Transportation simply fascinated me, I think about as much as math did for my former N. C. State professor. It was like getting paid to do a hobby. Finally, I had found the right field, and I wanted to know and remember everything about it. After that, the decision to continue for the Ph.D. was easy.

What a Family!

Of all the things I liked about college teaching, the part I absolutely loved the most was being in class with my students. Mainly what made this so special were the little things that transpired on a daily basis in the give and take between my students and me. I like children and young people and always have. Even as a small boy, my dream was to have a big family, and thank God, it came true. First, Sharon blessed me with Katie, Jeff, and Dave who in turn added two more great kids in John and Kendra, our son- and daughter-in-law. Now these children have given us the special gift of our four grandchildren. But never in my wildest dreams could I have ever imagined having a family of nearly 11,000 children, which is exactly what I got from teaching.

And this view, that these were not my students but members of my family, significantly affected my whole approach to teaching. My thought was that if Sharon and I were counting on other educators to teach our children and grandchildren the best they possibly could, then my mission would be to teach other parents' children like they were my own. Consequently, I gave students advice that was no different from what I would tell my children in the same circumstances. For example, if I wouldn't recommend a company as a place of employment to my daughter or sons, neither did I do so to other people's children. And I sensed that the students understood and appreciated this honesty and concern. In fact, they told me that I got away with telling them things and giving them advice that they never would have accepted from their parents.

When I think back on the thousands of students I taught, the vast majority makes me exceedingly proud. Of course, there are some who disappointed me. Regardless, it was a privilege to teach them, all of them, at least for the brief time we were together, and I feel so fortunate that they shared their lives, dreams, laughter, and experiences with me. One of the things I regularly did in my classes was to tell them that I respected them, trusted them, and believed in them, the types of reinforcing comments that students need to hear more often from teachers. I found when I sought the best in people, more often than not I got it.

At the same time, I recognized that we are all human and imperfect. Some students had a hard time doing what they ought to have been doing. So like any good father, I paid attention trying to pick up signs of behavior that threatened my students' success and happiness. And I think it is worth our time to discuss some of my personal findings, mainly for the purpose of trying to reverse the troublesome trends and help current students.

For starters, I learned a long time ago that people have to want an education more than their teachers want them to get one. Unless students approach learning seriously, the benefits will not be maximized. Unfortunately, too many don't see this and instead spend their time searching for shortcuts to make education easier, like seeking out the easiest A's, finding the less demanding teachers, and regularly asking for exceptions to rules. I call such students educational efficiency experts. In earlier days, people called them "lazy" and "operators."

Growing student apathy concerns me, and while I know that things like boring teachers and huge classes are contributing factors, again it is within students' powers to do something about it. For instance, the most important thing any student can do to improve his or her education is take classes from the school's best teachers. Yes they will make students work, but students will learn far more than in the easy courses.

More troublesome to me than apathy is an increasing trend in cheating, and even worse, the lack of guilt that seems to be associated with it. How do we get through to kids the important message that achievement without honor eventually comes at a high cost, a penalty that will primarily be borne by the dishonorable? I was lucky. My parents believed uncompromisingly in honesty, hard work, and honor, values that they, thank goodness, drummed into my soul and that I lived by. My students heard these same values from me and additionally my explanations why they were important to their lives. More importantly, I made sure I did everything I could to walk the walk and serve as a good role model. Life definitely is about choices. I just wanted them to make wise ones.

Northeastern University

In 1975 I took my first faculty job at Northeastern University in Boston. At the time, Northeastern enrolled the most students of any private university in America, but mostly it was known, and widely praised, for its highly successful cooperative education program. Virtually every Northeastern undergraduate worked approximately 21 months in their field while at the university. During the three and a half years I taught there, I exclusively taught transportation and logistics (T & L) courses in the business school and undergraduate and master's degree students. Why I am telling you all of this is to clarify later how my teaching evolved over time and as background information for a later discussion of why I taught.

Teaching at Northeastern was a lot of fun. Particularly appealing were teaching in a field I loved, working with small classes of 35 students or less, and connecting with young men and women loaded with good practical work experience in their majors. All of these things kept me happy and on my toes. A lot of people don't know what I really mean when talking about my field of transportation and logistics. Transportation courses prepare students, in due time, to manage railroads, trucking companies, water carriers, airlines, air freight companies, and even pipelines and mass transit systems, that is, businesses and public entities that provide freight and passenger services. Logistics, which some call distribution and that now has evolved into supply chain management, primarily addresses the movement and storage of inventory, so it comes at students more from a business-customer or user's perspective. I taught a variety of T & L courses, but my first love, the place where I did my dissertation, research, and service, was transportation. What fascinated me, and still does, are ships, trains, trucks, and planes. So I felt lucky to be in my element, found my work satisfying, and got off to a pretty good start as a teacher and researcher.

The University of Georgia

One day while I was sitting in my office, a colleague said, "Fred, do you know anyone in transportation who might be interested in a faculty job in Georgia? The University of Georgia has an opening." I asked him to let me see the ad. I was interested.

When people change jobs, I have found that most make a list of the pros and cons and rationalize the move based on how they were leaning in the first place. In 1978 I left Northeastern University for several good reasons, hardly any of which had anything to do with dissatisfaction with my previous job. In fact, Northeastern treated me very well while I was there. But Sharon and I discovered we weren't big-city people and longed for a beautiful small-town campus, shorter commutes from home to work, a good place to raise our children, and a home much closer to our parents, all of whom now lived in North Carolina. A good pay raise also didn't hurt. UGA hired me to assist with the building of the transportation and distribution program in the college of business. Subsequently, for 25 years until my retirement in 2003, I served on the faculty of Terry College of Business, one of the nation's leading business schools. The only exception was the 1989-90 year when I was a visiting professor at the Babcock Graduate School of Management at Wake Forest University where I exclusively taught marketing and logistics to MBA students.

During my 30-year college teaching career, I taught approximately 25 different business courses, about 150 different class sections, approximately 11,000 students, and freshmen through Ph.D. candidates. One of my classes had 3 students. About 35 were mass sections of up to 300 students. Most classes, though, held 25 to 60 students. Like people, every class section had its own personality. Some were exceptional and unforgettable in a most positive way. I still have recurring nightmares about two of them. The key was student attitudes, particularly those of the self-selected class leaders, most of whom actually helped me teach the class, a few of whom were hell-bent on fighting me every step of the way or making me look bad. Teaching different courses, different age groups, and different people kept me energized.

I was a Socratic teacher. This means that I preferred to ask a lot of questions rather than tell students what I knew, as many lecturers primarily do. In return, I expected my students to be prepared, answer questions, and think. The thrill was in never knowing what would emerge from their mouths. A colleague likes to think of this as teaching without a net. Sometimes I had to bite my tongue at some pretty ridiculous things students said. More often they stunned me with their wisdom and insight. What I particularly liked was their humor, which on many occasions brought tears to my eyes from laughing so hard. I'm not talking about making fun of people, laughing at them, or telling prepared jokes. Many of my students were just good stand-up comedians, which suited me fine, for I am also known to have, and use, a sense of humor. One of the best compliments I ever received on my student evaluations was "You are the David Letterman of academia." That made my day. There is enough humor in life without telling jokes.

Once, right after I had passed out an exam to 300 undergrad students, my graduate assistant, John Casten, said, "Look at the last row, Doc. I think that kid is asleep." Sure enough, he was. He had his arm on the desk, his hand was under his chin, and he was out like a light. So I walked up the aisle to row M, squeezed past a dozen students to reach the young man, and quietly woke him, much to the great amusement of all the students who were watching my every move.

Back down front, John asked, "What did you tell him?"

"I just said, you might want to wake up and take the test."

John looked at me and said, "That is not what I would have told him. I would have gotten in his ear and shouted, FIVE MINUTES LEFT!"

John would make a good teacher.

I once thought, during one of those mischievous moments that I so often had, about giving a multiple choice test, say 50-75 questions, where every correct answer was D. I never did it, but just thinking about the chaos that would have created continues to bring a smile to my face.

Well, it is one thing to teach a class of 30 using the Socratic method. In such an intimate environment, it is pretty easy to get to know your students quite well and get most of them involved in the discussion. And I did use this interactive method in most every class, even in classes of 120 students, after I understood how much more effective it was in stimulating learning than the more traditional lecturing approach. By lecturing, I am referring to the method of "I speak; you take notes." My practice, too, was to assign a good mix of essay exams, outside papers, group projects, oral and written case analyses, and other in-class presentations, virtually all of which I personally graded. Part of this goes back to the benefits of methods that worked at Classical High School and the Navy Supply Corps School. But I looked for teaching tips everywhere I could find them and picked up a number of great ideas from Harvard case teaching experts and even from the Oprah Winfrey Show. It amazed me how easily Oprah got people to join in the discussion, so

I figured, why not try it in class, which I subsequently did. A hidden objective was to give students plenty of good practice so that they would improve their research, analysis, writing, speaking, logic and other skills. I guess you could call it a forced agenda but an effective one, nonetheless. The bonus was that class became far more lively and fun.

Change Is Inevitable

Rarely is a teaching career stagnant. Over time, many things change, and dealing with this takes flexibility. When I joined the UGA faculty, I exclusively taught undergraduate and graduate courses in transportation and logistics, usually in classes of 25 or fewer students. By the 1980s the needs of the business school, the curriculum in my department of marketing and distribution, and my own personal priorities began to shift, and likewise, so did my teaching responsibilities. At first, I began to teach an occasional marketing class like principles of marketing, sales management, or marketing strategy mixed in with the T & L classes.

By the 1990s, the Terry College had grown significantly, classes by necessity became much larger, and pressure mounted to increase the number of undergraduates taught in mass sections of 250 or more students. This in turn brought on increased demands to assign more senior faculty, especially top teachers, to teach these mass sections, and I volunteered to become one of those teachers to help our students and my department. So for this and other logical reasons, I made a big decision to stop teaching in my field and concentrate on teaching marketing principles and marketing strategy. In hindsight, I know this was a bad career move because I was still actively engaged in transportation research yet had no well-suited classroom outlet where I could share my deep passion, and expertise, in transportation. You really do need appropriate course settings to make this a reality.

Some things are easy to forget but not my first class of 300 principles of marketing students, because I just didn't do it that well. By most people's standards, I did fine, but I knew I could, and should, have done better. In that class, I received the lowest student evaluation I ever received while teaching a mass section, and I taught dozens after that one. But I earned it. My problem was I didn't know how to use the Socratic method effectively in a lecture hall with 300 students who were accustomed to straight lectures. Senior professors were no help, either. All they told me was that it was impossible. "Just lecture," they said. If I had done that I would have been bored out of my mind.

Consequently, I decided to experiment as much as necessary to determine if I could indeed run a highly effective discussion class for 300. It took many hours of note preparation, an extensive and on-going search for current examples of marketing principles, the introduction of the first handheld, cordless mics in large classrooms on campus, and learning how to run the class like Oprah Winfrey did when she used to get so many people in her audience to speak, but everything finally clicked. In those classes toward the end of my career, I was drawing average student evaluation scores of 4.6's out of 5.0's where 5.0 is the best rating. In a typical 50-minute class, I was usually able to engage 30-50 students in discussion, and you know what? I learned a great deal from my students. By asking for their input and help, they actually helped teach the class, lessened all of our biases, opened our minds and hearts, and enhanced our mutual respect.

We've Been Robbed!

After much thought, I nevertheless feel that both my students and I were somewhat cheated by the mass-section experience. First, with rare exceptions, large classes compromise academic rigor and eliminate much needed practice. Gone were the essay exams because I couldn't afford to spend, or even endure, the 45 hours needed each time I graded a test, four of which occurred each semester per class section. No longer were there any individually prepared projects assigned, again for the same reason. And grading in-class participation in a class of 300 was most impractical. All of these things affect what students learn.

Of course, there were also benefits. Students were exposed to better teachers, many of whom were national leaders in their disciplines. Teachers like I were given the opportunity to work with far more students than would ever have been possible in smaller classes. At the same time, I believe I did a good job delivering course content, serving as a worthy role model, and helping more of them than would have been possible otherwise. Still, I do not find mass-section teaching a very good way to instruct students. A friend of mine calls teaching classes in groups of 250 – 400 "Stack 'em deep, teach 'em cheap education." And that is the main reason, no matter what university administrators give you, for using mass sections. They save money.

The down side, and it's a big one, is that large classes create convenient ways for students to shirk responsibility and hide in that anonymity. Students tell you they resent being a number, but many of them actually love it because big classes almost always mean less studying and homework. Another problem is absenteeism, which escalates because taking attendance is so time consuming that it typically isn't done. Another disincentive to students coming to class is red notes. These are class notes taken by an "A" student, typed, sold to a business, printed by that company, and sold to students before each exam. They're called red notes because the business publishes them on red paper so they can't be photocopied.

Do mass sections add to student apathy and the devaluing of education? Yes, particularly when students face boring lecturers day after day, which indeed happens in some classes. Mass sections explain, at least partially, why so many college students cannot write or speak or analyze like they are supposed to be able to do as college graduates. It happens when people don't practice enough and aren't thoughtfully, and frequently, critiqued by professors. But what still bothers me most is that in the mass sections I taught I had so little opportunity to get to know my students well like I wanted to, and needed to know them, and that is a huge loss to me, and I think more so to them.

Does Anybody Read These Things?

Most everyone who has been in college has had the privilege (burden?) of filling out countless teacher evaluations and then wondering whether anyone ever actually reads and acts on them. To put your minds at rest, let me assure you that at least one professor read his evaluations, yours truly, and I read every one that was ever written about me, thousands to be exact. And I was always tense when I read them. That happens when you want them to be perfect yet never are.

In preparation for writing this section of the chapter, I decided to reread about 1,000 of my previously submitted, anonymously written evaluations starting with my classes in 1978. My Purpose? I wanted to observe, and share with you, how they affected my teaching and me. The magnitude of their impact surprised me.

One of the first things I noticed is that the student comments fell into four broad categories: the positive reinforcement types, gut-wrenching critical comments, environmental complaints, and course improvement suggestions.

Obviously, my favorites were the positive ones, reinforcing messages like the following that I received.

"I had the class at 8:00 a.m.; not once did I feel the urge to sleep as a result of boredom."

"I never wanted to miss class."

"He motivated me--not only in business but in many aspects of my life."

"I remember how tough he was, but it was worth it."

"He let me see how much potential each student has."

"He has made me want to work harder."

"He allowed everyone to voice their opinions."

"Students are forced to use finance, accounting, and marketing which provides for a higher quality of education."

"I would love to have him as a second dad."

And there were far more like these, which in their own unique terms conveyed appreciation and respect and inspired me to keep doing this job as well as I possibly could. What they told me was that my game plan was working and that I should stick with it.

Inevitably, though, in the stack each quarter I would find a disheartening reminder that someone was dissatisfied, and I hated to read such comments. Here is a sample.

"Professor Stephenson is not an effective teacher. He shows favoritism, is not a clear and direct teacher, [sic, is] ambiguous, his tests are very subjective, so in essence, he can decide exactly what your grade will be. This is the most unfair class and the most biased and ineffective teacher I have had in my 4 1/2 years at UGA. He is just a bad teacher. Maybe he should have stayed in the military, because his education skills are horrible!!"

Comments like these would bother me for days, mainly because I couldn't imagine what I had done to bring out such punishing words and animosity. However, as much as I wanted to toss them in the trash can, I didn't and instead forced myself to sort through the harsh criticisms looking for legitimate concerns. Particularly painful was this student's claim of unfairness, for there was nothing in my teaching I worked harder to achieve than just being fair, something so fundamental to good teaching. This, then, is why I read all the evaluations from a class at one sitting, to look for patterns, good and bad. Fortunately, in this situation no other comments supported this student's unfairness criticism. To the contrary, five of them directly contradicted it such as the one that read, "He has the best sense of fair play of any professor I've had at UGA." This helped me calm down, put things in perspective, and allowed me to dismiss most of the former criticism, but still, did the student have a point about ambiguity? Could I have been clearer? Maybe. So I would then work on fixing that problem in the future.

One of the big conclusions I drew from teacher evaluations is that I generally learned more from the critical ones than from the reinforcing types. For example, this one confirmed that perception is just as important as reality. Second, if I thought I was actually going to succeed in making every student pleased with my teaching, I was mistaken. No matter what I did, no matter how hard I tried, in 31 years of teaching, never was everyone totally satisfied. To teach or lead anything, one needs a somewhat thick skin. And teachers also better have a sense of humor, common sense, and a darn good idea of what they are trying to accomplish in that classroom.

Another group of comments fell into the "environmental complaint" pile. By "environmental" I mean they asked me to change things beyond my control like "We need to be on a semester plan rather than quarters," "I don't like two-hour classes," and "The building needs better air conditioning." As Pop used to say, "I work for the bank, son. I don't own it." Interestingly, I took a lot of notes on which environments best facilitate teaching and while serving on committees at UGA, I was able to influence, at least in a small way, the design of Georgia's new Student Learning Center, a $39-million state of the art classroom, study, and electronic library facility that has become the second most used and popular building on campus.

One of the things I enjoyed about reading evaluations was the occasional evidence of student humor that poked fun at my human shortcomings. To the question "How could this teacher improve himself/herself to become a better teacher?" some responses read,

"Get rid of the accent!!"

"Speak Southern."

"If he could be about 3 inches taller, we could see him in the back of the room."

And I wish some students were more handsome, but that won't change either.

On a more serious note, let me tell you that having read all of my evaluations over the years, I have found them almost universally thoughtfully written, constructive, delivered with good intentions, honest, and helpful. For every offensive or unsubstantiated remark, there were hundreds that just tried to improve teaching effectiveness. The recent rereading of the comments left me with a very long list of fine-tuning adjustments that I made as a result of taking student evaluations to heart. All of which helped improve teaching and learning.

One said I preached too much and talked down to students. It is an easy, and wrong, even if unintentional, thing to do. This comment altered my course content, message delivery, and efforts to show more respect to my students.

Another said I had the tendency to deviate from the point and talk too long on a particular subject such as when telling stories to reinforce points. I concluded I was guilty of doing this and wasting time unnecessarily. It motivated me to be far more organized and aware of the clock, say what needed to be said, eliminate some material, and get back to the rest of the lesson more quickly. Incidentally, in all my years of teaching I only went to one class without carefully prepared class notes. That day I had prepared them as well but in my rush to take the train to work, I accidentally left them at home. One kid told me after class it was the best class of the quarter. My point is that good planning and organization are very important to good teaching.

A third said to stop when the period is over. This valid point led me to start class on time and end it on time. Everybody's time is important--theirs and mine.

Another stated that I tended to interrupt students when they were giving presentations or answering questions and that I needed to be less rude, more patient, and let them finish. This student, too, was right. So

I worked hard to cease doing this, but I have to tell you, there are only so many minutes in a class and in a semester. Sometimes teachers have no choice but to stop the unfocused rambling or absolutely inaccurate thinking of some students for the sake of the rest of the class and the teachers' credibility as well as to insure that the essential material gets covered that day and in the course. Comments like this one taught me that the management of the class was still my job; however, there are ways to do this more tactfully.

Frequently I was told to talk slower. Sorry. I'm from Rhode Island, where we all talk fast, and in my enthusiasm and excitement, I would sometimes get carried away. The point, though, was valid. My students weren't trained stenographers. It was my responsibility to give them a fighting chance to take notes.

Changing topics, take a guess which topic received more comments than any other. The answer is, by an overwhelming margin, tests and grading. A paraphrased summary is in order.

Dr. Stephenson, your tests are too hard, you should grade less harshly, and make the exams easier. My grade does not reflect what I learned in the class. I don't like, or do well on, essay exams. It is my opinion that you covered way too much material on this exam, there weren't enough exams during the course, and the test grading is picky. Stop using your red pen so much. It's tearing me apart. Your tests have too many questions, your tests don't have enough questions, your tests ask the wrong questions, and you didn't ask what I knew. I didn't have time to finish the test. Give us objective tests; your essays made me think too much. What can I do for extra credit? Your teaching assistant should not be grading our essay exams. Only you should do the grading. And I could add about 20 more of these.

My reaction to most of this was to examine the validity of each concern, alter the testing and grading process if it made sense, yet still maintain high academic standards. Testing is an area where I knew I had a much richer understanding of what these students could do and needed to do than they did. But even here, I made some adjustments based on their concerns. For instance, I subsequently graded every written paper and essay they turned in and no longer used my teaching assistant as a grader. Another change was to reduce the number of questions on some tests to make sure students had adequate time to finish exams. In some cases, I also increased the exam frequency to reduce the content coverage on particular tests. But guess what? None of these things altered grades much at all. What I never did was give grades away. I expected students to work and gave them the grades they earned.

This student comment sums up what I believe many students think about tests.

"I hate the tests, but then again I hate tests in every course!" So did I as a student. All I can tell you is that I haven't worried about tests since I started writing the questions. On the other hand, students should count their blessings. I figure I graded 40,000 tests and papers over my career, and of all the things I loved about teaching, grading was at the bottom of the stack. Nothing stressed me out more. It is tough, tedious, mostly thankless work. Nevertheless, I did it conscientiously because valid constructive criticism is how you coach students through an education.

Well, this conversation would be remiss without a discussion of textbooks, another issue high on the student-evaluation priority list. Are you sitting down? I discovered that few students like their textbooks. Any textbooks. Maybe that is because they have to read and study them. But in my courses, I worked hard to find stimulating texts. Once in a blue moon I would read a comment like, "Great text." But such contributions were buried beneath an avalanche of criticisms that the text was too dry, boring, too long, excessively wordy, dated, too hard, filled with unnecessary details--you get the picture and probably the memories.

One day a kid wrote on his evaluation form, "Dr. Stephenson should write his own book. The book was very weak on some points."

So I did. When it was done, I thought it addressed many of the criticisms in the preceding paragraphs.

What feedback did the students eventually offer?

"Good book--easy to read and understand."

"Comprehensive. The textbook is the most detailed text I've ever read."

"Text is too boring."

I rest my case.

Why I Taught

Despite these concerns, I loved teaching, whether it was transportation, distribution, or marketing or whether I was facing a few or many students. The classroom was my stage, my high for the day, my chance to spend time with young men and women I cared for and in whom I had great faith. It was my time to relax and have fun. Things went so well on some days that I left class sky high. There were days when I came to class down, ill, or tired to the point of exhaustion, and the students invariably picked me up. I can't really explain it. Perhaps it was similar to stories I have read about comedians who had to deal with much pain in their private lives but on the stage, in their element, they could tune out their problems and make people laugh, including themselves. Of course, not all of my days or results were good. I know what it feels like to leave for work happy and have my feet knocked out from under me. Rare were those days, however.

What made teaching work so well for me? First, I sincerely liked my students. Second, I am an outgoing person. Third, I wanted a job that gave me the chance to help people. A friend once asked me, "Seriously, Fred, how many students do you really think you reached?" My answer was, and I believe this is a conservative estimate, "Ten percent. But ten percent of 11,000 is 1,100 people, and I can live with that." What other occupation would have given me such an opportunity? Fourth, teaching gave me a way to leave something behind. My overriding message as a business-school teacher was that I wanted my students to succeed, that I believed in them and expected them to do great things in their own ways, that to get there they would have to set high goals and work hard, but that I wanted them to do it the right way. I challenged them to be the most honorable people they could be to make their families and friends as proud of them as possible. And I understood that this message had little chance of sinking in unless my students thought I truly walked the walk. So I tried to do just that and earn their respect.

Early in my career, I made a decision to strive to become the best teacher I could possibly be. There are so many jokes about teachers, such as "Those who can, do. Those who can't, teach." My belief is that, yes, many people can and do teach, but few do it exceptionally well. If you doubt this, start naming every great teacher you had from kindergarten through your last year in school. When I have asked this question among my Ph.D. colleagues, people who typically have had over one hundred teachers, no one has ever named more than three teachers. Maybe it isn't so easy. Excellent teaching requires talent, attitude, effort, purpose, diligence, and the courage to innovate and risk failure. Few ever make the top grade. But every teacher can improve if they have the desire and make the effort, which is the main theme of our book, *Extraordinary Teachers*.

One of my favorite quotes comes from William Arthur Ward who once said, "The mediocre teacher tells. The good teacher explains. The superior teacher demonstrates. The great teacher inspires." Thinking back to the great teachers you named, isn't this one of the key things that gave them distinction? Great teachers help students realize they are special. They convince them that they are capable of achieving goals that were previously considered impossible.

Student Blessings

Let me end this chapter with two stories about former students of mine that will also clarify why I taught and why others should consider this profession.

Tony

In 2001, Tony wrote me this note.

> Dr. Stephenson,
> My name is Tony, and I had your MARK 3000 class a couple of semesters ago. I will be graduating this May, and a little while ago I was thinking about my favorite classes that I have taken at UGA. I immediately decided that yours was my favorite. At the time I happened to be outside your office waiting on a class I have in Brooks 145. I was hoping to run into you so I could compliment you, but instead I felt led to write to you and really explain myself. I'll start with a story about one of my favorite memories of your class.

I can clearly remember on the first day of your class when you were describing the format of the class. You said something along the lines of, "This is a class of over 300 people, but it is still a discussion class. You will participate, so if you are uncomfortable using the microphone, leave now." I could tell instantly that I was going to enjoy the class. What was so funny was that right after your class, I had another class in the Fine Arts building that was about the same size. On the first day of that class, my extremely boring teacher said something along the lines of, "This is a class of over 300 people, so there's no way it can be a discussion class." Needless to say, I was completely unmotivated and actually ended up doing very poorly in there.

I learned that being a teacher is more about making the students care than about making them learn. You personify this quality. You have the God-given gift of being able to not only teach well, but also make everyone you teach love what they are learning. Had I taken your class a little earlier, because of you I would have become a Marketing major. Unfortunately, I was and am too ready to be done with school to double up MIS and Marketing, and last time I checked, UGA wasn't offering a Marketing minor. Regardless, I felt like you should know that I truly respect what you are doing for literally hundred's of people every single year. In short: Thank you. God bless and keep up the great work.

Until this note and our subsequent meeting, I am ashamed to admit that I honestly did not know who Tony was. Still, it confirms two things that are important. Teachers reach people they don't know they touch, so always give it your best shot. And what you do or say may seem insignificant to you but might be very important to them.

Scott

Scott, a senior in my marketing strategy class, appeared in my office one day, looked me right in the eyes, and got right to the point.

"I have a bone to pick with you. You made me spend my whole weekend thinking and learning."

He made this comment in reference to his take-home exam.

"Wow! What's the downside?" was the first thing I thought. Instead, I kept quiet.

Scott then explained how he had gone to the computer lab to write his exam and worked most of Saturday. "I wasn't able to get anything good done." Sunday, he again spent most of the day there with equally unproductive results. "It was very frustrating," he said. But on Monday, he told me it all came together.

When Scott was in my office, he actually was in good spirits. Then he added, "I don't know what I will receive on your test, but I have learned a lot. Even if it is a C, that's OK. I am getting so much out of class."

In this grade-crazy world we teach in, such comments are rare and truly appreciated.

At the time Scott and I were talking, I had yet to begin blind-grading his class's exams. Blind grading is a teaching technique I learned from another UGA colleague that works by asking students not to put their names on their papers to be graded but only their student identification numbers. The purpose is to eliminate grading bias. Then, when the grading is completed, you match the student identification numbers to names.

Reading and personally critiquing 52 marketing strategy exams for Scott's class eventually took me 15 hours. During that whole time, however, I kept thinking about Scott's comments and hoping, make that praying, that he would not be disappointed. And when I finally matched the names with the numbers, to my tremendous relief Scott had not only done well, but exceptionally well. He had earned a rare A+! I was so happy for him. To see this hard working, struggling young man who never asked for any special breaks hurdle the bar in such an extraordinary fashion gave me such a wonderful feeling that it brought tears to my eyes. And as I write this and remember that day, the dam has sprung another leak.

Scott later told me that he was so stunned and happy after getting his graded exam back that he couldn't think or talk all period. Then he said, "Of all my years in education, this is the high point."

I want you to know that it was also one of the best moments in my life as well, because I know that when a student like Scott flies over a high bar he has never before cleared and proves to himself that he earned it, he changes for the better. That is what I was after for all of my students. Then the sky is the limit for what those students can accomplish in life. This is why I refused to cut the standards. I really did have great faith in their abilities to excel. Some teachers give up on students too early.

These students and others are why I spent 31 years teaching. Like Ma, I loved them, and I think many of them knew it. More importantly, I have no doubts that more than of few of them loved me. And that is what life and family are all about.

TRACKER

Ever since Baldy, I have had a love affair with mountains. Whether I'm climbing them, gazing at them from a distance, or flying over them, mountains fill me with awe and joy. To deepen my faith, revitalize my soul and spirit, or simply calm down, I go to the mountains. Everyone needs such a place.

Having said this, I suspect you will be surprised to learn that between the ages of 20 and 48, I recall only climbing three mountains. One of them was Mt. Washington, the highest peak in the White Mountains of New Hampshire that I climbed with two Geneva Point Camp buddies in 1964. It's not that I didn't want to climb more peaks. Definitely, I did. But other priorities like a young and expanding family, my career, and civic and religious responsibilities took precedence. All the while, though, my heart continued to urge me to return to the mountains.

The Incredible Fred A. Birchmore

One day I read in our church bulletin that a local Athens, Georgia, resident, Fred A. Birchmore, was planning to give a talk about hiking the Appalachian Trail (A.T.). That struck a nerve because ever since my climb of Mt. Washington, where the A.T. crosses its peak, I had a nagging desire to hike that trail. This, therefore, seemed like a fine opportunity to learn more about the trail from someone who had hiked the whole thing. Consequently, our family attended the talk, and it was indeed fascinating. Afterwards, I introduced myself to Fred and shared my interest in the A.T. He then asked me if I wanted to learn more about it. "Yes," I replied. As a result, Fred said he would loan me a book that would either strengthen or weaken my desire.

Within days Fred delivered the book, a 1,000-page collection of stories about the first people to hike the entire A.T. When I completed it and again spoke with Fred, he wanted to know if I was interested in reading more. Again, I said, "Yes." Thus, he gave me volume II, another 1,000-page book, from which I compiled additional extensive notes. Next Fred gave me some great advice, the first of many pieces of wisdom this wonderful man and special mentor shared with me over the years.

"Fred, what are you waiting for? If you want to hike the trail, you need to quit thinking about it and start. Don't put your dreams off for a better day that may never come. Begin with day hikes to see how you like it. Then try a short over-nighter to see how you deal with camping out in the elements. If you still like it, take a long hike." And I followed that plan to the hilt. I was 48 when I took my first A.T. hike. It was November 17, 1991, and my daughter Katie and I did an 11-mile hike in Georgia. Then I began taking other day hikes with my sons, Jeff and Dave. During May 1993, Jeff, then 21, and I did our first overnight backpacking trip, a 3-day 28-mile hike, climbing from Amicalola Falls State Park to the A.T.'s southern terminus on Springer Mountain, then north on the A.T. to Woody Gap. Two months later, Jeff and I did a 200-mile A.T. hike from Georgia across the crests of the Smoky Mountains to Hot Springs, North Carolina. As I write this, I have now completed more than 1,200 miles on the Appalachian Trail, the latest a 228-mile hike in Vermont and New Hampshire that I did with Ken "Waypoint" Sowles in 2006. The intent of this chapter is to see if I can take you along with me on some of these adventures and share the lessons my backpacking life taught me.

First, though, I must tell you more about Fred Birchmore, the most extraordinary person I have ever known. Never have I met a better athlete, world-class explorer, higher achiever, more courageous, absolutely more accomplished, finer, more remarkable person.

The two most instructive books I have ever read are the *Bible* and *Around the World on a Bicycle*,[3] Fred Birchmore's true story of his one-

---

[3] The original book was published by The University of Georgia Press, Athens, Georgia, in 1939. It was reprinted in 1996 by Cucumber Island Storytellers, Montchanin, Delaware.

speed bicycle ride, mostly alone, around the world in 1935-36. With no weapon except great faith in his maker and the goodness of humanity, Fred crossed Europe, much of Egypt, the deserts of the Mideast, the wilds of Afghanistan, and Southeast Asia, the latter during the monsoon season. He survived attacks by wolves, a person intent on slitting his throat, cobras, malaria, raging rivers, and being stalked for three days by a tiger. During his life Fred has ridden bicycles 40,000 miles, hiked thousands of miles, walked down the Washington Monument on his hands, discovered ancient Inca trails and ruins in Peru, and built The Great Wall of Athens, a 600-foot long, up to 16-foot high, 3-foot thick stone wall that includes some rocks weighing more than 300 pounds.

What is most amazing about the wall is that Fred lifted by hand an estimated 72 boxcar loads of granite stones, placed the rocks on the wall using no mechanical power except his own muscles, mostly worked alone, and built it when he was 71-76 years old. If you ever see his wall and doubt that he actually built it without mechanical equipment, remove such doubts. I watched him do it. Fred Birchmore is 5 feet 6 inches tall. He weighs about 135 pounds. At 90, he could still do head stands. At 94, Fred and his wife Willa Deane still rise early each morning, walk 2-3 miles, eat breakfast, and go to the YMCA to work out. What an inspiration both of them have been to me as well as to my children and my UGA students whom I often took to the Birchmore's home to walk on the wall and listen to their extraordinary life stories.

I likewise recommend you read his other book, *Miracles in my Life: Tales of a Happy Wanderer,*[4] that documents not just his life but the accomplishments of his remarkable family. Through his books, teachings, talks, role modeling, and The Great Wall of Athens, Fred is my constant reminder of the capabilities within all of us to achieve unimaginable things if only we have courage, determination, and most importantly, persistence. Whenever I felt ready to give up on the trail or elsewhere in life, I drew inspiration from Fred. He taught me always to shoot higher than I believed possible, to keep going forward one step at a time, to stay positive and maintain my faith, and to plan, think, and be resourceful. I count this lawyer, college professor, International Exchange Scholar, author, lecturer, free lance writer for magazines and newspapers, collegiate boxer, acrobat, aviator, archaeologist, ornitholo-

[4] Cucumber Island Storytellers, Hockessin, Delaware, 1996.

gist, singer, coach, environmentalist, ecologist, stone mason extraordinaire, and good friend who came into my life by accident one day among my greatest blessings.

Appalachian Trail

The Appalachian Trail is America's oldest and most revered long trail, a 2,175-mile footpath that runs through 14 states from Georgia to Maine. Three types of people walk this trail: day hikers, thru-hikers, and section hikers. The latter two are backpackers, for they spend nights on the trail and must carry everything they need for days on their backs.

Experts who have hiked all three of the great American long trails have consistently stated their belief that the A.T. is more difficult than the Pacific Crest Trail or the Continental Divide Trail. The reason is that the A.T. has fewer switchbacks and many steep inclines and descents. And I can attest to its difficulty. So far I have found no really easy sections on the A.T. that I have hiked from Georgia to Front Royal, Virginia, across the 105-mile northern half of the trail in Pennsylvania, and in New England. By far the toughest part was New Hampshire and Vermont. But Pennsylvania killed my feet. The trail is flatter there than in the southern Appalachians and New England, but it is covered in sharp, slanted, and other sorts of rocks that slowed me down and blistered my feet. Climbs are not the only thing that makes the A.T. tough.

For most people, thru-hiking the A.T. is a 6-month effort, 180 days averaging 12 miles per day not including additional mileage in getting water or going to town for supplies. That is about what it would take me to do it all, but I have chosen to hike sections, for I am unable to pull six months from the rest of my life at one time. So I go when I can for a week or two and sometimes more. Keep all of this in mind when I say that Fred Birchmore and his son Danny did the A.T. in 101 days. Fred was 63 at the time and averaged 22 miles per day. His advice to me, however, was don't rush to the end. "The joy," he said, "in hiking the A.T. is in the journey." He needn't have worried. I did a 25-miler one day, and I cannot imagine how he averaged 22-milers every day for 101 days. I'm a slow old tortoise. To do the A.T., I estimate that

I would need to take 5.5-million steps. Later, this will put my blisters in perspective.

So what's the trail like?   Sometimes I have walked on old logging roads. At other times I have hiked non-stop for miles over rocks (picture a dried up creek bed). Mostly the A.T. is a dirt path about 1-2 feet wide, simply a groove worn by hikers and eroded by the wash of rain. Most of it is a pretty, peaceful walk through the woods, at least down South where I have done most of my treks so far.

What have I seen? Far more beauty and amazing natural wonders than I can ever describe in one chapter. Hiking in the southern Appalachian Mountains is like walking under a dark green canopy surrounded on all sides by lush vegetation of exceptional variety, my lungs filled with clean air, my attitude lifted by the fragrance of wildflowers and birds singing. Some days I have walked under hundred-yard-long rhododendron arboretums dripping with gorgeous white or pink blossoms. At other times I have gazed down from on high at a sea of low lying clouds that resembled an ocean of white water splashing the shore. Often I have been so close to nature and God's amazing wild creatures that I could almost touch them. For some the A.T. is a long walk, a chance to prove you have the right stuff. I see it as a life-enriching experience. Definitely, it changed me, I think for the better.

First 200-Miler

The best way to give you a feel for the A.T. is by reliving a few of my more memorable backpacking trips. I'll begin with the 200-mile, 18-day adventure Jeff and I took from Dicks Creek Gap in Georgia to Hot Springs, North Carolina. It was our maiden voyage, so to speak, and as such, it was a most instructive outing, one we still relish and laugh about. It also covered some of the highest terrain and most difficult hiking on the A.T. particularly in terms of vertical climbing per day. By this I am referring to altitude change rather than miles hiked each day. The former is a much better judge of the energy required, which was considerable.

While the scenery was fine, I have to tell you the discomfort was huge because I developed foot blisters on the second day and didn't get rid of them until day 16. Sometimes those blisters were stacked three high on top of one another. Furthermore, unlike our previous hikes where it seldom rained and if so, only for short periods, it rained long and hard for 7 of those days and because of overcast skies and high humidity, we stayed wet for 13 of the 18 days. Well, not totally wet. Fred wisely advised me to carry a set of dry clothes for camp and told me never to let them get wet. And it felt wonderful to strip out of soaking wet pants, shirts, socks and boots and slide into those dry garments each afternoon. The problem was, and it was a most challenging psychological barrier, that we had to get back into all those cold wet garments and boots early every morning. All I can tell you is that we did it, but we waited to the very last moment and started walking immediately to warm up enough to tolerate the discomfort. Body heat, incidentally, is what dries your clothing out faster than the sun. Hard exercise is what does it. That and quick-drying synthetic-fiber clothes. I learned the hard way about wearing jeans backpacking. When they get soaked, they dry very slowly, and wet denim wore the skin off several parts of my body where the fabric rubbed against them.

Never seriously attempt the A.T. unless you are willing to put up with the misery that is part of the deal. The trail's theme is "No rain, no pain, no Maine," and it couldn't be more accurate. And I would add the lack of cleanliness. Can you go a week without a shower or washing your hair? Often we don't have a choice. The A.T. is not for the timid or weak at heart. You better really want to do it, or you would be far happier staying home. And being uncomfortable is one thing. Blisters are painful, especially if they are stacked right on top of each other or located on the back of your heels.

It took years of experimentation using everything from Moleskin to duct tape, but I think I have found a solution to my blisters. During the Vermont-New Hampshire hike where it rained 21 out of 23 days and we stayed almost constantly wet, I had none. The key was light-weight boots, walking for days before the hike in sandals and/or bare feet to dry and toughen my skin, coating my feet each morning on the hike with a friction-reducing product called Body Glide, wearing an 80% silk thin liner sock under my medium-weight wool socks, taking my boots and socks off several times daily to allow the heat in my boots to dissipate, and applying Moleskin to hot spots before blisters appeared. This may sound tedious, but it worked. I was blister-pain free as a result.

Sleeping it off

One thing that makes the A.T. unique is its shelters. Most of them are open, three-sided buildings that typically sleep 7 people, and on average, they are located about every 10 miles along the trail from Georgia to Maine. I say "about" because shelters are located near water sources, which everybody needs and wants near camp.

Where you most often find water is in a gap or a downhill location. This is because water seeps or runs downhill, and springs and creeks are found far below the peaks or high ridges. The point is that shelters are irregularly spaced. Sometimes the next shelter is 6 miles from the last. In other places it may be 16 miles away. Most thru- and section hikers head for the shelters for protection from the rain, to sleep on dry wooden floors, to find water, to cook, to meet and socialize with friends, and to write in and read shelter books. The latter have three primary purposes: security, communication, and entertainment. Backpackers make entries in these logbooks to establish their whereabouts in case friends or family are looking for them. And messages written by hikers can be instructive, philosophical, and/or really funny. And since I don't carry a book in my pack because of its added weight, I look forward to reading the logbooks.

Once I read this in a logbook. "Definition of hiking the A.T--hike, eat, get water, swat flies, poop, sleep." Yep, that just about covers it. It's a crude but pretty short priority list. I'd add get dry and warm, high priorities when you are soaked and very cold as we were in New England. You never really know what you will read next. On that first long section hike with Jeff, an entry in the Hogback Ridge Shelter logbook announced that June 21st was Nude Hiking Day followed by "June 22nd is the rain date." Definitely that became a topic of discussion in the shelter that night. I also know for a fact that some people did it.

Tents and Chainsaw

For a lot of good reasons, sleeping is a big issue on the trail. Thru-hikers and section hikers know this and almost always carry a tent, tarp, hammock, or bivy sack. Many, however, prefer to sleep in the shelters because they save time and get them out of the rain. Trust me, it is no fun setting up and taking down a tent in the rain. But I have mixed emotions about shelters because I'm old and hard wooden floors, even with my 1-inch-thick sleeping pad, are uncomfortable. Another problem is whom you are sleeping with. Shelters are communes. Snoring and other noises are part of the total package. The good news is that long-distance hikers tend to be quite tolerant and respectful of others' needs and privacy. For instance, when men or women have to get out of wet clothes, we just shut our eyes.

Then there are the mice. Virtually all shelters have these pesky, scampering, chewing rascals that you seldom see in daylight but that race through the shelters all night. When you hear chewing in the darkest hours, it concerns you because those razor sharp incisors just might be cutting right through your expensive backpack. None have done that to mine yet, but mice have eaten through a lot of other pieces of my equipment, run right across my face one time, and bitten the tip off the nose pad on my glasses twice, fortunately not while they were on my face. Mice will eat anything. But for the record, they aren't rats, and they aren't big. They are simply annoying, clever, tiny gray field mice, and in the shelter, your constant sleepover buddies.

Personally, I like the privacy and comfort of my tent but hate carrying its four extra pounds all those miles when I am not using it, which is most of the time. My pack weighs 37 pound when fully loaded for a 6-day hike. It needs to be closer to 28-30 pounds. But it is nice to be able to read mosquito-free in privacy, which I can do in my tent using my flashlight. And it was definitely a relief that night when Chainsaw, the loudest snorer in human history, commenced his infernal racket. I guarantee you he could be heard at least 100-yards away.

Jeff made the mistake that night to sleep in the shelter with two females and Chainsaw, who at that point seemed like such a nice old man. Pretty soon it began. Then it roared. Shortly, I heard a lot of banging around, and I knew it was Jeff, trying to wake Chainsaw up and get him to quiet down. It didn't work. About 30 minutes of insufferable noise later, Jeff came steaming mad into my tent. But all night long that locomotive rumbled along. In the morning the two exhausted women broke camp early and in the process accidentally woke Chainsaw from his slumber. Then he chewed them out for waking him up. Folks, I snore some. Lots of people do. But if anyone tells you that you sound like a chainsaw, stay out of the shelters. Find a cave somewhere.

Who Turned off the Lights?

People go to bed early in shelters. There really is no choice, for what else are you supposed to do when it gets dark and there's no electricity? Once I came to a shelter with six young guys already in it, all lying down in their sleeping bags. No sooner had I gotten there than one of them said, "Guess I'll go to sleep." It was 6:30! And he closed his eyes as did all the other five thru-hikers. There was no way I was joining them. It's a rare day at my age that I ever sleep more than 8 hours, and looking at a 2:30 a.m. wake-up time was ridiculous. So I did my best to keep quiet but didn't sack out until 9. Still, at 5 the next morning, I was staring wide-eyed at blackness. And that's why I tend to break camp at sunrise. That and it is the best part of the day. Incredibly, the other six were still sleeping when I left the shelter. I used to be able to sleep forever like them, but you just wait, youngun's. One day you'll understand me better.

I told that story to open a short conversation on compatibility, a big consideration if you plan to hike the A.T. Whether we slept in the shelter or tent, my sons wanted to sleep until 9 a.m. I knew what time I was going to wake up. That's why my first trail name was Rooster. What was I supposed to do quietly each morning from about 5:30 until 9 a.m.? This is just one of many incompatibility problems that A.T. backpackers face. Others are how fast people can or want to walk, how many hours and miles they want to go each day, what they want to eat and when, how much talking they want to do, and who is going to go get the water or clean the cooking pot. It's a pretty long list and a good reason why many partners, even best friends and fiancées, split up and why others hike alone. If you want hiking companions, pick them very carefully. Either that or you better be willing to compromise. The boys and I worked on a number of our differences, argued a little, pouted some, but we did work it out.

Tracker

Trail names are a long-standing tradition on the A.T. Soon the boys changed mine to Tracker. Jeff is Pathfinder. People assume trail names for safety and other reasons. For instance, you may want to leave a note in a shelter book for a friend, but you don't want strangers to know who

you are. Now you might think that I got my trail name because I am
highly skilled in locating and identifying animals from their signature
footprints and scat, but the truth is that my boys named me Tracker
as a joke because of an incident at the family farm in North Carolina.
One day Inky, Fuzz, and I took a long walk down by the river where
I discovered beavers had been cutting trees and building dams. Inky
and Fuzz, the farm's two dogs, were my buddies. When I reported this
to everyone, the boys thought I was way too excited. Thereafter, every
time I went walking, the boys would ask me if I found any more beavers.
I've been Tracker ever since. As long as they love me and want to do
things with me, I don't care what they call me.

Surprises

Jeff and I saw some very impressive scenery on this first 200-miler
over Standing Indian Mountain, Albert Mountain, Siler Bald, Cheoah
Bald, and the 65-mile route along the high ridge dividing Tennessee and
North Carolina through Great Smoky Mountains National Park. We
observed much wildlife including the biggest salamander I ever saw, one
that I dipped out of a puddle with my cooking pot lid quite accidentally
while trying to collect water on a mountain in North Carolina. We were
rained on heavily as we ascended the ridge to Mollies Ridge Shelter and
wound up spending the night with 12 others in that packed facility.
While sleeping on the second deck, I awoke to an animal scratching in
the shelter, and when I finally got my eyes to focus, to my surprise it
was a skunk on the floor five feet below me. Everyone else was sound
asleep, so my reaction was to stay silent and hopeful, which apparently
worked, for after five minutes of nosing around, the critter, much to
my great relief, departed.

When I told my marketing class at UGA about this skunk encoun-
ter, a student told me that he had seen a skunk in that same Smoky
Mountains shelter. In his case, however, he awakened to find the animal
asleep on his stomach. I asked him what he did, to which he replied, "It
spooked me so much, I jumped up, the skunk flew into the air, it took
off, and thank God it didn't spray us." What I have learned since is that
it is not uncommon for skunks to live near shelters. I know another
lived near Blood Mountain Shelter in Georgia and frequently visited

the occupants inside. Yet, I know of no A.T. situation where skunks sprayed shelter occupants. Maybe they're waiting for you.

About half way across the Smoky Mountains and more than 100 miles into the hike, we heard rumors of great cheeseburgers at Mountain Momma's, a country store just outside the north end of the park. By this time we were so hungry for greasy food, anything with fat in it, cheese, and most any drink but water that we picked up our pace and were literally pulled for nearly 25 miles to our destination. And was it worth it! One of the most interesting things about backpacking is that it is such rigorous exercise that the typical backpacker burns 4,000 – 7,000 calories per day. Translated, this means you can eat most anything you want and still lose weight. On the trail Jeff and I ate a lot of peanut butter and honey sandwiches, Spam and Hormel spreads, peanuts, noodle dinners, chocolate candy, granola bars, and still on this trip I lost 3 inches on my waist, despite all the milk shakes and calories I consumed in town when we stopped for supplies. When we hit Mountain Momma's, we wore that grill out.

Fire!

There are times in life when you become aware that your kids have something very important that they can teach you if you will just pay attention. Such was absolutely the case one evening on this trip at Mt. Collins Shelter when a fireball accompanied by screams jolted Jeff and me from our daydreams. Something had gone drastically wrong at the camp site occupied by two college-age backpackers about 75 feet away. As quickly as we could get in our Tevas, we ran to the spot where we observed a 15-foot circle of fire and a young man on fire with visible burns on his arm. We worked furiously, especially Jeff who aggressively stomped at the fire. The young man's female companion was not burned but was highly concerned about her friend and traumatized by the accident. What took me most by surprise was how fast Jeff took charge of this situation, administered first aid as best he could with our limited supplies, and calmed both individuals down.

The fire's source was a serious error of judgment by the experienced male backpacker who attempted to ignite his camp fire by tossing white gas (camp stove fuel) directly from his fuel bottle onto the fire. When the flame hit the fuel, it raced back to the bottle's source in the man's hand. Although he claimed to have started fires successfully like this many times before, this is a prime example of backpacking risks caused by over-confidence and unsafe practices. That, however, is not my real message here. Without Jeff's quick response, there is no telling how much worse the consequences could have been, and I am still amazed at this inner strength and capabilities in Jeff that I never knew existed.

In life, there are pivotal moments when relationships change, and this was such an event. On that day, roles were reversed. I became the student and my son the teacher and protector. Jeff showed courage, a cool head, decisiveness, quick thinking, and leadership skills that most parents pray their children will have, but until then, I had never really witnessed them. And on this day, I knew he would do just fine in life. It was a turning point. After that, I started asking him far more often for advice and trusted his judgment more willingly. I learned to talk less and listen more, for he could teach me a great deal. And he most definitely has. Furthermore, Jeff changed my relationships with my other children because he made me see them differently, not as my children so much in need of my advice and protection, but as equally competent, resourceful individuals who wanted to help and teach me as much as they could. As sorry as I am about the man's suffering, I am grateful for what life taught me that evening.

Observations

Despite the rain, the hardships, and the frustrations of such an arduous journey, I came away very satisfied with our first big section hike and far more knowledgeable about many things. Mainly I had a great time because I shared the trip with my boy. I was so proud of him. He put up with pain, some minor crises, a lot of strenuous climbing, and 24 hours per day with my idiosyncrasies. The trip convinced me that I had the desire and ability to hike the entire A.T., and now I knew more about how to do it. And I did want to hike as much of the trail as I could. My thinking was that if I could handle the highest peaks in the South in the rain and heat of summer, then I most surely could handle just about anything the A.T. threw my way as well as most other challenges in life.

350-Miler

In June 1995, Jeff, Dave, and I started on what I intended to be a 500-mile section hike. Dave was 16 at the time. The plan was for the boys to accompany me part of the way, and then I would go on alone for the rest of the hike. Let's be honest. Dave was a reluctant backpacker. It was my fault. One of the first times I took him hiking, when he was about 12, we walked 18 miles, a very dumb thing to do on my part that almost turned him away from hiking forever. Anyway, Jeff urged him on, Dave joined us, and the three of us had a great time together. Even the rain gave us a big break.

Got Ya'

Much of what an A.T. hike is about is memories, and we have so many good ones from this trip. One evening we stopped at a shelter before a big climb the next day to the top of Roan Mountain. My plan was to start early in the morning to take advantage of the cooler morning air. The boys' plan was to sleep late and leave whenever. Keep in mind that they walk faster than I do, so I decided that I would leave early, and they could catch up to me on the trail, and they agreed. About noon, I finally reached the summit, a wonderful partial bald covered in acres of blooming Catawba rhododendron. As I proceeded to take off my backpack, I saw a young man standing about 150-feet away, and thought, "That's funny. He looks a lot like Dave." And then he yelled back at me, "Hey, Dad."

How could this be? There was only one trail to the top. Nobody passed me, and Dave was sound asleep when I left camp. Then I saw Jeff, and together they solved the mystery. When they woke up, another hiker in the shelter asked them where they were going that day. They said, "Roan Mountain." He said, "Want a ride? There's a road up there, and I'll be glad to drive you there in my truck. It's parked a half-mile from here." So they accepted the ride and got to the top ahead of me. How they teased me about this for the rest of the trip. Actually, it was pretty funny.

Track Meet

That night we stayed at Roan High Knob Shelter, at 6,285 feet the highest shelter on the entire A.T. Although it had room for 14 people, we were its only occupants. So we chose to sleep in the loft, which had a window covered by a piece of plastic. In the middle of the night, I awoke to two loud noises, the plastic flap banging like crazy in the wind and a lot of foot traffic. The latter sounded like a road race, which it turns out was a fact. All night long squirrels raced across the deck. Must have been mating season, I guess. Sort of killed the sleeping for me, however. The boys slept right through it. I believe one's comment in the morning was, "What noise?"

Southern Balds

I get asked a lot what my favorite part of the A.T. has been, and I always give the same answer: the great southern balds between Carver Gap and highway 19E, 14 miles to the north. Balds are grassy meadows right on the tops of mountains, and in this section we hiked across four magnificent balds: Round Bald (5,807 feet), Jane Bald (5,807 feet), Little Hump Mt. (5,459 feet) and Hump Mt. (5,587 feet), the greatest concentration of Southern balds on the A.T. The scenery was stunning.

If you ask hikers to name their favorite A.T. places, opinions vary considerably. Largely, it is a function of the weather and time of year that backpackers reached various trail points. We were on the balds in late June when it was so beautiful. My fondest memory that day was watching my sons ascend the long meadow up Hump Mountain's spine while a bank of clouds rolled in. I swear it looked like they were walking right into Heaven. It was the best spiritual moment I've ever experienced on the A.T.

Sadness in My Heart

Sharon met us that Saturday in the town of Roan Mountain, Tennessee, with bad news that my mom had fallen and broken her hip. All of us then drove to Burlington to see her. From Saturday through

Tuesday, Ma appeared to be getting better. I spent much of the morning with her on Tuesday, and my sister Eleanor spent the early afternoon with her as well. However, later that day while we were visiting with her doctor, a call came in about Ma. By the time we returned to the hospital, much to our sadness, she had passed away from a blood clot. It was June 28, 1995, three days after her 90th birthday.

In my trail diary, I later wrote the following:

"I will miss Mom. She was the kindest, most unselfish, considerate person I have ever known and a profound influence on me. I loved her as much as a person can love a mother, and I always knew she felt likewise toward me. I will miss her but never forget her. Also, I feel so blessed to have been her son. Mom has no worries about life after death. She is in Heaven already."

Perhaps it was she that was following that trail up Hump Mountain that day.

Trail Angels

When family tragedies strike A.T. hikers, the question becomes whether to continue the journey or return home to help loved ones. This was an indecisive point in my life, for I wanted to go on but also felt a strong need to help Pop. He, though, encouraged Jeff and me to get back on the A.T. and so did other family members. Thus, Jeff and I did that resuming our hike on July 7th. Due to other commitments, Dave returned to Athens with Sharon, and we definitely missed him as well as Ma. I still miss her.

The layoff in addition to hiking with a heavier heart took their toll on our physical and mental condition. In many ways, it was like starting again, and very quickly I developed a bad heel blister. That is why coming off a long descent on a very hot day, the creek ahead looked so inviting. What we longed to do was dive in and cool off, but to our frustration, the land was fenced prohibiting our access. About this time, a man appeared on the property, so I asked him if he would mind if my boy and I just sat on the rock by the river and soaked our aching, hot feet. He said, "Sure. Go ahead." So we did, and it felt wonderful. A few minutes later a woman emerged from the cabin and asked us if we would like some cold water. "Yes," we said, again grateful to these nice folks. Then she stated, "I've got some ice cold sodas in the house. Can I bring you one?" Jeff and I were looking at each other and wondering how much better could it get? Then while we were drinking the sodas, which tasted delicious after days of nothing but water and Tang, the woman said, "If you are not in a hurry, we are getting ready to have a steak dinner. We would love to have you join us. You can also take a shower in the cabin if you want."

That was it. I was sure I had died and entered a better world. Yet the most meaningful part of this story is that when we sat down to eat, this couple had divided their two steaks, their baked potatoes, and their salads in half. There was no extra food. I am not sure I have ever met two more generous, kind people than Gene and Betty, the first of many good caring Americans I have come to know on the trail. Thru-hikers and section hikers call them trail angels, and their good deeds are what we backpackers call trail magic, those unexpected and so much appreciated acts of kindness and generosity that people provide us. What a wonderful example these good Tennessee folks set for us.

Solo

At Damascus, Virginia, Jeff and I stuffed ourselves on restaurant food and said our goodbyes. Thereafter, I was going solo, and since there was not enough time left to finish the planned 500-mile hike, I was determined to reach Catawba, Virginia, about 240 miles farther up the trail. It was a strange, uncertain time waving goodbye to Jeff and heading up my first mountain alone, and I did experience sadness and some anxieties. One reason was that I knew that there were not going to be a lot of thru-hikers on the trail at this time of year. Most heading to Maine were long gone and in Northern Virginia or Pennsylvania by now. Still, I really wanted to go and plodded my way up the trail.

Hiking alone is different in a number of ways from hiking with a partner. It isn't just the absence of company. That tent, stove, water purifier, fuel and other items that we distributed among us now were all in my pack. Likewise, there was no backup if I became injured or got into trouble. Unless I met other hikers to work with, I was on my own. An advantage, however, is that solo hikers tend to see more wildlife. Since my boys usually walked ahead of me, they typically saw and accidentally spooked the animals before I got there. Now I saw them all including lots of deer and wild turkeys.

If you have never been present when wild turkeys take flight and blast through the low lying branches, you have something to look forward to. The first time they did that I hit the ground thinking that someone had shot a rifle. One of my fondest wildlife memories on this trip was coming over a hill on an old logging road and surprising two turkeys that in turn began running away from me down that road before they took off in perfect formation. It reminded me of the Navy's Blue Angels precision flight team. They lifted off side-by-side, one about four feet behind and to the left of the other.

Getting Scared

Not long ago I gave a talk to my granddaughter's fourth grade class on hiking the A.T., and one of the many good questions the students asked me was whether I ever got lonely on the trail. They also asked if I ever got bored. A third inquired if I ever got scared. The answer to all three is "Yes." It didn't happen often, but it indeed happened. For sure I was lonesome for the first 3 days after Jeff and I parted ways. And I have been bored sometimes especially when getting to a shelter early in the day. But one of the times I was most scared was the fourth day of this solo hike.

I was hiking so well that I decided to go another 10 miles that afternoon and stay at Mount Rogers National Recreation Area Headquarters. My guidebook said hikers could camp on the building grounds and order hot delivered pizza from the pay phone there. Unfortunately, as night approached, I got caught in a thunderstorm dead center on the crest of Brushy Mountain, several miles from my destination. I thought there was little choice but to push on along that ridge walking in two inches of gushing water since there was really no place to protect myself from potential lightning strikes, which definitely had me worried. Both sides of the trail were covered in dense brush and small rocks.

I am not sure exactly how far I hiked under such violent weather conditions, but it took longer than an hour to reach my NRA facility destination about 8:15 p.m. I had hiked 25 miles that day, alone, the last part in a most tense forced march. To my dismay, though, the grounds were devoid of people, the building was locked, and I was cold, soaked, and concerned about hypothermia, which is indeed a risk in the southern Appalachians even in the summer months. The worst part, however, was that the facility was near a relatively busy, dark road, which meant I would have to risk one of the worst threats to A.T. hikers. The golden rule is "Do not camp near a road." The reason is that you are too accessible to potential trouble makers, particularly drunks bent on doing mischief. I've never been bothered by troublemakers and it rarely happens to anyone on the trail, but occasionally it does happen.

Unfortunately, I had no real choice. That night I laid out my sleeping pad on the back porch and slept with one eye open until the cleaning lady finally arrived at 6 a.m. I didn't even get the pizza because the price was so high. The good news is that I survived to hike another day. The next day I reached Atkins where two great chocolate milkshakes and a fine hot meal restored my spirits. Life again was good.

Chestnut Knob Shelter and My Slinky Bedfellow

Chestnut Knob Shelter, one of the largest and most unique shelters on the A.T., will go down in Tracker hiking history as another night to remember. A former forest ranger's house, the shelter is a fully enclosed stone building perched right on the top of a mountain. I decided to stay there because another storm was brewing, and after the last big one, I was not going to take that chance. Besides, I was exhausted.

When I entered the building, I made a quick decision to put all of my gear on the first bunk by the door. This was great until I began reading the shelter book where an entry dated about 3 weeks earlier said, "I think there was a snake in here last night." I didn't think much of that until I read another message that again mentioned a possible snake in the shelter. Then a third said, "There was a snake in here chasing mice. I saw it, and it was on the bunk just inside the door." This got my attention because that was the bunk I was lying on, and the entry was two days old. Right then I picked up all my gear and moved it to the opposite side of the shelter where I stowed it on the lower deck. About 9 p.m. I was asleep. All by myself.

In the early morning hours, I awoke to a loud, unusual thump and when I aimed my flashlight toward the end of my sleeping bag, I spotted a black snake about 3 feet from my big toe. Now I knew it wasn't poisonous, but excuse me if I tell you I don't care to share my sleeping bag with any snake. What happened is that the snake had been working its way toward a mouse when it fell off the top deck to the one below. All I can say is that I was done sleeping for the night and finished with Chestnut Knob Shelter. I started hiking in the dark that day under the stars.

Bland and Wytheville

How far you hike on the A.T. and what your pack weighs are tied very closely to food and how much backpackers will carry before they go to town to get re-supplied. The trade-off is that the less food you carry, the more frequently you need to waste time and energy getting into and out of towns, and the more you carry, the longer you can stay on the trail but the heavier the load. Food is one of the heaviest things hikers carry, so my strategy typically is to try to go 5 to 7 days before going into town.

Towns are very crucial to long distance hiking because I need a post office to get my previously shipped supplies, a grocery for bread, some place to buy fuel for my cooking stove, a laundry to wash my gross smelling clothes, and a restaurant to get something I'm craving to eat. I also want a cheap motel so I can shower and sleep on a comfortable bed. All of this is why Bland, Virginia, sticks out. On a Saturday morning, I hiked more than two miles from the A.T. into Bland. My first disappointment came when I read a sign announcing that the only laundromat in town had gone out of business. Next I discovered that the restaurant where I planned to eat had been closed for sanitation reasons. At least the Post Office was still open so I got my shipment and walked to the motel, unfortunately, a business located up another mountain in the opposite direction from the A.T. Things were not going very well.

Under the circumstances, I decided to rest in town a little longer than usual and attend services next morning at the Presbyterian Church. I got there for the 9:40 service and learned the sign was wrong. The only service was at 11:00, which I later attended with about 20 other people. Our leader was Sam Cassell, a lay preacher. After the service,

Sam introduced himself and his wife Sis, and they invited me, this stranger, to lunch at their home if I had time. So I joined them for a wonderful home-cooked Southern meal loaded with the vegetables I so desired. Then they asked if I would be interested in attending their church picnic in Wytheville, which I also did and where I got the most cordial and sincere welcome from Joe and Liz Shumate and their congregation. I had the best time and enormously enjoyed the picnic and hay ride they took me on. Again, I was the beneficiary of A.T. trail angels and trail magic, and it couldn't have happened at a better time, for I really needed a dose of good food and fellowship. And I am still very grateful for everyone's kindness. I had a splendid day, and it really gave me a badly needed morale boost.

Mo Fats

One of my most pleasing times on the trail was the three days I hiked on this trip with Mo Fats. Mo, which is short for "Missouri," was perhaps the largest hiker who ever attempted to do the entire A.T. When he started in Georgia, he weighed 386 pounds not including his 50-pound pack. But he was diligent, and by the time our paths crossed in Virginia, he had lost 100 pounds. By the end of the season, he had backpacked all the way to the Delaware Water Gap and had dropped a total of 126 pounds. These two accomplishments were incredible, but why I want to tell you about Mo is that he epitomizes the great character and heart of the people I see on the trail. Most are truly special individuals.

The truth is that just about no one really hikes alone on the A.T. if they hike in prime thru-hiking season for that area. By this I mean that if you assume most thru-hikers start at Springer Mountain, Georgia, between March 1st and April 15th, you can estimate where they are likely to be at 12-15 miles a day and then hike where they are currently backpacking. But even if the thru-hikers have long passed the section you're on, you meet people like Mo, and together you share a few days or evenings. In the process, I learned a great deal about individuals from all over the world, different professions and beliefs, and various age groups. All helped me grow as a person.

Mo was one of the nicest people I ever met on the trail, and we spent a lot of enjoyable hours together. In truth, he hiked even slower than I, so typically I would go on ahead and Mo would eventually make his appearance at the shelter. One night, though, I got really worried because it was getting dark and he was very late. Thinking he might be in trouble, I yelled his name many times over but to no avail. Finally, I decided I better go find him, and just as I was about to leave I saw his cheery face coming toward the shelter. This is the way it is on the trail. We do get close and look out for each other. We are a family--a good family. And a number of people have gone out of their way to help me and take care of me. More will be said about them later.

Timber Rattler

One animal that strikes fear in A.T. hikers is the timber rattler, which along with the copperhead, make up the two species of poisonous snakes found on the trail. The reason people fear timber rattlers is that this snake's venom can kill you. Usually it doesn't, but it can. Copperheads, though more aggressive, usually just make you quite ill. What I knew before hiking the A.T. is that on average a thru-hiker sees one timber rattler during the entire 2,175-mile journey. You just don't know when. The first one I saw was in Virginia, and it scared the dickens out of me. The location was Sinking Creek Mountain, and I was alone hiking a section of trail that was covered on both sides with dark green, big-leaf plants about 18 inches high that I couldn't see under and that reached out to cover most of the trail. Suddenly a 4-foot timber rattler sounded its rattle and jumped directly onto the trail about 3 feet in front of me. It had been lying under the foliage next to the trail, apparently waiting for lunch. My immediate reaction was to back-track so fast that I about impaled myself on a tree 10 feet to my rear. I don't know how high my blood pressure went, but I was sure glad that snake jumped out ahead of me rather than toward me.

The two of us never took our eyes off each other, and neither did he stop shaking that rattle. Trail advice says that rattlers are not aggressive unless you step on them or threaten them. He also wasn't stupid and knew he couldn't swallow me. Snakes just want you to leave them alone and allow them to get away. So I waited patiently; however, he did not go away. Instead he crawled into a hole in a 2-foot high ledge ahead on the trail, a rock that I needed to step over. In that opening he coiled up, shook that tail, and waited for my next move, which I guarantee you was not going to be stepping up over that snake.

A big decision had to be made. Either I could wait for him to come back down the trail toward me or I could hike through the brush to my right and go around the ledge where he was currently located. The danger, and it was quite real, was that his mate or other rattlers could live in that dense brush and rocks on my alternative route. It took about 5 seconds to make that walk, five of the longest seconds I ever took doing anything. This was prime snake country, confirmed two days later when I saw another timber rattler. Further evidence came later from none other than the Crocodile Hunter himself who said on one of his TV shows that he had never seen more poisonous snakes (and they were timber rattlers) in any place in his life than where he was filming in the mountains of Virginia, near where I had been hiking.

Timber rattlers are beautifully marked snakes, so exceptionally camouflaged that you have to look hard to see them. And they're not the same colors. One was mainly green and the other was brown. When I show people the slide I took of the second rattler, most do not see the snake even though it is dead center in the photo and within 10 feet from where I took the picture.

What I got out of these thrills is that I need to scan the trail ahead regularly when hiking in snake country, use my hiking stick to hit the ground ahead of me because snakes sense vibration and should hit the stick first, and proceed very cautiously when hiking alone. I'm not afraid of snakes. I just don't want to surprise any more of them.

Homeward Bound

The farther you go on the trail, the bigger the problem you have getting home. On this trip, though, I got a lot of help from my friend, Harry Norris, President of Howell's Motor Freight. Harry runs his refrigerated trucking business off I-81 north of Roanoke and close to my ending point at McAfee Knob. When I needed help, Harry was there for me. He picked me up on the A.T., took me home where his family treated me very kindly, and arranged for one of his truck drivers, a good guy by the name of Danny Richards, to give me a ride home in his 18-wheeler during his run to Atlanta. Not many backpackers can say they rode home in a semi, but I can. It was like icing on the cake.

Animals

One key reason I hike is to see animals, and I have viewed many types including deer, rabbits, turtles, bob cats, skunks, raccoons, bears, owls, turkeys, snakes, lizards, mice, butterflies, bats, cattle, sheep, among others on my A.T. hikes. Surprisingly, I haven't seen a lot of birds, but I do hear them. I've also been annoyed, bitten, or stung by gnats, mosquitoes, flies, horseflies, hornets, yellow jackets, ants, spiders, and other pests. And everyone is concerned these days about ticks and for good reasons. In fact, I picked off 12 ticks on my 2006 hike in New England. Yet, all these creatures are part of nature, and if you are going into the woods, you need to coexist in their habitat.

What I try to remember is that I am a guest in their home and not vice versa. One night I was even sung to sleep by what sounded like a million frogs, and I needed their lullaby since my stomach was killing me. When I hit Catawba Grocery store, I was so hungry that I consumed a beer, a soft drink, 2 big hot dogs all the way, a bag of chips, and a pint of ice cream, and I liked it so much I reordered and ate the entire meal minus only the beer. Half way through the second serving, the waitress calmly said, "I've seen a lot of hikers do what you're doing. Most regretted it." Brother, did she hit the nail on the head.

My granddaughters love to hear my A.T. animal stories, some of which I have already told you. However, their all time favorite is my bear story. In late October of 2000, Steve "Snickers" Howard, one of my UGA students, and I took a 55-mile hike from the James River south to Troutville, Virginia. Steve had already completed the whole A.T. and in the process *gained* 15 pounds, the only person I know who added weight on the trail, in part, I guess, because he ate Snickers bars every day, even in his hot chocolate. You should try it. Break up the bar and add it to your hot chocolate. It's great. Anyway, on the first day of that hike, with full packs we climbed for 8 miles and set up our tent at Marble Spring Campground, a primitive camp site in a gap on the mountain. Our thinking was that with full heavy packs, it was unwise to try to reach Thunder Hill Shelter 15 miles from our starting point, especially on the first hiking day.

At 6:30 p.m. we began fixing dinner--Lipton's Noodles and Stroganoff enhanced with generous additions of butter and sliced pepperoni. Steve was an acclaimed trail cook, and I wanted him to teach me some of his secrets. I had just remarked how good the food smelled, especially the strong smell emanating from the just dumped in pepperoni. After Steve dished out our food, we began eating sitting opposite one another with the cooking pot in between. Suddenly Steve said, "Oh, my gosh, bear! Behind you." And I looked over my shoulder and saw a black bear of about 250 pounds looking right at us. It was just before dark in the evening of a new moon, and, no doubt, the bear smelled that pepperoni. Keep in mind that bears can smell food over great distances, something we should have thought of earlier. There were only two of us at this isolated campsite.

Immediately we stood up, closed ranks, raised our arms high, and began yelling to scare the bear away. It didn't faze him. Then he began stalking us. First he walked 15 feet to his right, stopped, and went back to his direct line toward us, but now he was 10 feet closer. By this time we had grabbed our flashlights, which luckily were near us. Unfortunately, they were tiny flashlights carried to minimize weight. Steve's at least had a high intensity bulb that enabled us to see the bear. The bear's next move was to his left. Again, though, when he returned to the line, he was closer to us than before. By now it was getting quite dark. While all of this was going on, we continued trying to decide what to do if he kept coming. Neither of us had ever before been approached by bears in camp, but we had heard that if they do that, consider the situation dangerous.

There's an old joke that says you don't have to outrun a bear, just one other person. This might have settled Steve's nerves but not mine. He was young and so much faster than I, and it was utter foolishness to assume I was going to outrun an animal that could go 30 miles an hour. Throwing our food at him similarly made little sense for that incites further bear incursions. Likewise, we understood that if the bear destroyed any of our vital gear, this hike was history. Mostly, though, we were just concerned about our safety. One thing we did was put on our raincoats to make us look bigger. All the time we continued making noise and trying to eat our hot food to get it out of the way.

Finally, after about 10 minutes of stalking us and getting to within 50 feet of us, the bear got down on all fours, growled, and charged right at us. Truthfully, if he had kept coming, it was going to be bad. There was nothing to fight him with--no rocks, sticks, or anything else near by. However, about 15 feet from us the bear ran a short distance up a tree where for about 3 minutes he hung on and watched us. Then he climbed down and went back to his starting point, began stalking us again, and then walked behind our tent and disappeared over the ridge. But we didn't have any idea what he would do next, and this was worse than seeing him in front of us. Our conclusion was we could not sleep here tonight. We needed to get away from that camping site.

Our decision was to break camp as fast as possible and head up the mountain. While I packed the sleeping bags and pads and broke down the tent, Steve watched for the bear. In that short interval, Snickers also somehow found a way to eat the rest of our hot food and put the stove and other cooking gear away. At 7:30 in the dark, we started hiking up the mountain. Steve took the lead scanning ahead and to the left for the bear. I followed looking for the bear to our right and rear. In the rustling fall leaves crunching under our boots, it was impossible, unless we stopped, to hear the noise of an approaching animal. Furthermore, it was spooky particularly when our lights spotted pairs of reflecting eyes, which might be a small animal nearby or the bear farther away. About ten times this happened, and we stopped and listened before proceeding again.

About 30 minutes into the hike, Steve's flashlight burned out. I suggested he put in his spare batteries. He then discovered he had forgotten to bring them. Luckily, my spares, a pair of double-A batteries, fit his light. Now though, we had no backups for the rest of our hike, a problem we would deal with later, but right now, we had far more pressing concerns. And so we just kept trudging up that mountain ridge.

Finally, we reached Thunder Hill Shelter, and no shelter has ever looked better to me. It was 12:15 a.m., and we had climbed 6,000 vertical feet that day, the most I have ever done in a single day with or without a pack. We were so relieved to be safe. And I can assure you I do not plan to cook a strong-smelling hot meal ever again in an isolated campsite like we did that day. We were very lucky that bear only did a bluff charge. Had he kept coming, we would have given him anything he wanted. We just didn't know whether he wanted the food in the pot or one of our legs.

The People

The Appalachian Trail is more than the adventure, the wildlife, the beautiful scenery, and wildflowers. Surprisingly, what most backpackers remember and value most are the people, those wonderful friends who share their lives, food, and fellowship with them on the journey. This is especially true of thru-hikers and trail angels. Annually thru-hikers create a special subculture, a family of people who deeply care about each other. The significance of this became very apparent to me by listening to their discussions in camp, watching the way they kidded each other around the campfire, and noting their obvious concerns about fellow thru-hikers they hadn't seen in some time. How I wished to be a full member of this family.

In truth, though, and for obvious reasons, section hikers tend to remain on the outside of this family. They are treated well but just not fully taken in by the subculture. The reason is that everyone knows you will only be with them for a few days. Plus, they know each other so very, very well. However, on my two most recent A.T. hikes, I have been most fortunate in that small groups of thru-hikers have opened their arms to me and taken me in, if not to 100% family membership, then very close to that level. And I loved and appreciated it.

Who Are These Hikers?

When people ask me who hikes the Appalachian Trail, mostly I say it is people between the ages of 22-32. A second key group is older people, a combination of retirees and others like teachers on summer break. The younger folks almost universally are people in transition--just graduated from college, just quit a job, or still trying to find that special occupation where they can fulfill their passions. Probably there is no better time to hike the trail than when you are young and relatively free of so many of life's responsibilities like full-time jobs, families, and mortgages. Also young people are more likely to have the necessary energy, stamina, and physical good health to succeed.

Many of the young people I have talked with on the trail have concluded, and rightly so, I think, that it takes more than money to motivate you to go to work willingly each day. Admirably, many of these young people are aspiring artists, musicians, or writers or want to serve mankind in some way that makes the world a better place. They're just trying to figure out who they really want to be or just who they really are. And sometimes I think I am able to help them figure this out. Mentoring is a good role for retirees like me.

Approximately 75% of the long-distance A.T. hikers I meet are males, but I think the percentage of females is growing. Some of the backpackers have lost loved ones and are trying to recover. Others are dealing with broken relationships. Our common ground is that we are seeking adventure and a unique experience. And we love nature. Another is our desire to be out where we can think more clearly, and indeed, one does a lot of good thinking on the trail. Most of us like challenges. We want to test ourselves, get in shape, and see what we're truly made of. Yes, it is satisfying to accomplish things most people can't or won't do.

To better understand the thru-hiker culture, let me share two of my more recent A.T. journeys with you. The first was a one week solo section hike I took in May 2003, in Virginia from the James River north to Waynesboro on what was the most painful A.T. hike I ever took, literally an endurance contest where I battled almost constant heavy rain, stayed cold and wet, and developed toe, foot, and knee problems. The second was my 2005 solo trip covering the A.T. across Shenandoah National Park, 107 miles south to north. On both trips, it was the people who made them so special.

Virginia Hike, May 2003

During May 2003, I set out on a planned hike from the James River to Front Royal, Virginia, a distance of 183 miles that would have taken me to the northern end of Shenandoah National Park. I abandoned the trail at Waynesboro after 76 miles due to severe bad weather and multiple blister and tendon problems. Never had I experienced worse

A.T. hiking weather--constant cold rain, low temperatures--and a lot of pain. When I heard that weather for the next week was going to be as bad, it just made no sense for me to do Shenandoah. I would wait for better weather and do Shenandoah then. It was a smart move.

Don't get the wrong impression. I did not say that my 2003 A.T. hike was not worth it. In spite of the weather and physical problems, I had a good time, thanks to the thru-hikers who befriended me.

One trail rule that was fully tested on this trip is the one that says there is always room for one more thru-hiker in a full shelter on a rainy night. Primarily, the shelters are there for thru-hikers, the people who need them most. Long-distance section hikers are next in line. When shelters are empty, it's fine for short-trip backpackers to sleep in shelters. But time and again people moved their bodies and gear to let me in, like the night Turn Around, a woman and thru-hiker from Saint Paul, and I came in soaked to the core and were given a place to stay in the full shelter. Another was Punchbowl Shelter where I met Mule, Pig Pen, Flower Power, Bearhugger and her dog Sampson. There was no hesitancy to share these shelters with me, a section hiker, and I appreciated it.

Then how can I forget the kindness of four young adults, Dirty Bird, FidoDido, Prince William, and Swiftsandal that evening at Maupin Field Shelter. These four thru-hikers welcomed this old man to their fellowship, came to me to see if they could help me in any way, and made the decision not to go farther as planned but to stay with me that evening so I wouldn't have to spend the night there alone. I learned much from these kind friends especially about their desire to become artists or teachers and how they wished those roads were not so difficult. Also, they told me they appreciated the encouragement Sharon and I were giving our son Dave as he pursued his dream and enjoyed his passion for drumming. They just wished more parents would be more understanding and encouraging.

Another thing they did that meant so much to me was extend an invitation to accompany them to town and to the movies; however, I just knew I couldn't match their trail speed and would only hold them back, as slow as I was hiking. And then when I got to town and a car honked at me, to my surprise it was Dirty Bird, this wonderful, lively female, and her hiking friends who offered me a ride in their car. I couldn't imagine how they got that car until Dirty Bird, said, "Cell phone. I called Enterprise and they picked us up at the trail." Very smart, these young people, and I just loved their attitudes and zest for life. Their energy was captivating.

Another was High Octane, a very fast hiker who still had time to slow down, walk with me, and offer help. And Twit, a man in his 50's whose hobby was running 100-mile marathons. And how could I forget Flatbread, a nurse and grandmother from Boston who got her trail name from her unique way of compressing bagels by running over them with her Jeep. If you are puzzled why she would do this, the reason is that backpackers only have so much cubic capacity in their packs. And she liked the high carbs and taste of bagels.

Renegade

Rumors began flying one morning on this trip that there was a trail angel ahead at the creek who was cooking custom-ordered breakfasts for backpackers, but I better hurry because he was leaving soon. My feet were in such bad shape by this time that even though my heart was willing, my body just wasn't. Yet, to my delight, he was still there when I arrived, and he offered to fix me breakfast. He called himself Renegade, and in the next hour he served me ice cold juice, a soda, pancakes, eggs, toast and jam, cereal and milk, and cookies, and all I wanted. And it tasted sooooo good, let me tell you. Then Renegade told me his story.

Each year for many years this blue collar trail angel drove to a spot on the A.T. in his camper and set up a fully mobile kitchen with gas grills, tables, chairs, coffee pots, and multiple ice chests and during every waking hour for two weeks when backpackers came through he fed them to the best of his ability and free. He told me he would accept a donation, but it wasn't necessary. He just wanted to help people on the trail. Again, I was so touched by the kindness and generosity of total strangers, in this case by a man who gave up his vacation time and spent his limited resources to assist others and me. This was now the third time I had been personally blessed by thoughtful Americans on the trail. Since then, Sharon and I have become trail angels back home, and we will continue to do so to assist A.T. backpackers. I know what it feels like to be the recipient of such wonderful blessings, and it feels just as good to be on the giving end.

Shenandoah National Park

In May 2005, I started at Waynesboro going north across Shenandoah National Park. Almost immediately, it began raining--an ominous sign after the downpours and cold I experienced in 2003. But an A.T. hiker keeps going because if you stayed home at the threat of bad weather, you would never backpack. Plus weather is so unpredictable. You never know what weather you'll experience. One time I hiked for 30 days on the A.T., and it rained one hour. It was so hot that I was praying for rain to cool my body down.

Under the circumstances, I stopped at Calf Mountain Shelter for the night, just 7 miles from my starting point. I arrived at 1:30 p.m. and went inside to dry off and warm up. There I met Waypoint, a retired engineer thru-hiker from Phoenix, and we hit it off almost immediately. Waypoint was hiking solo and had been on the trail since March 1st. Other thru-hikers soon joined us, Rainbow and Spartacus, for instance, a recently married young couple heading north. So while we sat in that shelter passing the time, we all got better acquainted. But I have to tell you it's boring to get to a shelter too early in the day. It convinced me that I needed to hike far more miles per day. It is much better to reach camp between 4-5 p.m. That would be my goal.

Waypoint told me he needed to get to Front Royal on May 31st to meet his friend. So the next day I asked him if he wanted to team with me to get there on the 31st and I in turn would give him with a ride into town, provided Sharon could pick me up 2 days earlier than planned. And this was the start of a fine relationship. It meant hiking 21 miles one day and 15+ another, but we thought we could do that. And we did. I can't imagine finding a nicer, more compatible hiking partner than Waypoint. We had so much in common from our retired status to past Navy service to our 100% commitment to hit every restaurant on Skyline Drive we could reach. Train, another thru-hiker of enormous good will and humor, thus started referring to us as "a couple." A couple of snorers was more accurate, but mild ones, anyway.

The rest of that hike was so much fun. What made it especially so were Waypoint, Just Mike, Train, Swan and her brother Buck (naked). Train got his trail name from carrying, and blowing, a toy wooden train whistle. The first time he did so, I couldn't imagine how a locomotive was near me in Shenandoah National Park. When I asked how Just Mike got his name, Train said someone asked him what his trail name was, and he said, "Just, Mike." So that became his name. And Buck got his name from taking a swim one day in his birthday suit. And so it went. We had so much fun night after night showing up at the shelters at various times of day, building campfires, sharing our drinks, and teasing each other about anything we could needle someone about. All of us could take it as well as dish it out. I think that is why I maybe fit in. That and having hiked about half the A.T., which they respected.

Waypoint and I determined that we weren't broke so we were going to get better trail food at every opportunity. Thus we hit every Skyline Drive wayside snack bar and restaurant. It was cheeseburgers and blackberry shakes at Loft Mountain and eggs, bacon, hash browns, English muffins, OJ, coffee, blackberry cobbler and ice cream (fantastic) at Big Meadows, and so forth. I guess you could say Waypoint and I grazed our way across Shenandoah. Remarkably, when I got to the northern end, all I had left in my food bag was one candy bar and 2 ounces of peanut butter and honey, which made it a perfectly planned hike food-wise. You want to eat everything in the bag so you can stop carrying it.

Thereafter, I was famous for talking about blackberry cobbler--which we tried to buy at every restaurant. Along the way another unusual thing happened. Thru-hikers gave me a beer twice in camp. That means someone carried the cans there in their packs. And Just Mike hauled a 4-pound bottle of blackberry wine that Train and he bought 6 miles up a mountain and presented it to me as a gift my last night on the trail. So we shared that and other goodies rarely ever available on the A.T. Now the empty bottle proudly sits on a shelf in my home. I packed it out 13 miles the last day as a lasting memory of the generous, kind friends and great times we shared together on the A.T. That is another golden A.T. rule we live by. If you pack it in, you pack it out. We try very hard to keep the trail beautiful.

I met several other special thru-hikers that last week in May 2005, people like Fatty, Montana, and Tomcat, all who shared their stories and advice with me. Interestingly, I met Fatty at Winding Stair Gap in North Carolina earlier in the year. He stopped at our trail-angel spot. One of my new buddies was Fiddlehead, a delightful young boy who was camping on the trail with his parents. The young ones are so fascinated with backpackers and the trail. What energy he had. The last day Waypoint and I hiked out with Mr. Clean, Sr., our most senior thru-hiker at 67. When we were waiting at route 522 for Sharon to meet us, we had one last gathering of many of my new friends. How I hated to leave them.

Shenandoah National Park was one of the best hikes I ever took on the A.T. I came there not expecting much, I guess because of my 2003 experience just south of the park and Skyline Drive, a road that I thought would produce considerable noise and some security risks. But it didn't. Rarely did we see the road or hear the noise even though we hiked close to it. And when you have hiked the higher, more dramatic mountains in North Carolina and Tennessee, I wasn't expecting the greatest views. But was I pleasantly surprised.

The A.T. in Shenandoah National Park was a beautiful trail, the smoothest, easiest to walk on that I have experienced. My thanks go out to the Potomac Appalachian Trail Club for doing such a wonderful job maintaining the trail and its huts. I really appreciate your efforts. Throughout my journey I was surrounded by beautiful and varied wildflowers and greenery. And the wildlife was just outstanding. Every backpacker in our group saw at least one bear, even Train and Just Mike who finally lucked out on the next to last day. On three different occasions, I saw a bear, all beautiful, healthy 250-300-pound jet black creatures and so many deer that were so unafraid of people. This was uniquely special to me. And I experienced trail magic at the picnic areas and overall such happiness. As an added bonus, I lost 10 pounds in 8 days eating everything I wanted and remained almost blister and pain free. But my fondest memory remains my new thru-hiking friends.

I hope by writing this that all of you over the years who have opened your hearts to me on the A.T. will understand what your kindness and memories mean to me. We had good times together, although much too brief, and I am so proud of you for accomplishing so much on the trail. I have great confidence in all of you to do very well in life and to find great happiness. Certainly you made my life better, and for this I will remain forever grateful.

Trail Dangers

My granddaughters always want to know what I most worry about when backpacking. Let me share a little more on this because it may surprise you.

First, I don't want to get lost and have been a few times such as on one foggy morning really early when the trail crossed a cow pasture and trails went every which way. I simply couldn't tell what was the A.T. and which were the cow paths. It didn't help, either, that the cows had knocked down the trail-marker posts. Another few times I got disoriented coming back to the A.T. from a side trail after getting water or staying in a shelter. It's sort of like those situations when you forget where you parked your car in a parking deck. If side trails were winding paths and/or you weren't concentrating either upon entering them or on the hike back to the A.T., it is easier than you think to turn the wrong way on the trail. Similarly, it is easy to take a wrong turn and get off the A.T. onto a side trail. The golden rule is to look for the white 2-inch by 6-inch blazes that go all the way from Georgia to Maine, and if you don't see one in 200 yards, go back until you do. But if you go south on the A.T. when you intend to go north, blazes won't help you. They're all white and not marked north or south.

I got lost twice during that 2003 hike, the first time after eating lunch at a spot near the trail. When I got back to the A.T., I had no idea whether to go left or right. So I sat there until a man about my age came by, and I asked him if the direction to my right was north. His response was, "I sure hope so because I have been going that way for two damn months." That's what friends are for. Incidentally, I had a compass, but the trail wanders so much that sometimes you are heading south on the way north to Maine. The second time I got lost was at a shelter. When I returned from the privy about 3 in the morning, the fog was so dense I walked right by the shelter. There was no use yelling because no one was there but me. Finally, I located the picnic table and got my bearings back to my sleeping bag. The whole time the shelter was less than 10 feet away. Incidentally, if you think every shelter has a privy, guess again. Most shelters do not have outhouses.

Perhaps it would be better if I just told you what hurt me or nearly hurt me the most while hiking the A.T. I already told you about blisters, snakes, bears, hypothermia, hooligans, lightning, knee stress, foot problems, and fire. However, what came the closest to seriously injuring me and almost killed me were falls, and there are several varieties that nearly did me in. Surprisingly, one of the most dangerous things on the trail is a wet, downward sloping tree root, especially if you have a little mud on your boot when you step on it. On several occasions my feet have shot out from under me on such roots, and each time I have landed hard on my leg or fallen down the embankment beside the trail. Easily I could have broken a leg or hip or cracked my head on a rock.

On other occasions I came close to falling from heights of 10 to 100 feet or more. In each case, I overestimated my strength and balance. One such time occurred at the end of the bear-escape evening when upon finally reaching the top of Thunder Hill, I attempted to plop down on a wall. The momentum of my forward motion intensified by my pack weight came very close to tilting me over that wall to rocks 20 feet below. The truth is I didn't know the drop-off existed because I didn't bother to look first. Even with the pack off, it is easy to overestimate your balancing ability after a strenuous hike, where muscles are rubbery. I know what it means to teeter on the edge of a precipice and have learned to be extremely cautious near drop-offs.

Some other threats might surprise you. Bee stings can be dangerous. Poison ivy can get you. Heat stroke is not out of the question. I am increasingly concerned about ticks and Lyme disease because I know someone who has it and how powerful the disease is. Like life, there are no guarantees on the trail, but good planning and common sense will do as much to help you succeed as anything I know. And if you worry too much about potential threats, you won't enjoy backpacking.

Other Places I've Hiked

The A.T. opened my eyes to many other splendors in this country and Canada. America the beautiful is no myth. With my children, I have hiked to the bottom of the incomparable Grand Canyon, stood on the tip of Half Dome in unparalleled Yosemite National Park, walked in the Virgin River through a good part of the Narrows in Zion National Park, discovered the unmatched variety of Grand Teton National Park, and sat under Delicate Arch in Arches National Park. Sharon and I have seen the unrivaled lakes and glaciers of the Canadian Rockies and felt humbled walking beneath the giant trees in Sequoia National Park. Likewise, I have had the privilege of hiking with each of my older granddaughters as they climbed their first mountains and officially became members of Grandpa's Hiking Club. All of these journeys left unforgettable memories made special by nature's magic and the delight of family laughter.

Why Hike the A.T.?

Why do I hike the A.T. where most every mile is a challenge? To obtain views no one but a hiker can see and become a part of that great natural beauty. To witness the radiance of morning sunbeams pouring through the trees, pristine valleys embellished by deer sprinting across a ridge, wildflower-covered balds, a rusty farm fence covered with hundreds of spider webs glistening in sparkling beads of moisture, and hawks gliding so effortlessly beneath my feet as I sit on a mountain ledge. I do it to listen to the owls and deer calling their mates in the night, observe cotton-like clouds drifting across dark azure skies, be soothed by the unmistakable sounds of steams trickling across moss covered rocks, and absorb the verdant colors of the lush mosaic carpet of thousands of plants mile after mile. I do it for the surprises, which are limitless.

I go to the mountains to escape the noise and insane rat race of life, slow down, minimize my worries, sort my priorities, define and strengthen my convictions and beliefs, put things in better perspective, and understand myself better and the world in which I live. On lofty peaks I come to grips with reality and my limitations and take solace in my strengths. There I distance myself from petty problems, petty people, and cynicism. The A.T. has taught me that most big problems, like high mountains, aren't insurmountable obstacles, just a series of smaller hills that can be scaled with diligence and patience as long as I continue to keep moving forward purposefully. It is there I find peace.

As previously mentioned, a big draw is the people I meet and enjoy so much, my friends, the long distance hikers and trail angels. I love the way they judge people not by their pedigree, education, wealth, job title, or resume but simply by the kind of people they are. If only more people would return to this simple, honorable way of treating others.

The real joy of backpacking is sharing the adventure. It is there that I have really gotten to know my children and learn to rely more on their resourcefulness. Hikes have greatly strengthened our mutual love and respect. And the pleasures we receive from reliving our experiences are priceless. For me the A.T. was the beginning of a better life.

Then most certainly there are the animals that taught me so much about their needs and expectations. "Just let me go about my business of finding shelter from the elements and nourishment," they whisper to me. "Just let me live my life in peace. Respect my home." And I have tried to accommodate all these requests and go to great lengths not to step on a spider or a snail or an ant, for they, too, deserve to see the next sunrise.

Wildlife, in turn, has treated me royally. Sitting alone on a stump one evening, I heard the click-clack of hooves on rocks and the splashing of water. A doe soon appeared no more than 50 feet from me, and I could tell at first she didn't notice me, so I just stayed quiet and still and watched as she nibbled the grass nearby. Finally, she raised her head and saw me. Yet, instead of running, she just seemed to understand instinctively that I posed no threat to her. So once again, she began eating, gradually working her way across the camping spot, and slowly walking back into the woods. I really liked that sense of trust.

At another site, a doe followed by a tiny fawn scampered across the space no more than 40 feet from me. In this case the surprised doe immediately escaped by running up a steep bank about 10 feet high. The fawn tried to follow but couldn't make it and looked with pleading eyes toward its mother. I then watched the beautiful sight of that doe coming back down the bank and putting her head behind her fawn and literally pushing and encouraging it successfully up the bank to safety. The thought of seeing more such incredible sights is motivation enough to return to the trail.

I go to the mountains to celebrate living, to live my dreams, to engage my passions, to satisfy my love of exploring. There I have the opportunity to reflect on my numerous blessings, especially my family, and all the things I too often take for granted at home like cheeseburgers, running water, heat and air conditioning, lights, showers, toilets, our comfortable bed, and ice cold drinks.

I go there because in this great nation I have the freedom to do so, to experience first hand how beautiful America truly is, and to share this magnificent scenery through my photographs with others. I hike the A.T. because it solidifies my faith in humanity and confirms the goodness of the American people.

Backpacking Advice

I'm no backpacking expert, but please consider what hiking has taught me.

If you think life is out of control, consider trying my hobby. Return to nature, to basics, to simplicity. Slow down and smell the roses. They're out there usually not that far away. The key is deliberately looking for them.

One of the things you don't want to regret in your old age is that you left some of your biggest dreams unfulfilled. And don't wait until 48 like I did to start living my A.T. backpacking dream. There are no guarantees that a better day or a more convenient time will ever come.

It is important, I believe, that people maintain balance in their lives. Diversify your interests. I see retired people who are struggling because all they ever focused on was work. What makes retirement so enjoyable for me is that I have more interests and passions than time. My intention is not to try to make a hiker and backpacker out of everyone, for if this happened, the trails would be swamped with people. All I'm suggesting is that you search for and find those hobbies or interests that you love to do or want to do and start doing them. It makes no difference to me if it is painting, sewing, or building cities out of Lego's. And don't let anyone make you feel guilty for taking some time in your life to do things totally for your personal benefit. If you don't do them, you put your health and relationships at far greater risk.

Take your kids and grandkids hiking or share one of your hobbies with them. Do it early in their lives and break them in easily so they will learn to love them as you do. I strongly encourage one-on-one experiences rather than Griswald family outings. If you really want to get close to your children and learn from them, put yourself in a co-dependent role without other distractions or competition.

Remember, the joy in the A.T. is in the journey not the finish. That is equally true of life. Don't miss each day's blessings in your rush to reach some long-term goal.

Let's all be trail angels of some sort.

Finally, remember this message from Fred Birchmore. "As long as you're climbing, you're not over the hill." I am hoping my hill is as high as Fred's and the one my 99-year-old father is still ascending. Life as far as I am concerned is just getting interesting. I don't want to miss anything good.

PROFESSOR

In January 1975, I joined the faculty of the College of Business at Northeastern University in Boston as an Assistant Professor of transportation and logistics. And did it feel great to return to full-time pay status after four years of graduate school in Minnesota. We really needed money. Likewise, we were thrilled to be moving closer to our families, something Sharon and I both really wanted to do.

Northeastern was known at that time as a fine teaching school committed to improving its research contributions and credentials. Aware of this, one of my University of Minnesota professors gave me some unsolicited advice. "You are going to a university that primarily emphasizes teaching. That means your teaching load will be heavier than at a research school. Just make sure you do your research so that if you eventually want to go to a research school that option will still be open to you." What he was telling me was that no research school was going to hire someone who didn't have a good publishing record. Following his good advice, I began my academic career working hard on both my teaching and research, and although there was no pressure on new faculty to do so, I additionally did my best to fulfill my fair share of the faculty's service responsibilities.

"Dr. Stephenson, I Presume"

Funny things happen to professors. Really. A few months after my arrival at Northeastern, the College of Business held a faculty social event, which Sharon and I thought my dad would enjoy attending. Thus, I invited him to join me. That evening at an appropriate time I introduced Pop to the dean who immediately turned to his left and said, "Professor Smith,* I don't think you have met professor Stephenson."

Immediately, this professor, a senior faculty member, grabbed my father's hand and said, "Welcome to the faculty, Dr. Stephenson, and is this your son?"

To which my dad calmly replied, "Yes."

Pop got the biggest kick out of the old professor thinking he was the professor and I was his guest. Later the dean told Pop, "You should have told him you were a professor of management science. Nobody really understands what that is, and you could have fooled people all night." Academia needs more deans with a sense of humor like his.

I just kept quiet and let Pop have some fun. I told you I looked younger than my age, and the same has always been true of my dad. I was 31 at the time. Pop was 68.

Teaching in Beantown

Big-city living, with its noise, traffic, mobs of people, congestion, hustle, impatience, and shortage of green space, was a cultural shock to a small-town guy like me. While I loved being near Fenway Park and my beloved Red Sox and attending concerts by the Boston Pops, driving was an absolute nightmare--in a class by itself. Only those who have driven in Boston and elsewhere will fully appreciate what I am about to say. If you were courteous as my mother taught me to be and let another driver into the traffic line ahead of you, invariably every car following that one would get on the bumper of the one ahead until you aggressively blocked some-body's entrance. That's how you ever got anywhere in Beantown. You were compelled to get more forceful or spend the rest of your life waiting for that rare courteous individual to let you in line. Boston had to be the tail-gating, fender-bender capitol of America in the 1970s. Furthermore, double parking was the regional sport. Boston's driving behavior annoyed me so much that I developed a David Letterman list of the top-10 driving rules in Boston. My favorite was red light 1-2-3. What that meant was when the light turned red, the next three cars were permitted to sail through it, which they seldom failed to do. In one way Boston driving

---

* Fictitious name.

was so ridiculous it was funny. In another way it was deeply troubling. You can tell a lot about people from the way they drive.

Northeastern was located in the city at the edge of Roxbury and near South Boston, two towns that were the center of Boston's racial tensions in the 1970s. This became a bit scary at times, like that late evening when my car generator died in the center of some abandoned buildings on Huntington Avenue. My choices, both bad, were to leave the car and run to a gas station about a quarter mile ahead to seek car assistance or stay in the car alone waiting for help. Both had mugging risks. I got out of this threatening situation OK but not without a few uninvited gray hairs and a lot going through my mind. Still, I thoroughly enjoyed my teaching. As previously noted, Northeastern was a co-operative education school that drew hard-working students who earned and learned their way through college, many paying most of the costs themselves. When you do that, you tend not to waste your educational opportunities. One of them actually calculated and told me exactly how much he was paying for each class hour, and in those terms, I got his point. He truly understood the cost of cutting class and didn't, and I understood the cost of bad lectures and tried to avoid giving them.

Time to Go Anyway

As noted in the "Teacher" chapter, Sharon and I nevertheless decided to leave Boston and Northeastern University for The University of Georgia in 1978. Several good reasons motivated the move, hardly any of which had to do with displeasure with my job. Northeastern treated me with kindness and great respect, and I will always appreciate knowing that the senior faculty decided to promote me to Associate Professor even though I had previously notified them that I was leaving. That was a class act if I ever saw one.

Mainly Sharon and I wanted to leave Boston and end my long commutes and very long hours. We needed more control over our lives. From the time we had purchased our first home in Franklin, a suburb 28 miles from my office, I had been getting up at 4:45 a.m., catching a train at 6:00, and often getting home at 6:00 p.m. or later, all of which left me feeling trapped and exhausted much of the time. That wasn't living. It was survival. And while Boston provided considerable cultural and other advantages, it was a rare day that I was going to drive back into the city a second time during the same day to attend such an evening event, especially not looking at a 4:45 a.m. start the next morning.

You might ask why we just didn't move closer to Boston. The answer is money. The closer to Boston you get, the more your home costs, and we just didn't have it. Consequently, we sold our 1,600-square-foot single-family home with no garage and moved to Athens, Georgia. There we bought a 10-room brick home with a two-car garage (5 bedrooms and 3 full baths) for $10 more per month than what we paid in Franklin for principal, interest, taxes, and insurance. Property taxes in Boston were off the chart. They still are. People don't call Massachusetts "Taxachusetts" for nothing.

For the next 25 years, I hardly ever spent more than 15 minutes going to or coming home from work. In fact, the first time I drove that 5 miles home, I just sat in my car saying "Thank you, thank you, thank you." I couldn't believe it. It took about 15 years for the Athens rush minute to turn into the rush half hour slowing me down. However, in the three and a half years I worked in Boston, I estimated I wasted 2,000 man-hours commuting to work. Well, not totally wasted, as I was able to read on the train. Tied up might be a more accurate interpretation because commuting eliminated a lot of time I could have been using more productively for any number of better purposes. For instance, exercise. With the time I saved commuting to my UGA job I played racquetball four times a week and improved my health and attitude considerably. Also, I returned to a place where driving-courtesy and patience were more a way of life. Boston definitely helped Sharon and me sort out what was most important on our personal priority list.

UGA

My professional goals didn't change when I joined the faculty at the Terry College of Business at The University of Georgia but certainly faculty expectations did. UGA's faculty, more than 1,500 strong, was filled with high achievers especially with respect to research. As a top-tier research university, UGA was a full-fledged member of the academic big leagues. Northeastern's objective was more successful research productivity from its faculty than had been experienced in the past. UGA would not hesitate to deny you tenure if you didn't publish enough times in the top refereed academic journals in your field and show strong evidence of developing a national reputation. In other words, UGA would fire you for not achieving research excellence. Deans don't like to say "fired," but a spade is a spade regardless. When you are denied tenure, you can't stay on the faculty. So I well understood that to have a chance to do all the things Sharon and I wanted to do, tenure was something I definitely needed.

Many people outside of academia don't understand that tenure is an up or out decision and usually a one shot affair. Furthermore, at UGA getting tenure wasn't easy. Five other junior professors and I began our careers at approximately the same time in the department of marketing and distribution. Two of the six eventually obtained tenure. Fortunately, I was successful.

UGA's tripartite mission is to teach, to serve, and to inquire into the nature of things (to do research). Faculty guidelines state that professors seeking tenure must establish excellence in two of these three areas. Since none of the six of us had contracts specifically assigning faculty time to service responsibilities, our leaders concluded that junior faculty members needed to prove excellence in teaching and research. When the decisions were ultimately made, however, the only thing that really determined our fate was research.

Mushrooms

The six of us in our department correctly concluded that we had a problem. If we were going to satisfy the research requirements, we needed to pin down what the bull professors in our department expected us to accomplish to earn their tenure votes. Bull professors are Professors, a title bestowed for earning the most senior faculty rank. Faculty members start as Assistant Professors (like the six of us were) and get promoted to Associate Professors and then to Professors. Although we had a general idea of their research expectations, much uncertainty prevailed over how many articles were required and in what journals. Accordingly, we held a private meeting where the six of us shared what the bulls had told us individually and tried to draw some consensus research objectives. It didn't work.

Early in our discussion it became obvious that one bull had told someone one thing; another was stating a different expectation. This is not unusual in academia because different faculty members have different standards. Also, department professors might see it one way, the college tenure and promotion committee might see it another way, and the dean might disagree with both of them. I've known people in academia who received above average pay raises (determined largely by department heads and deans) and were rejected for promotion or tenure (both primarily decided by a faculty vote). So you can appreciate our anxieties. The more we talked, the more frustrated we became. Then, out of the blue, someone shouted, "It's like we're a bunch of mushrooms. They keep us in the dark." "Yeah, and fed s@#t!" another fired back. That did it. Instantly the six Assistant Professors became the Mushrooms.

As fate would have it, the next day when I was walking my children home from the swimming pool, I spotted a cluster of five mushrooms by the side of the road. This gave me an idea. Immediately upon arriving home, I grabbed my camera and returned to the spot where I got down on my stomach and captured the mushrooms for posterity's sake. Then we made six enlarged copies, framed them, and gave one to each Mushroom. On the front were the signatures of the other five Mushrooms so the owner would never forget his cohorts. I hung my copy on my office wall for all to see, but like the other Mushrooms, I maintained our vow of silence. No one outside the group was to be told the photo's origin. It was our inside joke.

Not long thereafter my department head noticed the photo but apparently not the names and said, "Nice photo. I like it. Did you take it?" I just said, "Thanks" and "Yes." It took several months for the bulls to solve the riddle, and when it happened, my department head stormed into my office and told me in no uncertain terms that he didn't think it was one bit funny. Well, the Mushrooms sure got a lot of laughs out of it every time we saw the photo in another Mushroom's office. It's still humorous. Through much of my career, I kept that photo on my wall as a reminder of my responsibilities to junior professors.

Publish or Perish

I'm sure you've heard the expression "Publish or perish." It's an accurate term that defines university priorities and professors' fates, at least at most universities. For more than 50 years, U.S. universities have placed an ever increasing amount of emphasis on academic research. I'm talking about publications, scientific discoveries, genetically improved crops, etc. Definitely there are many good reasons why faculty should do research especially when its results significantly benefit society. There is also considerable value in expanding knowledge. Personally I found that research stimulated my mind, kept me current and informed, sometimes provided answers that I thought I was the first to uncover, and gave me confidence, energy, and even pride. To stand before my students or an audience discussing not what I read in a book but what I actually discovered was very satisfying. So I absolutely believe in the desirability of professors doing research and remaining life-long students. If we want our students to approach learning seriously, we need to model that behavior.

There is, however, a downside to academic research. It has become an obsession at universities, one growing in intensity, and much research today is not done for the most admirable purposes but because everybody else is doing it. It's a "keep up with the Jones's" mentality and a deeply entrenched academic culture, an intolerant religion that is not to be questioned. What I have witnessed too often in America is universities pushing research more from their compulsion to enhance their reputations, status, and rankings than for bettering mankind. So much of what is done is image making.

Business Schools

As my career progressed, I observed a disturbing trend in business schools. An increasing number of faculty members seemed more interested in hits, that is, in having articles accepted for publication, than in the impact of those publications in helping business leaders or society. That bothers me. I am not saying faculty didn't care about the impact of their research, for they did. Nor am I implying that a lot of those articles didn't help people. It was just that administrators and bulls could far more easily measure the hits than the effects, so this is what they primarily chose to do. Unfortunately, to a large extent research has become a self-fulfilling academic game, the objective of which is to see who can score the most and gain other academics' respect and approval. Now I am not speaking for all the academic disciplines across a major campus. I am not sure what the other schools like law or arts and sciences do nor why. I didn't work inside those college environments. All I can report is what I learned as both a student and professor in my environment--business schools, and a lot of it greatly concerns me.

My mistaken impression when I was in graduate school was that the target for most research produced by business professors was business executives. Furthermore, the primary objective of such articles was to assist them in leading and managing their companies more effectively. The truth is that the target of most academic research is other professors. I draw this conclusion because very few business executives read the academic journals business professors rate most highly and that they are required to publish in for promotion and tenure. I wish this was not the case, for faculty members can't help business people who don't read what they write. Yet what is more troubling to me is that this does not seem to bother very many of America's tenured business professors enough or they would do something about it. When I have asked business leaders why they rarely read academic journal articles, the most common complaints are that the articles are irrelevant, too difficult to understand, too academic, too theoretical, outdated, boring, too long-winded, prove something that was obvious, or tell them something they already knew.

Early in my academic career I learned that if I wanted to reach business executives and help them, two very good ways were to participate in programs that executives attend and publish in media that business people read like *The Wall Street Journal*, trade magazines, and airline magazines, the latter of which are read daily by tens of thousands of air warriors. First, please recognize that there are academics who have made strong contributions through such avenues including colleagues of mine at every university where I have worked. They understand the importance of this argument. Likewise I applaud the efforts of deans like the Terry College's George Benson for their leadership in expanding their colleges' executive outreach programs so successfully. However, it has been my experience that business faculty at research universities are not highly motivated to publish in these media outlets. One professor actually discouraged me from trying to publish in the *Harvard Business Review*. According to him, it wasn't a fully refereed academic journal, *even though it was the most heavily subscribed to business journal of its type in America at the time.*

Actually, bull professors don't mind if junior professors do such things *provided* they publish sufficiently in the top academic journals. One warned me not to do those other things because the effort would take time away from the quality research I needed to do. Consequently, since there are insignificant rewards for such publishing endeavors, especially in terms of enhancing one's promotion and tenure chances, most faculty members don't send articles to these widely popular business media publications or do much executive-education teaching. The bottom line is that most people do what the reward and punishment system encourages them to do. It's human nature. Faculty members in academia are no different that way than people in other professions. It's a leadership priority/reward system problem.

For the sake of clarity, when I say what counts are articles published in "top refereed academic journals in one's field," "top" means a very small group of the toughest journals to publish in and "refereed" means the articles will be critiqued and approved for publication, or rejected, by panels of reviewers who evaluate and pass judgment on submitted papers. Unlike a magazine where an editor can decide an article's fate, academic journals use judges. "Academic" implies original research and considerable rigor using sophisticated research methodologies and statistical analysis. "Field" refers to a professor's academic discipline such as transportation and logistics, accounting, marketing, management, or legal studies.

An assumption within the hallowed halls is that if professors satisfy the reviewers (usually three academics per submitted paper and professors in the authors' fields from universities other than the authors' schools), the journal editor subsequently publishes their manuscripts, the authors successfully do this enough times, and other academics cite the authors' articles in their own articles, the authors are excellent researchers. Keeping score of hits in big journals and keeping tabs on whether professors are becoming recognized by other professors as experts in their particular stream of highly focused research is the career determining name of the game.

Calling It Like I Saw It

In wrapping this up, here are some things I want you to think about. Research governs faculty life and puts excessive, I think unnecessary, pressure on non-tenured faculty. Many of them in turn see little choice but to reduce some of their teaching and other efforts in order to find time to publish and survive. When this happens, the quality of teaching and outreach are negatively affected. Although I did most of my research because I wanted to, some of it I did because I had to. It was the chief determinant of my pay raises and academic future. Because research decides who gets the money and status, professors tend to do less of what their hearts often tell them to do and more of what insures academic success and financial security.

It is common knowledge that tuition and other college costs have been rising faster than the national inflation rate. A key reason is university research priorities. High powered research is expensive. It costs a lot of money to recruit assistant professors with excellent research potential right out of graduate school and/or associate and full professors with proven research credentials away from other universities, people moving to the new school for big salary increases and chairs, and this has a major impact on labor costs across the faculty. When newly recruited professors' salaries exceed the incomes of currently employed Professors, almost instantly the latter demand and expect to receive equity pay boosts. This in turn produces two consequences. Top researchers will either successfully obtain pay raises, or they will abandon their campuses for greener pastures--other universities willing to cough up more money. Then the drill starts all over again. My point is this. If universities weren't so driven by the research imperative, they could hire some fine professors for less.

Honestly, I don't have a problem with people making big bucks in academia or any other profession if others are willing to pay for it. That is free enterprise. Where I draw the line is when students, parents, and taxpayers are paying more for quality educational services than they need to spend. I am convinced we are not getting our money's worth because for every significant benefit derived from academic research, there are far more cases of research that has marginal, even questionable, benefits for mankind. Perhaps that is the price of seeking high quality research--the idea that you have to pay top dollar to help the cream rise to the top. I believe, though, that we need to restore a greater level of common sense in academia and return to doing research for the right reasons. Too much of it is aimed at self-serving interests. We'd be better off spending more of that money on students and teaching.

Getting Hits Is Harder Than You Think

While I already told you I earned tenure, I struggled to get it. The college tenure committee vote was 4-3 in favor. And I must warn you that in the future it is only going to get harder to earn tenure in America's business schools because the level of required sophistication has increased, and more people than ever are competing for roughly the same number of article slots. Top-journal article acceptance rates are low (often less than 10%), time frames for publication are long (sometimes 2 or more years), and tenure decisions are typically made early (at UGA about five and half years from your hiring date). One recent change is that many faculty members will never even reach their tenure decision date. Our college decided to make a decision typically after a faculty member's third year about whether he or she has the right publication stuff. If its conclusion is negative, that person will receive a terminal contract.

As I neared retirement, I participated in a retreat with a group of accomplished young faculty members from across our campus, almost all non-business professors, and was shocked when virtually to the person they announced that their spouses and they had made the decision not to have children until they had tenure. It made no difference whether the young professors were female or male or that they wanted children. To give you an idea of how times have changed in academia, when I was non-tenured, the thought never crossed Sharon and my minds to wait for tenure before starting our family. In fact we had two children before we finished graduate school. These young faculty members were in their mid-to-late thirties. I only hope that when they finally decide the time is right for children, it won't be too late.

Passing and Failing

At UGA I was promoted to Associate Professor and received tenure for publishing in the top journals in my field of transportation and logistics--what I was told I needed to do when I was hired. Later, the bulls in my department, most of whom were successful researchers hired away from other universities and who joined our faculty after I did, told me that to become a Professor, I needed to prove I could publish in top marketing journals. Marketing was not my field, but since my department was the department of marketing and distribution and since every other tenured professor in the department was a marketing professor and the bulls wanted to be "fair" to everyone, I got no empathy. For a while I thought about trying to do what they asked to satisfy my desire to obtain the respect that came with being a Professor. Then a combination of common sense and bull-headedness told me to forget doing that. My expertise was in transportation. That is where I knew I could help people the most. The rest of the story is that I did not do what they expected, and I was never promoted to Professor.

Professor Jokes

During my 29 years as a professor at Northeastern, The University of Georgia, and Wake Forest University where I spent the 1989-90 year as a visiting professor at the Babcock Graduate School of Management, I heard my fair share of jokes and insults hurled at professors. One of them was "When are you going to get a real job?" "I wish I got my summers off" was another, which I translated, accurately I think, as "What a racquet you guys have." The one I thought was pretty funny is that Ph.D. stands for "piled high and deep," which was often accurate.

Fess up. Did you ever crack jokes at a professor's expense? And you never told a lawyer joke either, right? Well I told professor and lawyer jokes before and after I became a faculty member. And I was on the receiving end of countless "Fred" jokes, which was OK. I figure that if you can't laugh at yourself, something's wrong. Still, I can fully appreciate why many people might see a professor's job as one of the cushiest occupations imaginable. I'll admit it definitely has its fair share of perks. And I truly did love being in class with my students. But the job wasn't perfect by a long shot. I measure this is by the number of things I did in my profession that I really didn't enjoy and some of the people I worked with professionally that I could have done without. Like every job I ever held, academia had its up and downs. That's life, folks.

The bad parts of the professoriate were the non-ending meetings, too few of which created long-lasting value; the monotony, stress, and boredom I spent grading papers and exams for thousands of hours; and in the more recent years, dealing with an ever increasing number of whining people, not all of whom were students. I also grew increasingly annoyed by the university's ever present, ever evolving agendas--the feminist, multicultural, diversity, inclusiveness, gay-lesbian-bisexual-transsexual, etc., platforms[5]--and the speech police, politically-correct crowd, and a few professors who thought more highly of themselves than everyone else did. To be perfectly honest, each of these irritations accelerated my decision to retire in August 2003, at age 60. The last few years of my job just weren't as much fun as the earlier ones used to be. And if you remember what Frank Smyth at Geneva Point Camp said, "Work needs to be fun."

"How Many Hours Are You in the Classroom Each Week?"

My department head once told me the story of the day his pastor asked, "Fred (not related), how many hours a week are you in the class-room?" Fully understanding the reverend's intent, he responded, "Five. How many hours are you in the pulpit?"

What everyone needs to understand about professors' jobs and all others is that the most visible part of a job is rarely its only part. Sermons may be the regular time each week you see your clergy in action, but they have many other things to do as well. The same is true of classroom teaching, the most visible part but far from the only responsibility that goes with a professor's job.

Actually, what professors do is heavily linked to the defined missions of their respective institutions. At research schools, people spend a lot

---

[5] For one of the most enlightening and comprehensive articles I've ever read on such issues read Robin Wilson, "Divided Loyalties at UMass," *The Chronicle of Higher Education*, November 23, 2001, pp. A8-A10.

of time researching. But many other things influenced how I spent my professional time. As I got more experienced and senior, I did a lot of mentoring and public speaking and wrote two books. That's one thing I really liked about being a professor. Academia gave me a lot of options to customize my job. The reason Fred only taught 5 hours a week was because, as our department head, his added administrative responsibilities took many hours. Several things dictate how professors spend their time. One blue print doesn't fit everyone nor should it.

Teaching Loads

The typical faculty teaching load in my UGA department currently is 2 classes (two courses or two different sections of the same course) a semester, or in other words, 10 hours of class time per week. By comparison, at a pure teaching school where research is a low priority it is not uncommon to find teaching loads of 4 or 5 classes per semester and 3 or 4 different preps. "Preps" refers to the number of different courses taught: the more preps, the more planning time needed. Regardless, the one thing institutions have in common is that jobs are structured by administrators to try to insure that professors do a full week's work for that pay check. Sounds like business or any other profession, doesn't it? As I reflect back on this, I estimate that I worked an average of 45-50 hours a week over my career. Some weeks I worked a hundred hours. For two years I averaged 70 hours a week. Overall, 45-50 is an accurate, and to me, not an embarrassing effort.

There isn't much question that if I had worked more hours at my job, I would have greatly enhanced my promotion and pay opportunities. The downside cost, however, was more than I was willing to pay. One reason I took an academic job was to be able to spend more time with my family, which I did. Becoming a professor was a conscientious decision that Sharon and I made together. By comparison, some of my faculty colleagues were, and are, workaholics. Sometimes I wondered if they ever slept. One wrote 4 books a year, year after year. We need people like them, and I congratulate each for their hard work and success. Most of them deserved the money they made as well as the status and perks they obtained. But I also know professors at the opposite end of this normal distribution who didn't or still don't give an honest week's work, the consistent under 40-hour crowd. At UGA that club has far fewer members than outsiders might believe. I worked with a group of high achievers all across the UGA campus, people with a lot of ambition, ability, and professional pride.

Ask Sharon

Sharon understands what a faculty job encompasses. She was there when I was grading papers at 4 in the morning or spending many Saturdays doing research while neighborhood dads were playing golf. I laugh at the number of people who asked me over the years if I went to most of the athletic events on campus. Rarely did I attend university games of any type. It wasn't so much from a lack of desire but just a lack of time. Something had to give. Also, I didn't have the luxury of leaving my job at the office. When I went home, it accompanied me. This was true even on most vacations we took, which weren't many. For most of my career, I kept pad and pen handy. Universities paid me to study and think, and many of my best ideas occurred when I was doing things like mowing the grass, driving my car, or even waking up in the middle of the night and thinking about things. And with a memory like mine, I knew I better write them down right then before I forgot them.

"What Else Do Professors Do?"

What then do professors do when they are not in class? Network in the faculty lounge? Prepare speeches? Read the *Wall Street Journal* cover to cover? Nap? Speaking of naps, I should have taken more of them. Sometimes I would get so tired grading papers that I would wake up with a strange line dragged across some kid's exam. That happens when you pass out from exhaustion and boredom. Academia, though, honestly kept me busy. Class preparation took a lot of my hours. For a new course, I would often work about 5-10 hours to deliver each day's lesson the first time. Few faculty members I know matched this effort, but I did it because my goal was to be an exceptional teacher, not just a good one. Obviously, the prep time decreased during the subsequent semesters when I taught the lessons, but even then I would invest time updating my class notes and revising my class plans.

At least 5 hours per week were spent counseling students. For 4 years in a row I taught between 800-900 students annually. Suppose for a moment that even a small percentage of them wanted to talk with me weekly, as they did.

Preparing exams and other assignments likewise took time. It's hard to remember any occasion when I delegated the responsibility of writing or selecting exam questions to a graduate assistant. It just didn't seem fair to my test-taking students. Also, I graded virtually all of those tests. Over the years I also wrote hundreds of letters of recommendation. On average, it took about 2 hours per student.

Another aspect of my job was faculty governance. While at UGA, I served on more than 125 department, college, and university committees, often as the chairman or secretary. A lot of my committee hours were spent hearing and judging appeals from students or looking into admissions, curriculum, and athletic policies or reviewing job candidates, promotion policies, and countless other matters. For eight years I served as the faculty advisor to the UGA Transportation Club.

Many hours were likewise spent doing research, writing books, and doing professional service. On average each published article I wrote involved approximately 200 hours of my time. My textbook alone took me 3,500 hours and 5 years to write. During its preparation, I read more than 2,000 documents. Service efforts included helping the business community through consulting, creating and running executive education programs, testifying before the U.S. Congress, and touring Georgia while trying to stimulate economic development. One year I gave 28 different speeches across Georgia and the United States. I wrote all of them. And yes, I spent a lot of time answering the phone and an ever increasing pile of email messages.

Don't Neglect the Home Front

While all of this was going on, I was likewise trying my best to be a good husband and father, serve my God and church, and help the kids in my community. Much to my regret, sometimes I really dropped the ball and shortchanged my family. And I am truly sorry. In truth, I was trying to do something very unrealistic. I wanted to be great at everything I did all the time, and I see now that it was impossible. With my less-than-brilliant abilities and only 24 hours a day, there just wasn't time to succeed at all of them simultaneously.

As I look back at this from a retiree's perspective, frankly, I don't understand how I actually got as much done as I did. The best answer I can come up with is that I selectively chose my priorities, staggered them when necessity demanded it, and got very little sleep. Never could I have done what I did without Sharon who unselfishly took over many of my responsibilities at home and assisted me wherever she could. It must be a very tough row to hoe to succeed alone in this complicated and challenging world. It is much easier when you have a trusted life-long partner, and no one could have been a better one than Sharon who believed in me and in what we were trying to do together.

"You Guys Are Overpaid!"

Many of our critics think professors are overpaid. Some are; most aren't. First, as a business professor, I was well compensated and appreciate it, but I don't feel guilty about it because I know I earned it. I didn't come from a family loaded with money or connections. Actually, I pursued a Ph.D. against some bad odds. Second, if people think faculty pay is excessive, they could have done the exact same thing I did. Why didn't they do so? Third, I wasn't one of the higher paid members in my department, and I never determined the pay levels. Fourth, a lot of faculty members, such as in English and History, earn low salaries. Since professors aren't paid the same amounts based on seniority and title, many of my colleagues in liberal arts and other schools are grossly underpaid relative to their efforts and contributions.

I suspect some of our worst critics did not choose academia because the path is not easy. To become a tenure-track faculty member at UGA, first I earned an undergraduate degree, worked five years, and next attended graduate school for 51 straight months until I completed my Ph.D. That was less time than most people take, which is usually 6-7 years for the doctorate. During graduate school Sharon and I dropped to poverty income levels, incurred high educational costs, delayed the start of my career until I was 31, and while others were buying homes and building their net worth and retirement funds, we struggled to keep our heads above water. Ten years later we finally paid off my doctoral educational debt.

In truth, not everyone has the ability or desire to earn a Ph.D. "But, you get this salary for working, what, 9 months?" Not really. If I had taken my summers off, I would never have gained promotion nor received tenure or the income we needed to support our family. One of the great myths about professors is that we spend our entire summers goofing off at our lake houses. Those days are over in academia unless faculty members are tenured and independently wealthy. During the first 20 years of my academic career, I never took a summer off. We had kids to feed and bills to pay, and I was determined to be successful.

Market forces determine faculty pay levels. Supply and demand, the type of institution that is doing the recruiting, the cost of living in the university location, and candidates' credentials and potential set the going rates. In this sense, pay levels are reached the same way they are determined in other sectors of the U.S. economy. I chose my field of business because I really liked transportation and wanted to teach it. The fact that it paid higher than most other academic areas at universities was more a matter of good luck and timing than anything else. Had I loved history more than transportation, I would have earned my doctorate in history. Faculty pay did not motivate me to choose my field nor cause my history and English colleagues to choose theirs. We simply followed our passions. Unfortunately, so many loved history and English that they flooded the market keeping a low ceiling on starting, even subsequent, salaries. At one time UGA was receiving more than 200 applicants for some liberal arts faculty positions. In my field, I doubt that 5 new Ph.D.'s enter the entire U. S. market annually.

Get Rid of Tenure?

If there is anything more controversial in academia than tenure, what is it? When tenure began in the late 19th century, its purpose was to encourage independent thought under the cloak of academic freedom--protection from political and other types of interference caused by those who disagree with professors' intellectual findings. The more controversial aspect, though, is job protection. Faculty members who are granted tenure earn the right to remain on a university or college faculty for the rest of their careers unless there are compelling reasons to remove them. The public assumes this means an absolute guarantee of life-time job security. That, however, is not entirely accurate since universities can and do occasionally dismiss tenured faculty members for reasons such as budgetary constraints or program retrenchment. I saw this happen.

The public, though, is correct in assuming that removing a tenured faculty member is very difficult. Likewise, there is a high degree of truth in the criticism that tenure gives incompetent, lazy, abusive, or negligent professors unwarranted job protection and in the process blocks other people from taking their places and making far greater contributions to education. What isn't correct is the belief that campuses are loaded with protected unworthy professors. I found very few people worthy of this disturbing characterization.

Most academicians I know adamantly support continuing the tenure system. I am not so rigidly inclined. Proponents fear that abolishing tenure would eliminate the open forum environment and free expression of ideas on campus. This in turn would restrain the advancement of knowledge and learning.

There are several things I agree with here. There are administrators who would not hesitate to abuse their power to get rid of professors who disagree with them. It's a small minority, but faculty members only have to meet one at the wrong time. Another argument is that without tenure, it would be easier to penalize or silence faculty members saying things that offend alumni, donors, or politicians. That, too, is true, and I have seen outside people make the attempt. No doubt, the abolishment of tenure would also accelerate the replacement of some higher paid tenure-track faculty members with much lower paid non-tenure-track instructors.

Tenure, however, is not what is keeping the wrong types of people at universities as much as an increasing number of threatened and filed lawsuits. And lawsuits and their accompanying bad publicity have a paralyzing effect on university administrators even when the university is innocent of wrong doing. I understand the sources of this paranoia, but not fighting for what is right is wrong to me and sends a bad message to everyone. It also encourages more frivolous lawsuits.

What Open Forum?

On the other hand, if you believe tenure insures an open forum on the American university campus today, think again. Ideally, institutions of higher learning should be places where diverse views are equally welcomed and treated with consideration and respect, but they aren't. My experience is that you can say most anything you want until you offend the speech police and the politically correct crowd. There is much close-mindedness and intolerance on college campuses today, and a lot of it is done by the staunchest defenders of free speech. Yes, they will fight for free speech unless they disagree with your thinking.

A good example is attempting to question customary approaches to affirmative action. You can support the belief like I do that all of us will be better off if our faculties and student bodies more clearly reflect and honor the diversity in our people, but if you challenge the status quo of admission policies, it won't take long to see what the response is, and it isn't pleasant. Or try telling business students that the foundation of your character and ethical principles is your Christian faith. That would likely get you an appointment with a dean or higher-up administrator, even though in my case it is true. My point is that academic freedom seems to have a very selective application, and academia's current "corporate" culture, determined chiefly by the faculty, governs what that "open" forum tolerates and blocks. And on university campuses today, we should be talking openly and honestly about many important issues that are unofficially, yet effectively, closed to discussion.

Having said all this, I do not think that the continuance of tenure is essential to the health of the American university. My biggest problem with tenure is that it has become the most central issue in academic life, a much too important early career decision that causes excessive stress to untenured faculty and provides too much of an invitation under the cover of academic freedom for abuses by tenured as well as non-tenured professors and even graduate teaching assistants. That was not tenure's intent. I'm an old fashioned guy who has enough faith in the competence and motives of my bosses and colleagues and in my own capabilities that I never felt compelled to need tenure. But when campuses have a tenure system, you better get tenure or you're unemployed.

Modern Day Campus Realities

Permit me to probe the depths of current campus life by reiterating three stories that represent a sample of events I personally witnessed during my last ten years as a professor at The University of Georgia. In this chapter it is not my intent to overtly criticize UGA, for I taught at two other universities, attended three colleges and universities, and talk with enough professors and students at additional institutions of higher education to know that what I saw at UGA is quite typical of campus life elsewhere. I am telling you my UGA experiences because it is better to speak from first-hand experience than to generalize too much, and I do believe people need to hear these stories from someone who lived them.

Equity Pay

Equity pay complaints are a recurring theme in campus life today, and from the beginning let me state that equal pay for equal work is a principle I fully support. When circumstances are identical and people are equally productive and successful, individuals should be equally paid and treated fairly. Always throughout my life I have tried to pay people who worked for me this way, and I have encouraged and backed those who needed to fight for fairer treatment. A specific case in point is a female staff member in the Terry College who thought she was underpaid for her responsibilities and contributions. When in-house steps failed to resolve the problem, she hired an attorney, took her complaint to the courts, and obtained higher compensation.

Then there is the opposite side of this issue. A group of female faculty members in the Terry College filed a complaint with UGA officials arguing that they were underpaid relative to their male faculty counterparts. A university-wide faculty committee of men and women professors was appointed to investigate the situation and recommend any needed pay adjustments. What the committee determined was that pay discrimination indeed existed in the case of one professor; however, the victim was not one of the complainants but a male faculty member who was found to be significantly underpaid. That individual, much to my pleasure, was I, and as a result, my pay was increased. Not once in my entire life have I ever filed an equity pay complaint even though at the time this event happened I knew that I was underpaid for my contributions.

My point is that there are some legitimate equity problems in academia that need to be fixed, but not every complaint has merit, and in fact many don't; furthermore, occasionally even white males are the victims of discrimination or oversights.

Honoring Those Who Gave All

During the 2000-2001 academic year, I was secretary of the UGA Facilities Committee that discussed a proposal to try to establish a memorial on campus honoring former UGA students, faculty, and staff who gave their lives in military service to America. This was not my idea, but I wholeheartedly supported the memorial. Apparently so did the rest of my committee because the measure passed unanimously. In our thinking, this was the least we could do to honor individuals who had paid the ultimate price on our behalf. Our next step was to present the proposal to the University Council, UGA's leading faculty governance group, for clearance that would allow further development of plans for the memorial. We did not ask for funding or a specific site for the memorial. However, in a stunning surprise, the Executive Committee of the University Council by a 7-6 vote rejected the motion. One of the most vocal opponents was Laura Chason, a graduate-student representative on the Executive Committee. As printed verbatim in *The Red & Black*, an independent student newspaper, this was her argument.

> A war memorial by its nature is going to exclude someone on this campus--females, non-Anglo males, African Americans, homosexuals and international students. It's a step backward for the University (at a time) the University is working hard to create a diverse environment.[6]

---

[6] Lacey White, "Monument Proposal Causes Stir," *The Red & Black*, March 16, 2001, p. 1.

Ms. Chason further stated, according to the article, that war memorials across the country have been criticized because they promote one gender and one nationality, thus having the potential to develop into a site of controversy. In the article, writer Lacey White stated that those who voted opposition to the memorial were mostly female faculty. I identify the opposition because Ms. White apparently thought the information was important to her story.

Actions like this one say much about life in academic circles. First, the Facilities Committee did not recommend a memorial honoring war. We recommended a memorial honoring individuals, our UGA people who served our nation and died while in the armed services of this country, and that is a huge difference. To further argue that the memorial would exclude females, non-Anglo males, African Americans, and homosexuals displays considerable ignorance about military history and ingratitude toward many people from these alleged excluded groups who died in military service. I also found it absurd to imply that the memorial only honored the deceased military personnel, specifically, deceased men. Any military death is a shared family burden. I know this for a fact because I watched my grandmother's expression at Memorial Day parades honoring her son Wilson and others like him who died in the U. S. armed services trying to help the citizens of foreign nations like France, where Wilson died. Memorials that honor fallen heroes equally honor their families who also paid such a deep price.

Really, by the time this event happened, I should not have been shocked that a student would express the opinions that Laura Chason argued that day. Off-the-wall comments from students are a fairly regular occurrence in the hallowed halls of ivy. That the faculty agreed with her in this case is the incomprehensible part. It verifies how far some faculty members are willing to go to defend 100% inclusiveness and show their anti-war sentiments. Also, the memorial episode should make it quite evident why it is so hard to get much done on college campuses because no matter what is proposed, someone is perceived to be slighted. It's ludicrous to me that students and faculty members think that everyone deserves to be a part of everything or that entity is therefore unacceptable.

For the record, a memorial was eventually cleared by the University Council. At that time it was called a peace memorial. A few years later a memorial garden was completed honoring members of the UGA community who died in defense of democracy and their country.

Tilted Left

In recent years I have read many articles about the political leanings of faculties across America and the accompanying issue of whether this slants the content of what is being taught to our students in detrimental ways. Several such articles are provided in the footnote in case you want some background reading.[7] The essence of their content is that the vast majority of faculty members at numerous universities across the land are registered Democrats and only a miniscule number, often less than 10% of professors in some colleges, are either registered Libertarians or Republicans.

The concern is whether an environment that is tilted so far left results in the presentation of biased perspectives, indoctrination of students, coercion to share professors' views, limits on conservative thought, and harassment and/or retaliation against conservative-thinking students and faculty. What I do know from the media is that some faculty and students are claiming just that and providing evidence.[8] Counteracting these latter charges are faculty members and writers who not only deny such allegations but also declare that the far right is very

---

[7] John Leo, "The Absent Professors," *U. S. News & World Report*, September 23, 2002, p. 14; "One Faculty Indivisible," editorial, *Wall Street Journal*, August 30, 2002, p. A8; Jill Carroll, "Keeping Your Politics Out of the Classroom," *The Chronicle of Higher Education*, May 27, 2003; and Phyllis Schlafly, "Confronting Campus Radicals," *The Washington Times National Weekly Edition*, January 26 – February 1, 2004, p. 31.

[8] For instance, see George Archibald, "Discrimination Against White Male Found: Accused of Using 'Hate Speech'," *The Washington Times*, September 24, 2004, pp. 1 and 12; Jason M. Crawford, "Liberal Bias Permeates UNCG," *Greensboro News & Record*, July 29, 2003, p. A6; Valerie Richardson, "Conservatives' Coming out Day," *The Washington Times National Weekly Edition*, February 9-15, 2004, p. 15; Julie Bosman, "The (No) Free Speech Movement," *Wall Street Journal*, March 14, 2001, p. A2; and Suzanne Fields, "Students on Campus Weigh in," *The Washington Times*, June 2, 2003, p. A19.

well represented in professorial circles and equally guilty of doing its share of indoctrination. In particular, they argue that conservative faculties in business schools and economic departments mislead students about capitalism.

Honestly, I can't tell you exactly what the percentage is of professors in the Terry College of Business who are registered Republicans. After talking with colleagues, if I had to make an educated guess, it would be that our college's faculty is split about 1/3 Republican, 1/3 Democrat, and 1/3 Libertarian. And so far I have been unable to identify one hardcore right winger. Thus, if anyone thinks the vast majority of the professors in the Terry College are registered Republicans, that is absolutely not the case. Furthermore, in my 25 years at UGA, I never heard of a single complaint lodged by a student or anyone else against a professor in my college for taking an extreme, biased, and erroneous position on capitalism. If that had happened, given our efficient grapevine, I am quite sure I would have heard about it.

Therefore, while I strongly believe that my business school, which also contains the economics department, is the most conservative of our 15 colleges and schools at UGA, I adamantly disagree that strong liberal leanings across my campus are counterbalanced by equally represented right-wing ideologues and ideology. For one thing, I can't identify another college or school on campus that might have a pro-conservative leaning. For another, Terry College professors represent less than 7% of the UGA faculty. Evidence to support the contention that plenty of professors on my campus lean hard right is absent.

Really, what faculty and administrators think politically is not the central issue in this debate. Professors are free to believe what they want and vote for whomever they choose, rights I absolutely support. The crux of the matter is not what people think politically but what instructors teach students in their classrooms and whether that is done in an open, fair environment that encourages divergent opinion and thought or suppresses them in favor of rigid, like-minded thinking. Can faculty teach without engaging in diatribe and indoctrination? Will they clearly distinguish between facts and their personal opinions when they discuss issues with students? Will instructors treat students fairly and not penalize or harass the ones who disagree with them? Do they welcome students to share divergent views in class? The concern is that if most professors on a campus tilt left, that perspective consciously and unconsciously will permeate the classrooms, teaching, and institutional decisions. And it will bias the thinking of the university's students and graduates on many important issues.

My experience is that there is not a lot of tolerance for non-liberal views on my campus. How do I know this? First, I watch, listen, and pay attention, and one of the things that amazed me was how often I witnessed faculty members in informal and formal settings just assume that all of us think similarly on the issues, that is, we lean far left like they do. If you are a conservative thinker, as I am on many issues, it is much easier to keep your mouth shut and just keep doing your job rather than create a scene. That didn't stop me on several occasions from letting my liberal colleagues know that I disagreed with their opinions, and I told them what I believed and why. Typically what that produced were looks of disbelief followed by periods of dead silence.

Students, furthermore, personally related in-class incidents to me of Bush bashing; insults against the United States; slams against business, capitalism, executives, and men; and other unsupported demagoguery that offended these students. Especially they resented instructors presenting their opinions as facts when these students had evidence to the contrary. Sometimes they witnessed classmates doing the demagoguery, but it was obvious to them that the instructors supported the abuse and encouraged the inappropriate behavior. In another case, I know a female student who told her father, a UGA faculty member, that she had two choices in her English class: write papers that agreed with her instructor's feminist agendas and get good grades or say what she really believed and get lower scores.[9] So do abuses take place on my campus by faculty members with agendas? Most definitely.

Let me clarify one final point. I believe only a small minority of professors on my campus deliberately and purposely use their classrooms as an agenda-based bully pulpit. Most do their best to present balanced and accurate information. But if students receive a regular dose of unintentional diatribe, and I do believe there is too much of that going on, over time this has a collective, undesirable effect. There

---

[9] For another example, read Lawrence Biemiller, "Citrus College Suspends Instructor Accused of Giving Credit for Antiwar Letters," *The Chronicle of Higher Education*, March 28, 2003.

is no place for such abuses in academia, and they need to end. Our job is to give our students access to multiple sides of the issues and let them draw their own conclusions. That's what being educated means.

Why I Became a Professor

People have often asked me why I became a professor. Mainly it was because I wanted to help people and have a job that suited the lifestyle Sharon and I wanted for our family. We agreed not to let the pursuit of money and material possessions govern our lives. I used to tell my students that going to work every day is hard unless you enjoy what you do, and I did. But also, the job needed to pay enough to support my family and allow Sharon to be a full-time mom, which she, as well as I, thought was important for our children, especially when they were young. During my life I have met some people who had a lot of money but not enough time to enjoy it. Many more had time but not enough money. Others lacked both money and time. Academia looked like it would give us a fair amount of both, and indeed, that turned out to be true.

University life additionally gave me considerable scheduling flexibility. As long as I met my classes and got the job done, people didn't care if I worked a 9 to 5 shift, and this let me do a lot of things I loved. In some ways, though, my weekly schedule was actually more confining than a business executive's which permits him/her to cancel and reschedule meetings. You don't tell 350 students to reschedule classes. At least I never did. So I took very few consulting or academic trips during the weeks I was teaching because there was no way to get back in time for my classes. Beyond this constriction, however, I often had the choice of taking my afternoons off to coach Little League baseball or kids' soccer and hit the office after supper or early in the morning. I also made it a high priority to exercise regularly. About the only time I punched a clock during my entire academic career was one summer when I worked for a consulting firm.

Was I ever envious of my more wealthy friends such as the many executives I met in the trucking industry? Sure. I'm human. I also craved the excitement of the business world and missed being involved with freight and equipment. Those things fascinate me. I have to tell you that academia is not the most stimulating working environment I ever had. Compared with what I did in the Navy, the ivory towers were rather mundane. However, I learned something very important over the years. Life is full of tradeoffs. I know for a fact that many of those trucking CEO's I worked with over the years wished they had the scheduling freedom I had and envied my ability to take extended backpacking trips with my kids. Many likewise craved my job's lower stress levels. It was quite a revelation to realize that they envied me, and it settled me down.

One benefit I appreciated in academia is that professors have many good work-location options. Institutions of higher education are found all over America. Some are located in big cities. Others are in small towns. If you know what you want, you can look for jobs in a preferred geographic region, where the climate better suits you, or near your extended family. I know one professor who picked his school primarily because it was near some of the best hunting and fishing in the country. The schools are there if the jobs are open and your credentials are good enough to convince them to hire you.

So I know I made a good career decision to become a professor and am even more grateful that the jobs were available and that my qualifications enabled me to obtain them. Could I have found a better profession and job? Perhaps. I have never spent much time thinking about it because I knew I would never know the answer. Life simply doesn't give any of us the luxury to explore every option. Furthermore, I wasn't searching for utopia. I just wanted some very good options. And I am pleased to say that the career I chose and the universities that employed me fulfilled my objectives. It was very rare day when I didn't want to go to work and I wasn't happy when I came home.

Would I Do it Again?

Given all that I have learned, if I was beginning my career today, would I once again become a professor? I am not sure. A lot of things in academia have changed during the last three decades, many in troubling ways that make me question whether my values, priorities, interests, and capabilities match what academia is currently looking for in new faculty members.

During my 29-year life as a business professor, I saw the introduction of personal computers; a vast array of amazing and unimaginable software products; electronic calculators that replaced slide rules; the addition of ethics, international business, and management information courses to the curriculum; tightened budgets; and procedures to insure greater faculty accountability. Change, which was ever present, sometimes made my life better. At other times it offended or threatened me. Always, it forced me to decide whether I would adapt and reinvent myself or find another job that better matched my interests.

Today's business schools have become high-tech professional colleges that teach computer skills and the use of cutting edge technological and communication tools. This was particularly evident when I was teaching MBA students who knew spreadsheet software and other computer tools embarrassingly better than I did. Likewise, faculty research requires far greater skills in statistics, computers, software applications, and sophisticated methodologies. I very much support what is going on in academia to teach such skills, for they are necessary for students and professors to succeed in a highly competitive and challenging world. It's just that I am not a high tech guy, and I can't help who I am, what I love to do most, and what my priorities are even though they became more misaligned with academia's plans and strategies over time.

Academic Dinosaurs

You might say that I am one of those old dinosaurs, a throwback to the days of traditionalist teachers who loved the daily ebb and flow of being in the classroom with their students. It was just so enjoyable talking with them, discovering their dreams and talents, and laughing with them as we shared lighter moments. One day a student told me that he really loved attending my class. I responded that I really enjoyed being there because students like him kept me young. "Not true, Doc," he replied. "We take classes from lots of professors, many younger than you, but they're old farts." How I would miss such unanticipated and delightful moments if I didn't become a professor again. Unfortunately, as institutions continue to expand the use of technology, this will lead to a reduction in face-to-face interchanges between professors and students, and I can assure you that students will feel that loss as much as their professors. I wish I could tell you otherwise, but that is the direction higher education is heading. In fact, on-line education is a growing trend in academia--a college degree at home on your computer.

Another point needs to be made. If institutions demand that tenure-track faculty members produce the highest quality research and more of it, by definition they have rewritten the academic job description and altered the types of people they will hire to give each new professor the best chance of career success. This means that instead of hiring the more extroverted types better suited for teaching, they will recruit the more introverted ones who seek the solitude of their offices and labs. Already this is happening.

One of the deepest regrets in my career is the loss of some of our most wonderful young faculty members, terrific male and female mentors and role models who were forced to leave our faculty in large measure because they put their students' interests ahead of their own, dedicated too much time to teaching, and failed to gain tenure. I am not saying they didn't do high quality research. Usually, they did but just not enough. As a father, I prayed that my children would find teachers like them, for I knew how important their impact would be on my daughter and sons. However, the recruiting changes I just covered pose a real dilemma for people like them and me. There is no guarantee universities would seek candidates with priorities and characteristics like ours. Understanding this, I seriously doubt that I would gain tenure the next time around at a place like UGA doing the things I did during my academic career.

Odd Man Out

I guess by now it's pretty obvious that for most of my life as a professor I felt like a step-child, the odd man out, the fish swimming up stream against a swift academic current. It's not that I didn't share many commonalities with my colleagues, things that I believe define the types of individuals most attracted to the professoriate such as our love of learning, an insatiable curiosity to discover new things, the desire to share our findings with others, high ideals, a sincere desire to improve society, and a belief that our work is important, for I did. It's just that I found so many differences between us.

Different in Many Ways

I regret to admit that I was not as close to a lot of my faculty colleagues as I imagined I would have been when I was an aspiring Ph.D. candidate. In those days I assumed that my closest colleagues at work would become my best friends away from the office. Except in a few cases, ones for which I am most grateful, that never happened, and it's disappointing. The truth is that I was more comfortable around my students, colleagues in the business world, and family and outside friends. It's nobody's fault. I just didn't have enough in common with most professors.

Most of the ones I worked with at UGA were more passionate about research than teaching. I favored teaching. Many professors were far more comfortable working alone on their research than being in front of classes or the public. I was just the opposite. Carmen Tesser, a colleague in romance languages, once wrote, "Most of us who 'profess' for a living came into the academy because we were the nerds in our schools. In my field, we were the ones who preferred reading and thinking--both solitary endeavors--to the social interactions associated with youth."[10] I love to read and think, but nerd doesn't describe me. A large number of professors love the theoretical aspects of their work. I'm an applications-oriented guy who likes to roll up my sleeves and solve problems. A high percentage of professors like to satisfy and impress other professors. I was more interested in earning the respect and appreciation of students and business people by helping both.

Differences are even more pronounced when I examine personal issues and beliefs. I am a conservative thinker in a sea of liberal-minded professors. I believe in God. Many don't. I am a veteran, a former naval officer who comes from a family whose sons and daughters regularly served their country and did their duty to protect this nation. It's a very rare day that I meet a professor who is a veteran or has anybody in their immediate family who was or is in the armed forces. I am a proud American who believes this nation's purposes and intentions are

---

[10] Carmen Chaves Tesser, "Great Myths of Successful Teaching," *Extraordinary Teachers: The Essence of Excellent Teaching.* Fred Stephenson, Editor. Kansas City: Andrews McMeel Publishing, 2001, p. 169.

for the most part very good. Some of my colleagues blame America for just about everything.

I'm additionally an individual who tended to question some of the popular campus agendas rather than just rubber-stamping them. Those that made sense got my support. If they did not, I challenged what we were doing. Most of my colleagues either acquiesced or supported them wholeheartedly. When people appointed me to committees, I told the truth about what I learned. On many occasions, I felt they regretted my appointment and opinions. None of these things I did to antagonize my colleagues. What guided me was my desire to promote high standards, insure fairness, support and reward merit over special considerations and unjust preferential treatment, encourage excellence and achievement, work for real substantive results not style points and image building, make realistic decisions in light of budgetary and other constraints, and always try to do the right thing regardless of personal cost.

Playing Right Field

Actually, playing right field wasn't so bad. Sometimes, in fact, it was very satisfying, especially when others recognized what I was doing and appreciated it. One such occasion was when the president of a business organization in another part of the country wrote me about his experiences in higher education and said, "I don't want to tread on your ground as a professional educator because I am not one. However, I believe one of the problems we have today is that school is aimed so much at teaching aptitude and not much on attitude. I have to take an ethics class in the program I am in. I wish they had one on common sense and positive attitude. Your perspective is so different than that of any college professor I have ever met. It is hard to imagine you didn't get kicked out of UGA at some point in time. I guess that is why you identify so well with business leaders."

By now it should be obvious that I am out of sync with main-stream academia. Sometimes I feel like saying, "I was one of them, but I wasn't one of them."

Proud of my Colleagues

Still, when I weigh all the pros against the cons in my life as a professor and particularly while a faculty member at UGA, I do want you to know that the good substantially outweighed the bad. I had a rewarding life. For sure, I experienced my share of failures and disappointments, several self-inflicted, but I learned a lot, helped change some things that I thought needed fixing, met many fine people, and made a difference in some people's lives. All of these give me a deep sense of satisfaction. It was a privilege to have had the opportunity to work at three fine universities and with many truly outstanding faculty members, staff members, and students. Sometimes I wish I had made additional and more significant contributions to society in this capacity, but overall I am pleased with my effort and results. The academy gave me the flexibility to handcraft my career in ways that matched my interests and utilize more of my strengths and skills. Throughout, I remained the CEO of my professional life. At times I paid a price for the privilege, but at least it was my call.

As you can tell from what you have already read, I believe the academy needs to address some serious issues, the most important of which is to restore a more open-minded campus environment. Certainly I hope people in high places will take what I have said to heart and improve things. However, at the same time I am very proud of the significant contributions that our universities and colleges have made. Similarly, I have great admiration for hundreds of professors I have known over the years for their numerous outstanding achievements.

Space limitations only permit me to mention a few of them, but I do want you to know Prof. Richard Hill, Emeritus Professor of Chemistry at The University of Georgia. Dick is one of those rare individuals who excel at just about everything. He is an extraordinary teacher[11] as well as a top researcher and a prized mentor to many students and faculty members. Never have I met a colleague with more dignity, integrity, and character. I am very grateful to be his friend and for being a recipient of his wonderful counseling.

---

[11] To learn more about Professor Hill and his teaching philosophy, see Richard K. Hill, "Why I Teach," *Extraordinary Teachers: The Essence of Excellent Teaching*. Fred Stephenson, Editor. Kansas City: Andrews McMeel Publishing, 2001, pp. 27-33.

Another highly respected UGA colleague of mine is Patricia Bell-Scott, Professor of Child and Family Development, who taught others and me so well by her example, fairness, wisdom, and leadership. No one I know was ever better at explaining complex issues in more clear and convincing ways than Patricia. And she always did this with such grace, dignity, and tact.

A third person who profoundly influenced my career and me is Dr. Ronald Simpson, Professor Emeritus and former Director of the Institute of Higher Education and before that, Director of UGA's Office of Instructional Support and Development. An exceptional visionary and leader, Ron was most instrumental in elevating teaching to a higher plane and moving UGA to the national forefront in instructional improvements. In my early days at UGA, a time when I often felt alone and abandoned in my quest to improve teaching on a campus dominated by research advocates, Ron entered my life, kept me motivated and focused, and introduced me to so many other faculty members across campus who shared my teaching beliefs. All three of these individuals, so successful in what they did, always remained such humble, down-to-earth people, which I think is so admirable.

Finally I think of my esteemed colleague and friend, Dr. Joe Bouton, Professor of Crop & Soil Sciences, the finest researcher I have ever known. Joe specialized in perfecting new strains of forage and pasture crops, and one of his end products was Alfagraze, an alfalfa variety that significantly increased use of the crop for direct grazing. As a result, he changed farming and ranching in countries worldwide. One day while I was hiking on the Appalachian Trail in Virginia, I met some ranchers near the trail who, when learning I was a UGA professor, made the connection between the university and Alfagraze, a product that had benefited them substantially. They couldn't praise Joe Bouton enough for developing this product that had so improved their lives and business. In their eyes, Joe was a certified hero. It made me very proud of Joe and The University of Georgia. What an outstanding contribution he made through his research.

It would have been a shame to have missed getting to know people like Dick, Patricia, Ron, and Joe, and I'm so glad I met them by becoming a professor. For some, life as a professor was a match made in Heaven. That was not quite my situation, but I can assure you my life as a professor taught me a great deal and produced some excellent results.

ADDENDUM

Selected Professorial Accomplishments and Honors

Dr. Fred Stephenson is Meigs Professor of Distribution, Emeritus, The University of Georgia.

For his contributions to teaching and learning, he received more than fifty UGA teaching honors including twice being selected as a recipient of The University of Georgia's highest teaching honor, the Josiah Meigs Award for Excellence in Teaching (1988, 1997). On two occasions, he was also named the top teacher in UGA's Terry College of Business (1983, 1993).

Dr. Stephenson developed the idea and served as editor of the book *Extraordinary Teachers: The Essence of Excellent Teaching* that was published in 2001 and is used across America to help teachers improve their teaching regardless of subject or grade level taught. The book was republished as well in China. He is also the author of *Transportation USA*, a principles of transportation textbook. Prof. Stephenson has published in the leading academic journals in his field of transportation and logistics such as the *Transportation Journal* and the *Journal of Business Logistics*.

In 1988, he received the Terry College of Business faculty award for Outstanding Contributions to Service, thus making him the first Terry professor to win two of the college's top three faculty honors in teaching, research, and service, the other being his two teaching awards.

Dr. Stephenson is Conference Director and one of the two founders of the Terry College of Business's *Trucking Profitability Strategies Conference*. Now in its twenty-second year, TPS is recognized by many as the leading educational conference in North America for trucking company presidents, CEO's, chairmen, owners, and other senior executives.

For six years (1994-1999), Dr. Stephenson served as Conference Director for *The NTTC Executive Strategies Forum,* an annual conference that addressed the needs of senior trucking executives in the North American tank truck industry.

In 2002 he was selected as Elon University's Distinguished Alumnus of the Year.

LEADER

It's hard to think of a period in my life when I wasn't entrusted with leadership responsibilities. As a child, I occupied the first chair of the soprano section in the Grace Church Boys Choir. Subsequently I became president of my junior high school student council, president of my church's Methodist Youth Fellowship, president of the sophomore class at Elon College, president of the Geneva Point Camp family, president of Elon's junior class, president of the Elon student government association, and president at the age of 46 of a business, a corporate travel agency. Sometimes I was elected to these positions. At other times I was selected or appointed. To me it didn't matter for each leadership position equally told me that others believed in me and I needed not to disappoint them.

Over the years I've led choirs, a Navy household goods office, two Navy disbursing offices, a bakery, sports teams as a coach, university and church committees as their chairman, classes as a teacher, even backpacking trips with my family and friends. In these capacities I led a wide variety of people including students, hikers, military personnel, U.S. civil service workers, Philippine civil service employees, business leaders, professors, athletes, teenagers, adults, kids, truckers, business men and women, assistant coaches, males, females, and university staff personnel. I am also co-leader with Sharon of the most important organization with which I have ever been affiliated--our family.

When you think of leadership, am I wrong in assuming you first think of individuals who lead other people? That is what first comes to my mind--how to inspire and motivate followers to help me accomplish what my organization needs to get done. Yet, as I have thought more deeply about leadership, I quickly concluded that leadership is far more encompassing. Personally I have led conferences, panels, debates, classrooms, research projects, night operations at a freight terminal, programs, ideas, movements, book writing efforts, athletic teams, and plans. Additionally I have led fundraisers, civic battles, struggles for better public schools, athletic comebacks, home improvement projects, purchase decisions, a Ph.D. dissertation, a bowling league in high average, a softball team in on-base percentage, a basketball team in scoring (one game only and it was a fluke), and change. Once I even had a leading role in an opera. And for most of my 63 years I have led a life--mine--a most important responsibility. Most of these leadership experiences just sort of happened as the occasions presented themselves during life. There was no grandiose plan. On the other hand, there clearly was a pattern. The more I led, the more I wanted to lead. In truth, I enjoyed being the leader and learned I had some aptitude for it.

The other thing I concluded was that I never led anything perfectly. In hindsight I always thought of things I could have done better. And I did want to improve and lead more effectively in the future. Consequently, I became a lifetime student of leaders and leadership. And as I learned from my leadership experiences, observing good and bad leaders, and hearing what others knew about the subject, the teacher in me compelled me to share what I discovered with anyone willing to listen. Hopefully you are one of those people, for the rest of this chapter is an attempt to do just that. I make no claims to be a leadership expert. As I said, I'm just a good leadership student. But I can tell you that my experiences have been diverse and interesting. In the process, they taught me many lessons that I shared with my college students to help them lead better. I'm hopeful that this chapter's contents might help my readers as well. In any event, I think you will find many of the stories interesting.

Running Monopolies

Not many people willingly admit they ran monopolies, but I led three of them in the U.S. Navy and am not ashamed to admit it. The first one was the Subic Bay household goods office. Then I ran the disbursing offices first at Subic Bay and later at Quonset Point. The reason I call all three monopolies is because that is essentially what they were.

When customers have no choice but to use your services, isn't that a monopoly? If military and civilian customers in the Philippines wanted to receive or ship their household goods, my office was the only alternative available. And if they wanted to get paid, obtain a travel advance, and get reimbursed for expenses incurred on navy business, I was their single source money provider. No bragging intended, it was simply a fact of life. However, it just didn't seem right to me so I took on the mission to alter those offices so they didn't operate like monopolies. By changing some things, such as our attitude and the way we did business, I thought we could make our operations far more customer-friendly.

The first thing that needed adjustment was our office culture. By this I mean management and employee attitudes. Accordingly, at my Subic disbursing office I began making decisions as if I managed a bank in the highly competitive U.S. banking industry. There, if bank employees didn't make customers happy, the latter took their money and business to another establishment. A high priority thus became teaching my employees to treat customers like there were other service alternatives. The goal was greater empathy and a changed mind-set. The result was better treatment of our customers. I have become convinced over the years that no leadership task is more important than setting the cultural tone for an organization and then practice what you preach. The leader's attitude sets the example for everyone else's.

Another conclusion is that leaders need to pay attention to what is going on around them. I don't mean that leaders should micro-manage everyone's business, for that irritates employees and tells them you don't trust them. What I am talking about is removing one's derriere from the office chair and getting out among the employees and customers. Do some observational research watching the interactions between employees and customers. Spot check operations and become more visible and accessible. Come down to the employee level, get more human and personable, and let them know you care about them and the work they are doing. Nothing meant more to me as a follower or junior employee than for a big boss to make the effort to come to my location, show interest in my work, or say thanks.

While out there, watch the body language (especially facial expressions) and listen to the dialog between employees and customers. This is what I did in my monopolies and was shocked at times by what I saw. For instance, at the main office of the three disbursing offices I managed in the Philippines, we had a bad queuing problem--long waits for customer service that frustrated enormously my military customers who often stood in line an hour, often missing lunch, to satisfy even the simplest of their disbursing needs. Gatekeepers were the primary cause of this problem. Customers could not go directly to the people handling their pay records because long-standing office practices (that I inherited) placed just two disbursing clerks at the customer-service counter. To get to the right clerk, a customer had to go through one of these two gatekeepers.

Keep in mind that my office served 7,000 military personnel. Gatekeepers worked very well to increase my employees' efficiency, but they stunk in terms of customer service. This was one of those moments when a leader must decide who is more important, customers or employees. Actually, both of them are very important if you expect to succeed, but at that time, my customers needed the most consideration, and I needed to change what we were doing.

In short order I devised a plan to remodel the office, construct an 80-foot-long counter, put almost all the disbursing clerks directly at the counter, and identify each clerk in a manner that allowed customers to go directly to the person handling their pay records. It took six months to complete the office renovations and even longer to remove the office grumbling, but the results were outstanding. From that day forward, the wait time for service dropped to practically nothing, customers were smiling again and very complimentary to my personnel, and my employees in turn seemed much happier being at work. It's amazing what happens when frowns and anger are replaced with smiles and gratitude.

Quonset Point

When I became disbursing officer at Quonset Point/Davisville, I inherited other problems. There I worked with U.S. civil service workers and military personnel and served a broad mix of military units from air wings to naval construction battalions (Seabees). One day soon after assuming my job, I observed a long line of visibly upset customers waiting for service from one of my civilian clerks. Right out the office door that line extended. So I understood their growing, warranted impatience. However, this problem nearly escalated from irritation to physical abuse when, with a customer at the counter looking directly at her and the long line right behind the enlisted man, my employee sat down at her desk six feet away, faced the line, and began to eat her lunch. I just about had a heart attack.

Immediately, I asked her to follow me to the back of the office where I inquired what she was thinking, eating directly in front of the line.

"It's my lunch break."

Maybe so, but I expect my employees to use common sense.

Leading U.S. civil servants, especially a group as senior and as set in their ways as many of my employees were, wasn't easy. Some of them were terrific workers. Others limited their efforts to what was in their position descriptions and not one thing more. I did my best to remedy this particular situation by putting more clerks at the counter. However, I had bigger problems to fix.

Barbara*

Quonset Point taught me that the most important single individual in an office is the receptionist, the person who is the initial contact point with the highest percentage of your customers. I'm talking about the person who answers your call the first time you ever contact an organization. It's the person whose attitude and responsiveness define what your organization stands for and how it will treat customers. In my office, the person I inherited in this job was Barbara, and she left much to be desired.

The first week I was on the job, her phone rang, and this is what I heard come out of her mouth. "Yeah, what do you want?" Nothing else preceded those words, and the tone could not have been more condescending. Barbara introduced me to the trials and tribulations of working with "C-" grade employees and the rigidity of U.S. civil service guidelines.

Have you ever fired a worker? So often my students would recommend firing someone during our case analyses of business problems. And I almost always followed it up with the question, "Have you ever

_____

* Anytime you see this symbol, the name is fictitious.

fired anyone?" Most had not and had no idea how upsetting and difficult firing people can actually be. Even when you are fully justified
in firing someone and do so, some employees typically spread inaccurate rumors about your motives and you. This in turn creates morale
problems and fears about who your next victim will be. Many of your
employees are certain their name is on the ticket.

Not many bosses enjoy firing workers. When somebody really
deserves it, it's not so tough, but I was unemployed once and fully understand the stress that puts on a family, and this gives me quite a bit of
empathy. Therefore, I generally tried everything I could not to fire an
employee, as I did in Barbara's case where I counseled her and provided
suggestions on how to improve her performance. Still, nothing got
better. Barbara needed to go, and I needed someone in that job who
cared more about people. Yet I couldn't fire her because she never gave
me clear enough grounds to do so. Barbara was the classic mediocre
C-minus-grade employee worker. She knew civil service protective rules
enough to just squeak by. Barbara did the minimum, but well run offices need far better effort and results.

I devised a plan. If I couldn't remove Barbara one way, I would
personally rewrite every civil service position description in my office
(14, if I remember correctly) and eliminate her job during the reorganization. Four months later, I got the changes approved, got some
deserved pay raises for my best employees, and informed Barbara that I
was sorry, but as a result of the office reorganization, her job was being
eliminated. She would have to leave. And she did when that blessed
Friday finally arrived.

Monday morning at 8 a.m., however, she was back in the office.

"What are you doing here?" I asked.

"I have seniority over Agnes* so I took her job."

Agnes was one of the best workers I had, a young lady with a great
attitude who never stopped trying to take care of customers and helping
her fellow workers. She just hadn't worked for the U.S. civil service as
long as Barbara. Welcome to the world of civil service work rules and
leadership reality. I lost Agnes and never got her back. Barbara was with
me until I left the Navy. At least she wasn't the receptionist.

Here's something young people often miss. Most of the time when
you lead, you inherit the prior personnel and problems. It takes time

to hand pick your own people, and sometimes the environmental forces like civil service rules and that ever moving clock refuse to let you do what you know is needed. A good leader tries to fix things, but some things just aren't easily fixed, especially with an entrenched, protected work force.

They Deserved the Money Yesterday

Compared to the huge backlog of military travel claims I inherited when I took over leadership of the Quonset Point disbursing office, Barbara was a minor problem. I don't know about you but I hate being yelled at for things I didn't do. Very quickly after taking over the disbursing job, though, I began receiving angry complaints from military commanders and enlisted personnel desperate to be reimbursed for out-of-pocket money they had spent on temporary military duty assignments. Many of these people hadn't been paid in 6 months, which was not only totally unacceptable but truly unfair. In particular I was greatly empathetic to the lower ranked enlisted personnel because they earned so little, worked on budgets often below the poverty line, and really needed the money they were owed.

The problem was that we did not have the personnel in our 3-person civil-service-run travel claims group to eliminate the backlog rapidly. The supervisor told me that she had a pile of more than 1,000 travel claims, and it wasn't shrinking because the same number of new claims came in each day that the unit processed for payment. Somehow I had to solve this problem.

My first stop was my chain of command. There I asked a senior officer for funds to pay my civil service workers overtime pay so they could attack the pile of claims.

"Can't do it. We don't have the money."

"Can we hire some temporary workers?"

"No. Same reason. No money."

"Then what do you suggest we do?"

"Use your enlisted men. Work them 24-hours a day if you have to."

For the record, at that time enlisted men made about half the pay that U.S. civil servants earned for the same job responsibilities. Furthermore, the previous day I had attended a staff meeting where the commanding officer told all the junior officers that we needed to do everything possible to encourage our best enlisted men to re-enlist. Privately, I thought, "So let me get this straight. You want me to tell my most competent people that they should re-enlist so I can work them 24-hours a day at pay that is one-half what their civilian counterparts make?" Enlisted men do not get paid overtime, either. I'm sorry, but I had too much respect for my enlisted men and am no hypocrite. There was not going to be an easy answer to this problem unless I personally came up with a workable plan. Fortunately, I did.

After I returned to my office, I called my master chief to my side and told him what I learned and that we still had to eliminate the backlog. He was a very caring guy and immediately understood the need. Then I said, "Chief, I want you to put together a small team of enlisted volunteers to eliminate the backlog. I want you to lead it, and I will assist all the way until we solve the problem. When the team works, I will be there as well helping to process the claims."

Within hours, the chief reported that he had his team of volunteers, and we agreed to attack the pile of travel claims starting after work that evening. Within a week and a half, the stack was down to zero and new claims were being processed and paid in one to two days. DKCM Robert Archer and our men did a fabulous job earning well deserved accolades from numerous commanding officers and personnel. We also set up procedures to minimize the problem in the future, such as by gaining assistance from military units to preprocess paperwork while away on temporary duty so that our office could expedite payment when they returned. We even got the units to send us employees when they returned to Rhode Island to help us finish the job faster. Most of these travel claims came from military personnel who spent 6 months annually supporting U.S. government scientific efforts in Antarctica.

Ironically, after a few days of our team's processing of claims, Chief Archer said, "Sir, you don't need to help us any more. We've got it under control." I think that was his polite way of saying, "Just let the experts do it, boss. You're in the way." And I probably did slow them down because they were the experts, and I was learning as I worked. Nonetheless, I am convinced that offering to help my enlisted men was crucial to the successful result. If leaders are going to ask workers to give up their family time and off duty hours to do an important job, then the least they can do is share the burden.

The other important thing a leader must do is give the employees the credit. I strongly recommend that you put your appreciation in writing so there is a permanent record helpful to the employees in-volved--something they could show a future employer. Verbal recognition is fine in the present but virtually worthless in the future. And if you receive a letter of commendation, keep those letters of praise in a file that you can easily locate. You never know when you might need them to prove you have a great attitude, work hard, and have a success-ful track record.

You might be interested in knowing that we got little thanks from the civil service travel claims unit. Mainly they resented us stealing their work.

My point in sharing these military examples with you is that leaders need to recognize problems early and make plans and decisions to solve them. They need to set priorities to determine who or what needs the most attention and address those needs. It is important that leaders set good examples and establish the corporate culture of the organizations they lead in ways that help customers and give their employees pride. But likewise understand that no matter how good a leader's intentions, not everyone will jump for joy at his or her decisions. Given this reality of life, I suggest leaders just do the right things for the right reasons. Make sure your intent is honorable. That is what good leaders do, and it sure makes sleeping easier.

Get Involved!

In 1976, I was invited by my Northeastern University colleague, Jim Molloy, to consider testifying at the U.S. Senate hearings on regulatory reform of air transportation. He told me that the Subcommittee on Aviation of the Committee on Commerce, Science, and Transportation was planning hearings during the winter of 1977 and wondered if we should testify. That question arose because Jim was an airline consul-tant with considerable expertise in commuter airline operations, and he knew that I had done my doctoral dissertation in the air freight area and was very interested in the future of cargo and passenger aviation. My initial reaction was, "Are you kidding? I'm just a young professor." But the more I thought about it, the more I concluded, "Why not?" This is America, and I grew up listening to politicians prompting citizens to get more involved. Thus, we agreed to go forward with the idea. We just weren't sure how.

Jim said he worked with a law office in Washington and would inquire about the process for testifying before the Senate. The committee was considering two pieces of legislation, Senate bills S. 292 and S. 689 that if enacted would seriously alter the economic regulation of the domestic airline industry. S. 689, informally known as the Kennedy-Cannon bill, was named for its sponsors, Senators Howard Cannon and Ted Kennedy. Formally it was called the Air Transportation Regulatory Reform Act of 1977. S. 292 was an alternative bill introduced by Senators Pearson and Baker. Beyond that, I had little idea of what work lay ahead of us.

Attempting to take a leadership role in regulatory reform of transportation was revealing in so many ways. I am unsure where I got the idea that any citizen could testify before Congress, but we soon learned otherwise. People like us ordinary Americans could request the right to testify, but the committee's staff made the ultimate decision. Naively I also assumed that taxpayers would cover the costs of travel when and if we spoke to the committee. Eventually Jim's company, Tramco, Inc., covered every cent of the cost because the government provided none. When we talked with Jim's Washington attorney, he told us that we needed to send the committee staff our finished prepared testimony. Only after they read it would a decision be made whether we would be permitted to address the Subcommittee on Aviation. Several hundred hours of labor later on Jim's and my part, voluntarily and free I would add, we shipped our prepared statement to Washington.

During the winter the staff counsel called Jim and told him that we were scheduled to appear before the subcommittee on the morning of March 22, 1977, the second day of the hearings. The other speakers scheduled for testimony that day were Robert Crandall, acting director of the U.S. Council on Wage and Price Stability, James C. Miller, III from the American Enterprise Institute for Public Policy Research, and Hon. Charles L. Schultz, chairman of the Council of Economic Advisors. I was stunned. These were nationally prominent figures. We were also told to forward 65 copies of our prepared statement.

On the day of our testimony, Jim and I flew to Washington and arrived at the Dirksen Senate Office Building and the hearing room. As I opened the heavy doors, before me I saw a room full of people, the press tables filled to capacity, cameras and mics everywhere, and that famous dark-stained semicircular wooden backdrop so familiar to me from seeing it many times on national-news TV programs. The whole experience was surreal and intimidating. Never can I remember having more butterflies. I just seemed so out of place.

For more than two hours the subcommittee of U.S. Senators including Howard Cannon, Barry Goldwater, and about 10 others listened to the statements and responses of Mr. Schultz, Mr. Crandall, and Mr. Miller. Chairman Cannon then called for a brief recess before Jim and I would begin our testimony, a line-by-line critique of S. 689. During the interlude, I polished my comments and tried to steady my nerves. Following the 15-minute recess, the chairman called the hearing back to order. To my amazement and frustration, virtually all the press had departed as well as all but 4 senators. While I had assumed the missing people were taking a break, in reality they had departed the hearing room for good. I was not a happy man.

When I thought about it later, I recalled that the committee chair had made sure each senator on the subcommittee had previously been filmed by the press asking a question, I suspect as much for the constituents back home as for learning the facts. Then I recalled that the TV media works on sound bites--10-second news clips of a hearing before they show some other news story. Two conclusions I drew that day were that keeping up appearances is a big part of the Washington political scene and that Jim and I were not going to be on the CBS news that evening.

Regardless, we had a job to do, and Jim and I did fine with our opening statement and answers to the subcommittee's inquiries. Yet I remained angry for some time. It was unimaginable to me that senators on a subcommittee at what is still considered perhaps the most important hearings on interstate transportation in nearly 100 years had not even bothered to listen to us. Thus, I wrote a letter to Senator Ted Kennedy in which I fully expressed my displeasure with his colleagues.

Remember, Ted Kennedy was both a senator from my state of Massachusetts and the co-sponsor of S. 689. And I told him that I thought even senators owed people like us the courtesy of hearing what we had to say, especially after politicians like his colleagues and he regularly urged ordinary citizens to shake their apathy and become more involved. I also made it clear that Jim and I had made this effort because we sincerely believed the outcome was so important to America's future. And I informed him that I personally had invested hundreds of hours of my time to do this job right.

Not long thereafter, I received a letter from Sen. Kennedy saying that he thought our testimony was some of the most valued at the hearings, that he appreciated our contributions, and that his staff had personally briefed him on our testimony afterwards. Then he asked if Jim and I might be interested in doing additional work relative to airline deregulation, which we declined to do. All the time I was thinking, "I know senators are busy, but they still should have been in that room. Each senator has about 100 people working for him and Sen. Kennedy, you're looking at my entire staff. I'm it. And I also have a fulltime job besides this project." But I didn't say that to him. However, given the lack of attention we received on our trip to Washington, I had temporarily lost all motivation to do more work for people who were "too busy" to listen. To me that was a serious leadership failure on the Senate's part.

Interestingly, despite what happened and our frustrations, I learned some important lessons from our citizen-leadership experience. It did matter that we participated in the airline deregulation hearings and expressed our findings and conclusions. Our arguments, based on what I still believe was sound logic, favored deregulation of the domestic airline business. The first significant outcome of the hearings was that deregulation of the domestic air cargo industry, without which FedEx and others would still be flying small jets wingtip-to-wingtip instead of large cargo jets by the hundreds, was approved as a test case for airline deregulation. The growth of commuter airlines likewise came out of these hearings. And deregulation of the domestic airline industry was approved paving the way for the deregulation of trucking and railroads, moves that have produced significant benefits to carriers and many customers.

In sum, the hearings we attended moved transportation and America away from economic regulation back toward free enterprise, increased competition, greater efficiency, and often lower prices for consumers. The airline deregulation hearings we participated in continued for 14 days of testimony and into May 1977. Thousands of pages of printed testimony and statements attest to the thoroughness of the effort. Practically everyone who was anyone in U.S. aviation testified or submitted prepared statements. But what I know is that only two business transportation professors took the initiative to testify during that entire process. And I feel very good that Jim and I were those two people. It makes me proud that we contributed to the regulatory reform of aviation and that our efforts made a difference to help America.[12] The effort never paid me one cent, but it was the right thing to do and was well worth it.

First Learn to Follow

If you want to lead, first learn to follow. That is not a problem for most leaders I know because virtually everyone in my acquaintance started near the bottom rung of the ladder and worked their way to the top. We didn't have another choice. During the climb, we had to learn to take orders and directives and deal with the decisions, good and bad, of higher ups that affected us, which for me was just another good learning opportunity. Actually, I knew so little starting out that I needed all the instructional help I could receive, and indeed I learned

---

[12] See Frederick J. Stephenson and James F. Molloy, Jr. Testimony and prepared statement, U.S. Congress. Senate Committee on Commerce, Science, and Transportation. *Regulatory Reform in Air Transportation.* Hearings before the Subcommittee on Aviation, Senate, on S. 292 and S. 689, 95th Congress, 1st session, 1977, pp. 316-336. A few years later I returned to Washington to testify before the House of Representatives on behalf of manufacturers' representatives. See Frederick J. Stephenson. Testimony and prepared statement. U.S. Congress. House of Representatives Committee on Energy and Commerce. *The Sales Representatives Protection Act.* Hearings before the Subcommittee on Commerce, Transportation and Tourism, House, on H.R. 3496, 97th Congress, 1st session, 1981, pp. 138-165. This, too, was a worthwhile endeavor.

considerably from being on the receiving end of messages and working for both good and bad leaders. Early in life I made a vow that I would try to remember to do the things I appreciated as a follower under good leaders and do my utmost not to repeat the mistakes that cost some leaders my respect. The truth is that it's hard to be empathetic if you've never suffered from people who were oblivious to your needs or worse, who understood them but cared less.

One of the more interesting thoughts I had while formulating this chapter was that it was indeed a rare day that I wasn't a follower and leader simultaneously. I'd be leading one group or project and following other leaders on different ones, or I was leading some people but answering to a leader senior to me. For instance, as an ensign in the Navy, I worked for a lieutenant and simultaneously led the enlisted people in my unit. And I think that is true for most people almost all the time. Even a CEO typically works under the leadership of the chairman of the board. But to lead well you have to think of that follower's needs below you. You need to care. On numerous occasions I reflected on what motivated me as a follower and determined that this same approach might just motivate those I was leading.

The great benefit from following is that it exposes us to all types of leaders and hopefully to great mentors who can make all the difference in the world. In this regard I was most fortunate to have worked for and with many exceptional leaders. As a boy, my Grace Church choir director, Fred Cronhimer, was a firm but quiet teacher, a man willing to put his reputation on the line counting on young boys to deliver outstanding musical performances. Mr. Cronhimer was the first leader to show me the power of conveyed trust and respect. He acted like he was absolutely positive that I would perform in an exceptional way every time I sang solos, yet I know now that he must have had doubts. Not once, though, can I recall him talking to me directly about his concerns, expectations, or lack of faith. I in turn was convinced that Fred Cronhimer would never put me in a position where I was unprepared to sing well. He never gave me any reason to doubt that he would teach me exactly how to succeed before each performance. What was most important is that I knew he believed I would do well so I believed it with equal confidence.

People are slow to follow those who do not convey both competence and confidence. Followers will hesitate placing their trust and energies--maybe their lives--behind leaders like this, and for good reason. On the other hand, they will go to extraordinary lengths to accomplish the goals of a capable leader. A good analogy is the great high school football coach who teaches so well and understands the game so fully that his players just know that as long as there are seconds still left on the clock, Coach *will* find the way to win, and so often that is exactly what happens. Leaders accomplish very little alone. Therefore, they must convey great faith, spoken or otherwise, to the followers so that the latter believe they can successfully complete any task, like scoring that last second touchdown.

Frank Smyth, the head chef at Geneva Point Camp, turned a major baking operation over to me, a 20-year-old, and all he quietly said was, "You know what you're doing so go do it. If you need me, you know where I am. If anything goes wrong, you tell me first. I don't want to hear about it from somebody else." At that moment I had more motivation to excel than any previous time in my life. Frank, like Fred Cronhimer, thought I would succeed. More importantly, both men gave me the opportunity to do so.

To lead, one must sometimes be willing to take chances with people who perhaps are not yet totally ready. And when the appointed ones make some mistakes, as is almost inevitable, good leaders handle the setbacks calmly and with patience. Not once do I remember Frank yelling at me for making a mistake. He already knew I was embarrassed by my error and would do my best never to repeat the same mistake. Frank taught me so much about professionalism and pride. Until people really care about what they are doing and really crave respect and honor, not a whole lot of good is likely to result. Good leaders are able to successfully instill this pride in their followers.

When I was 10 years old, Beatrice Ward, the choir director at Mathewson Street Methodist Church in Providence, chose me to play the role of Amahl in Gran Carlo Menotti's opera, *Amahl and the Night Visitors*. Two things are significant here. I had never previously been in a play or opera, and I was going from no experience right to one of the two leading roles knowing that everyone in the opera was counting on me. If I didn't come in on time and on pitch, it could bring the opera to a halt. In fact I saw that happen during one performance when an adult soloist missed his lead. But of equal importance, I learned that in an opera, actually many people are leaders, for I, too, was constantly keying on the singing of people who came before me. They tipped me off to get ready to sing, and so I learned once again the importance of following even when you lead.

The point is that in good organizations, you better have good leaders at every level, for if one of your lowest level leaders drops the ball, the consequences can be severe for the entire organization. By the time I exited the opera business, I sang the lead as Amahl for three years. In my case, the key to good leadership in this capacity was preparation. We practiced my part so much that even to this day I still know some of the music well.

Good Leaders Taught Me Many Things

I really appreciate everything leaders have taught me. For instance, when I as an ensign and the newly appointed Subic Bay disbursing officer, CAPT Renfro, my executive officer (XO), called me to his office one day and asked me a straight disbursing question. Without getting into the particulars, he said that someone had requested that my office do something, and he wanted to know if we could do what the customer wanted. I was 99% sure we could do it, but not 100% positive. However, since this was my first meeting with CAPT Renfro and I didn't want to look unsure or make a bad impression, I said, "Yes, we can do it."

It was a trick question, one I suspect the captain used on his new disbursing officers to see how they would react, and he didn't like my answer. "No, we can't legally do that and don't ever guess when it comes to disbursing matters. If you weren't sure of the answer, you should have just told me so and that you would check the manual and get back to me with the answer." He didn't chew me out, but I knew he meant business. As a result, I used that advice wisely for the rest of my life. Even as a professor in class I made it a point not to say things that I wasn't positive were correct. I would simply tell them that I would find the answer and report back to them. Perhaps leaders do need to test their followers somewhat more to "keep them honest." But I also learned another important lesson from my XO. He didn't hold my error against me.

At Geneva Point Camp I was fortunate to serve my first year under Charles "Skipper" Sewall, an exceptional man who showed me the importance of leading by example. Mr. Sewall was an excellent role model who additionally taught me the importance of staying down to earth regardless of one's title and leadership status. His warm smile, sense of humor, and fairness were centrally responsible for the respect and trust others and I held for him. Always I found him to be firm in his convictions yet encouraging. Skipper, who was centrally responsible for the Winni Spirit culture that meant so much to the camp family, had a good plan he lived by.

CDR John Veazey, my immediate boss at Quonset Point, taught me the importance of properly evaluating people. It was his opinion that no leadership job was more crucial than taking the time to do an accurate and thoughtful annual evaluation of each person working directly below you. "Don't delegate that job to anyone," he said. "Too much is riding on the outcome, especially pay raises, promotions, perhaps even a career." He further insisted that the writer of that evaluation sit down with each critiqued employee to review the appraisal and give the individual an opportunity to respond *before* the evaluation was passed on to people in positions of higher authority.

John told me that a leader owes every evaluated employee the right to attempt to correct errors while there is time to fix them, that is, before someone higher up the chain has finalized a pay, promotion, or punishment decision. Also, he told me he didn't really enjoy talking with individuals he negatively evaluated, but he owed it to them. It was the fair and honest thing to do. It all made great sense to me, because there is nothing more frustrating to a follower than learning too late that an evaluation wasn't right and nothing can be done to correct the error. I've been on the receiving end of some of these mistakes, and I never quite had the same trust or respect for the person who prepared the review.

Choose, Delegate, and Get Out of Their Way

Speaking of trust in people, the Navy Supply Corps is amazing in terms of the different tasks it assigns its junior officers. My senior officers constantly gave me collateral duties expecting me to do things for which I had little or no training. For instance, I served as the chief inspector of a hazardous materials accident on an aircraft, a site inspector of facilities, an officer of the deck, a prosecuting attorney in an absence-without-leave court martial trial, a special event planner, and an auditor of the Navy chief's club. The downside of these assignments was that my lack of knowledge and experience often made me quite uncomfortable. I felt like I didn't know enough about the work assigned. The greatest benefit was that my senior officers showed faith in my judgment and abilities. As a result, I gained a lot of self confidence as well as good leadership experience.

I doubt the Supply Corps and Navy would take such risks if they didn't believe they had recruited and commissioned competent people. And that, too, is a key trait of good leaders. They know how important it is to choose and hire the best people. Every chance to hire a new person should be seen as an exceptional opportunity because that is how you will build a team that can accomplish great things. Speaking of choosing good people, no one did this better than the famed Antarctic explorer, Ernest Shackleton, in my opinion one of the greatest leaders in history. Because of his brilliance in selecting a compatible and skilled team of about two dozen men from the 5,000 who applied for the job, all of the members of the *Endurance* survived one of the most harrowing journeys ever recorded.[13] It has been said that Shackleton could talk with a person for five minutes and derive a deep understanding of that man's character strengths and capabilities. Few leaders have such a

---

[13] If you are a student of leadership, I highly recommend you read a book about Ernest Shackleton. Two very good ones are Alfred Lansing, *Endurance: Shackleton's Incredible Voyage to the Antarctic*, New York: Carroll & Graf Publishers, Inc., 1959, second printing, 2000 and Ernest Shackleton, *South: a Memoir of the Endurance Voyage*, New York: Carroll & Graf Publishers, Inc., 1998, sixth printing January 1999. Each book tells a remarkable story of men who overcame incredible odds to survive.

gift. Good results begin with good people, and good people start with leaders with excellent judgment.

You've Got to Be Able to Communicate

Good leaders are effective communicators, but sometimes the way they communicate is opposite to what everyone suspects. The Navy has a formal chain of command that directs people to work their way up that chain for approval and then down that chain with the decision to the followers. However, if this was the only way naval personnel communicated, not much would get done. This is because one doesn't always have time to get permission to do something. Some decisions have to be made almost instantaneously. Thus, I delegated a lot of authority and decision making to my deputy disbursing officers, chiefs, and section leaders who were experts at communicating informally. Here's one example.

My Quonset Point disbursing office left a lot to be desired in terms of office design, functionality, and appearance, and I knew our staff could serve the customers better if we improved the facility. One day I mentioned to my chief that we needed to renovate the office, and we needed to do it fast. But we had no money. The chief told me he would take care of it, and that is exactly what he did. I went home one Friday and returned Monday morning to a completely repainted office. How did that happen? One chief talking to another chief was the answer. He told me that our office did a lot of favors for the construction battalions at Davisville, so he called in a favor from a Seabees unit, and it painted the office one weekend free of charge. Again, that made my civil service workers unhappy because that work was only "supposed" to be done by U.S. civil service painters, but if I had waited for the funding and all the booked job assignments ahead of us to be completed, I would have been long gone from the Navy before the job was finished. Many things get done in the Navy over beer at the chief's club. Thank goodness.

Take Care of Your People

It's more than a little intimidating to be a young ensign in charge of chiefs and enlisted men, old salts loaded with real world experience and expertise, especially when they know you are a 90-day wonder. Before I became an officer I was warned by several former enlisted men, two of whom were family members, that my enlisted men were going to eat me up. Perhaps so, but I would not let that happen if I could do anything about it. And this is where a leader's attitude plays a crucial role in leadership outcomes.

My enlisted men were not my enemies. They were the people who would make me either succeed or fail, and I needed them to give me all they could to insure the former happened. Here's the problem in the Navy and as I have learned in business as well. Young officers and new managers, typically possessing something many of the followers don't have--a college degree--show up at work one day, uninvited by the followers, not only to be their boss but at pay levels that are hard to stomach for people who have been working diligently and producing well for years.

The common mistake made by many of these young college grads is that they think they have to act like they know far more than the real world expects them to know right out of the blocks. If you're one of these young managers, keep in mind that your older employees and colleagues were also young once, and many of them have children going through the same initiation ceremony that you are enduring. Many young people fake their knowledge and come across as know-it-alls, which then sets them up to fall flat on their faces. How? I have seen seasoned employees help these young leaders fail by withholding vital information that could have stopped the latter from looking ridiculous. My point is that if people act like they know it all, followers will let them prove it. So don't pretend to know more than you do. Actually, followers would like you to ask them for help.

Having been warned by my friends and family, I took a different tact that went like this. Shortly after arriving on the job I called the senior chief into my office for a man-to-man (actually more like a son to father since he was almost twice my age) talk. And I said, "Chief, if I work my butt off in disbursing, I will never have the technical expertise you have with your nearly two decades of disbursing experience. So this is what I propose. You run the office and take care of disbursing. I will take care of you and the men." He said fine, and we had a good working relationship thereafter. The chief held up his part of the bargain, and I think I did my job as well fighting for my enlisted men when they were right even when I knew I would get slammed by my own leaders.

One event can make a huge difference in leader-follower relationships. Mine came the day a commanding officer (CO) requested my disbursing personnel do something that we should not do. This was confirmed by my chief. I therefore made an appointment to see the commanding officer to argue against the request. And I did this and was chewed out for the effort. Fortunately for me the office door was left open while I was getting "corrected" and one of my enlisted men heard the whole conversation, which he subsequently shared with the rest of my crew. Soon it became apparent to me that they knew I had fought for them and had taken the heat. Yes, I lost the battle with the CO. What mattered is that I knew my men were right and fought for them. And they greatly appreciated it. In my opinion, not enough leaders fight for what is right or for their people, and that is why followers do not give leaders their best effort. Self-centered or timid leaders get little respect.

Saving the Trains

A few weeks after buying our first home in Franklin, Massachusetts, the selectmen of our community proposed to end the subsidy for commuter rail service. It was the summer of 1975, and there was no way that I was going to allow this to happen without a fight. One of the chief reasons Sharon and I bought our first home in Franklin was because the town had this public transportation alternative. From the beginning, my intention was to use commuter rail to travel that 28-mile one-way distance to my job at Northeastern University in Boston. The selectmen, that is, the governing trio that ran Franklin, believed that it was time to cease paying the town's share of the train's operating subsidy, less than $40,000 a year. For a lot of good reasons, that made no sense to me. So I went to work to change their minds and keep the trains operating.

My thinking was this. Many people in Franklin worked in Boston, highway traffic was bad and only going to get worse, and since the town had public transportation, now was not the time to ditch it. To the contrary, 1975 should have been a great time to improve it. From my studies of public transportation during graduate school, I knew that outlying communities that had commuter rail services had a substantial leg up on those that didn't, an advantage that attracted home buyers and produced higher property values. However, to those people in my town who didn't use trains, such as the three selectmen, that argument meant nothing. Trains were just an economic drain. Had I known in advance of the selectmen's intentions to terminate the subsidy and train service, Sharon and I would not have moved to Franklin. We were a one car family and intended to stay that way.

Immediately I developed and began distributing a petition to save the trains. My goal was to obtain 500 signatures from citizens in my community supporting the continued funding of the subsidy. Then I would present this petition at the town meeting hoping the citizens would vote to continue train service. To expedite this endeavor, I visited local businesses, many of which agreed to allow me to leave the petition in their stores to facilitate collecting signatures. My pitch to the business owners was that if trains drew people to Franklin, their businesses would gain additional customers and sales, and to the contrary, they had a lot to lose in the long term if service was terminated. That seemed to work for about 2 days, when suddenly, virtually all the businesses in Franklin changed their minds and removed the petitions. When I asked why, most played dumb, some said they changed their minds, and one honest guy told me, "We do what the police chief recommends, and he wants the petitions out of our businesses."

That taught me a great deal about local politics and power brokers. But the chief of police was not going to stop me because I thought I was right. Together with another train backer, George Franklin, we got 500 signatures and through the press, presented our arguments to the Franklin people. When the vote came up at the town meeting, we also won our case. The community voted to continue to fund the subsidy for another year. That saved train service to Franklin and gave us time to continue the fight. Annually thereafter, while my family continued to live in Franklin, the subsidy was renewed.

If you visit Franklin today you will find some of the best commuter rail service not just in Boston but in America. This is far different from the decrepit 40-year-old cars that froze our butts off. In a move I never anticipated the U.S. government spent $10,000,000 improving the Franklin-Boston right of way, totally modernizing the track, stations, and equipment. Train frequency increased, service improved dramatically, and demand escalated substantially. And that first home we bought for $39,000 in 1975 is now worth over $400,000.

When you visit the commuter rail train station in Franklin, don't look for the plaque that says, "In 1975, Fred Stephenson and George Franklin, two concerned citizens, went above and beyond the call of duty to save commuter rail service in our community." It isn't there, but the record is in the archives of the press if you search hard enough. All I know is that if we had not led the fight at that time, hundreds, if not thousands, of beneficiaries would have been stuck in highway traffic today and with property values far below current levels. Ironically, when I left Boston, it was a good thing the trains still existed. There were many people, particularly the police chief, who wanted to run me out of town on the rails. They failed. Sharon and I left when we wanted to go, and we drove our car in the opposite direction. The trains only went east to Boston, and our dreams had moved south.[14]

Entering the Business World

During the winter of 1989 I became the president of a start-up corporate travel agency, a business that had purchased innovative technology capable of quickly determining the lowest airline ticket prices for all the airlines flying between any two points in America. When I was approached with the job offer, I told the owner that I would accept the post as long as he would allow me to complete my academic year. I had a contract with The University of Georgia that I would not break even if it meant forgoing the job opportunity. Honoring my contract was something I owed the university, my colleagues, and my students.

---

[14] In my book *Transportation USA*, Reading, MA: Addison-Wesley Publishing Company, 1987, chapter 17 "Personal Transportation Management, Strategy, and Decision Making" is dedicated to helping individuals make smarter personal transportation decisions that could save them considerable money and improve the quality of their lives. Pages 480-482 define in dollars and cents how using commuter rail from Franklin to Boston saved Sharon and me more than $6,000 per year in the 1970s. I encourage you to read this chapter.

The business owner told me that this would be fine. He only needed me in Atlanta about twice a week until then. Consequently the deal was struck, and it was a most generous one in terms of compensation.

I made the choice to leave academia after deliberate discussions with my family and attorney because it made a great deal of sense at the time. My airline research had convinced me that airline pricing was gouging business travelers in non-competitive markets, businesses were looking for ways to reduce ticket costs, and the owners of the company had a highly differentiated product that would help solve the problem. Simultaneously, this was a period of time when I felt underappreciated by UGA, I was getting bored with the repetition of university life, and this opportunity was extremely attractive. It was a lifetime chance to build a company the right way from the ground up.

Any time you make such a drastic change in your life, I highly recommend you seek good legal advice, and in my case it was worth every dollar it cost me. I found it from Greg Garcia, my friend and most competent Athens lawyer. Among the crucial things Greg told me was to see if I could get a leave of absence without pay. "Protect yourself in case the business doesn't work out so you can return to UGA and not lose your pension. A lot of start-up firms don't succeed." And I was granted this leave-without-pay option and took it. Next he told me to avoid accepting fiduciary responsibility if at all possible because many start-up firms' financial problems lead to legal problems. By fiduciary responsibility, I am referring to not accepting financial responsibility and being a signer of any checks. Again, I heeded his advice. Third he advised me to make sure the company provided board insurance and if it didn't, don't join the board because board members are increasingly being held legally liable. I was promised that the company would purchase board insurance. It never did, however.

Let me tell you what I learned from this experience, and I did learn a vast amount of useful information from my short life as a leader in the executive offices of a start-up company in America. First, I must have had a brain lapse to believe I could serve effectively as president of a start-up company on a part-time basis. Your presence is needed every day to get the company off the ground. Second, when you are not present, somebody does your job, and if he or she succeeds, why do they need you? Third, I came down with a severe case of sciatica, a debilitating back-pain problem that severely limited my effectiveness. I am convinced today that my medical condition was primarily stress related.

It pains me to say this, but I have come to grips with the reality that I do not perform exceptionally well under duress. I don't like to admit it, but it is the truth. And you need this strength to run a high risk business. Fourth, it is most important that the CEO/owner and president are on the same page not just business-wise but priority wise. Unfortunately, we weren't close enough. Fifth, this was a high tech company, and I was not a high tech guy. Therefore, it was difficult for me to understand, explain, and demonstrate the technology, and I needed to be able to do this extremely well. I could show the dollar-saving benefits of the product, but that was inadequate.

Before I ever planted my feet full-time in the president's job, I was replaced and reduced to a vice president's position with a half cut in pay. My original contract had guaranteed me $150,000 per year for a minimum of two years. Lesson six is that a no-cut contract like I had is worthless if a firm is small and financially troubled. There is not much point in suing a business that is asset depleted. So I didn't. Instead I submitted my resignation and joined the ranks of the unemployed. Always I will remember Sharon's comment when I told her I had resigned. With a smile on her face, she said, "I've never been married to anyone who was unemployed before." Thank goodness I have a supportive wife. All I can tell you is that I was prepared to work at McDonald's if that was necessary to put food on the family table until I could resume my UGA job during the 1990-1991 academic year.

Here are some other lessons for aspiring leaders learned in the school of hard knocks. Running a business is far more complicated and difficult than it seems. I don't care if it is a huge business or a small one grossing under $500,000 a year. What I tried to do--go right to the presidency--is far more risky than beginning a career at the lower levels of management and working your way up through ever increasing positions of responsibility until by the time someone asks you to lead the company, you have prepared yourself well and can successfully take the next big step. So be patient. Next I learned that businesses and their leaders can be sued even when they are totally innocent, and when that happens, you have two primary choices neither of which is particularly attractive: settle out of court, which to me is essentially the same as admitting guilt when you were innocent, or fighting the lawsuit, which can cost a fortune in legal fees and far more if you lose the case, which is always a possibility. Lawsuits are one good reason why I was warned about not taking fiduciary responsibility and staying off boards without board insurance. They could have financially ruined our family.

Another very important thing I learned is that having great products, which we did, is no guarantee that your company will be profitable. Related to this is the knowledge that in high-tech fields, nothing is secure or permanent. Your firm's products can become obsolete over night. In our case, the internet and electronic pricing--something we knew nothing about when our firm was launched because they didn't exist--right now let people obtain discount airline tickets--what we used to market--essentially for free. People don't pay money for services that they can get for nothing. Next I developed a much deeper understanding of and appreciation for people who get rich as owners and leaders of businesses. They take great personal risks, and when they do succeed, they have earned the right to be rewarded well. The potential for big rewards better be there if we expect people to accept such high financial risks and stress.

Finally, I learned a painful lesson about bringing friends into a business. I believed in what we were doing, I wanted my friends to share the rewards by working in the company, they trusted me, and the company and I let them down. When things go great in a business, everyone is happy. When things go bad, relationships become strained, and of all the things that I regret about my corporate journey, hurting my friends is the one I am most sorry for.

How should I summarize my leadership role in business? Nothing taught me more about business, but definitely it was my least successful venture in a leadership position. The good news is that I am glad I did it. It was important to try, for if I hadn't done so I would have been second-guessing myself forever. And it produced a bounty of instructive teaching points that I frequently shared with my business students to help them avoid some of the errors I made. Absolutely, it taught this old professor a strong dose of personal and business reality. Experience does that for you.

I Was Country When Country Wasn't Cool

Two of the leadership efforts for which I am most proud were my efforts on behalf of better teaching and Trucking Profitability Strategies, a conference I help found to improve the trucking industry and help trucking leaders across North America. As previously discussed in the "Teacher" and "Professor" chapters, when I came to The University of Georgia in 1978, it was heavily engaged in enhancing its reputation as a world-class research university. However, in its drive to accomplish this objective, UGA unconsciously allowed teaching to diminish in importance. For a lot of reasons, I thought this was a bad mistake and began working to try to improve teaching university-wide.

One thing I knew I could change quickly was my personal teaching effectiveness. So I became intensely committed to becoming an out-standing teacher. Then I began giving talks on and off campus about the need to remember the university's original and most important mis-sion--to teach our students well. Next, starting in 1979, I began voicing my teaching concerns and suggestions more passionately during college and university committee meetings, such as when I was a member of the faculty concerns committee and the undergraduate program com-mittee. A turning point in this effort was my appointment to the UGA instructional advisory committee (IAC) in 1983. This was a recently formed faculty committee whose purpose was improved teaching across the campus.

The way one brings about positive change is active involvement--not just joining a group but taking an active role in its leadership, direction, and accomplishments. Before I left the IAC in 1986, I had served as the chairman of the Meigs (Award) subcommittee and chairman of the full instructional advisory committee. And I know we got a lot accom-plished in those three years to solidify the need for far better teaching across the campus. The fight, though, was only beginning. For three years I chaired the UGA committee to establish a fund for instructional excellence. And I continued until my retirement serving in various leadership roles advocating teaching improvements not just on campus but also beyond our Athens campus. I did this in several ways: serv-ing on numerous occasions as a teaching mentor to faculty members at UGA, giving numerous speeches on behalf of teaching, becoming a founding member of the UGA Teaching Academy, and conceiving the idea and serving as editor of *Extraordinary Teachers: The Essence of Excellent Teaching*, a book that has been used nationally and internationally to motivate teachers to improve their teaching and which provides the means to do so.

It was not easy taking a bold stand for improved teaching at a major research university, yet I knew it was a cause worth fighting for. Not everything I set out to do was accomplished; nonetheless, many objectives were met. Today at UGA there are more than 30 different programs run by the faculty and university administrators to improve instruction and hundreds of instructors and thousands of students who have benefited from these programs. Nearly 70 UGA faculty members have been honored with the university's highest teaching honor, the Josiah Meigs Award for Excellence in Teaching. And if one plans to receive tenure at UGA today and in the future, you are expected to do your job well in the classroom.

To know I played a role in the good things that have happened for our UGA students and their parents makes me feel good. It is also very satisfying to see the increased interest in teaching across America, a movement that UGA significantly helped accelerate. And for years I have especially enjoyed singing the song that Barbara Mandrell made famous, "I Was Country When Country Wasn't Cool," because when it comes to promoting better teaching, that song fits me pretty well. Good leaders don't wait for the top of the curve. They buck the skeptics and obstructionists and start trends. It doesn't particularly matter to me if what I am doing is popular. If it makes sense, then I work on it.

Trucking Profitability Strategies

In 1985 I was asked by Kittsu Greenwood, associate director of executive programs in the Terry College of Business at UGA, if I had any interest in working with her to develop a program in executive education. My response was affirmative. As noted in previous chapters, I always thought helping the business community should be a high priority for any business school. Kittsu then asked me what I knew the most about.

"Airlines and air freight."

"How about doing a program for the airlines?"

"I don't think so. First there are few of them, and when they need advice, they will spend $200-grand and hire professors from MIT or Harvard."

"Then who in transportation needs help?"

"Truckers. The industry was recently deregulated. It has thousands of firms. And many of them are having difficult times adjusting to a much more competitive market."

"How about a conference for truckers?"

"Maybe. I'm just not sure the industry needs another conference. Transportation already has many programs truckers can, and do, attend."

Shortly thereafter we arranged a small luncheon meeting in Atlanta with a handful of trucking company presidents. Our purpose was to determine if there might be interest in an executive level conference for trucking leaders. In no time at all one of our guests said, "I get a brochure a week about a transportation conference. We don't need any more." And that's the way it went with much pessimism expressed. Seeing no real enthusiasm for what we were considering, I told them that I appreciated their joining us for lunch, so enjoy it. Personally, I thought the issue was dead in the water.

During lunch, a trucking president remarked, "You know, I go to a lot of conferences and none really does me much good. Maybe there is one session that addresses trucking needs, but the rest are irrelevant. The meetings are much too broad in scope and general. If there was a conference that entirely focused on trucking issues, I might be interested in attending." Later another remarked, "I run a family business and my kids are not interested in succeeding me. What am I going to do?" Those two comments were the catalysts that led to one of the most beneficial endeavors I have ever been a party to.

Encouraged, Kittsu and I created a conference just for truckers that targeted the highest level of trucking leadership--owners, CEO's, chairmen, and presidents. We named it Trucking Profitability Strategies (TPS). That first year, 1986, we sent out 6,000 brochures and 34 people attended from Georgia and three neighboring states. In 2006, we held our 21st TPS conference, a program that drew leaders from more than 36 states and 4 Canadian provinces. Annually, TPS sells out. The reason, I believe, is that we have a strong reputation for delivering take-home value. Today, TPS is considered by many as the premier educational conference for leaders in the nearly $600-billion North American trucking industry.

Definitely, I didn't make this happen alone. Over the years I have been helped enormously by a fine Terry College staff; sound advice, leadership, and support from Kittsu Greenwood during her 17 years of administrative management of the TPS conference prior to her retirement and from her successors, Donna Wilson and Elizabeth Wiley; nearly 100 men and women who have served on our TPS board of advisors; hundreds of speakers who brought their honest and pertinent advice to Athens; and thousands of attendees who contributed their ideas and questions. Throughout the years I have remained the TPS conference director. My reason, though, for telling you all of this is to share what I learned about leadership from this most worthwhile enterprise.

First, good leadership starts with good ideas and good decisions. Three of the best ones we made were first to choose a big niche market, trucking, that had a real need. It is almost always a mistake to try to be all things to all people. Success comes easier if an organization stays focused. Second, we chose a timeless theme, Trucking Profitability Strategies, that will never become obsolete. Regardless of a company's profitability, there is always room for improvement. Third, we targeted the highest level of leadership, people who recognize and appreciate the need to learn and likewise have the immediate power to make a decision to come to the conference without needing to seek higher management approval.

Another important thing we did was share the ownership and responsibilities for TPS with our trucking executives. It happened during the third year when we created a board of advisors that was given chief responsibility to plan the next year's program and help me book the best speakers we could find. As a result, we determined what our attendees most wanted to learn and who they thought had the best credentials to teach them. Consequently, we quickly started booking the most respected leaders in the trucking industry, top Wall Street trucking industry analysts, and a variety of exceptionally qualified speakers. And it paid off handsomely. One of the most remarkable sights I have ever seen in any classroom setting is the seriousness for learning that our trucking-leader attendees show annually. I find it so instructive that these highly successful people seldom cut class, but college students with so much more to learn cut class with abandon. In addition these executives take copious notes because they intend to use them.

My job during the past two decades has been to guide the operation from behind the scenes and let our board chair, program chair, past board chair, and board members lead the program and sessions. Essentially what I learned about leadership is that far more can be accomplished by pooling the energies and talents of many leaders than by guarding one's turf. There was far more to be gained from establishing a great team of dedicated and resourceful leaders--a marriage of the best parts of business and academia. In the process I have met many of the finest business leaders in America and Canada, people of great character and achievements, and they taught me more than I could have imagined about what it takes to lead businesses and turn profits in a highly competitive trucking industry that today has more than 500,000 companies among its ranks. And they also reminded me of the valuable role business leaders provide to this nation, for without these men and women and their companies, most households would not have the jobs, incomes, homes, and standards of living that they currently have.

In starting TPS, my intent from day one was to run a conference that gave people considerable take-away ideas. This in turn would motivate their continued annual conference attendance. What is most satisfying is that while I do not know precisely what TPS has accomplished or how valuable my role has been in this whole endeavor, I know that many people have taken TPS ideas home and implemented them successfully to improve their businesses and personal leadership and management skills. The most fun has been watching small marginal companies grow into much larger more profitable ones. This makes me feel confident I did something worthwhile that has helped America, which has always been one of my main objectives in life.

Leaders and Pretenders

The world is filled with leaders, at least according to their titles and job descriptions. However, life taught me not to assume people are good leaders simply because of the impressive leadership positions they fill. There is a big difference between holding a leadership position and actually being an effective leader in that position. In fact, some of the best leadership examples I have ever come across involved people who held no leadership title but who on the spot stepped up to that role in a crisis. An example is a private who took charge of a platoon in battle when his leaders were killed.

Another thing I learned is that being a great leader in a previous capacity is no guarantee of equal success in the next leadership opportunity. For instance, you may inherit a team of workers who loved the person you replaced and resent your presence. Sometimes you come into a corporate culture that is far different from what you imagined or desire. On other occasions, one or two key people can sabotage your efforts to lead. Sometimes, though, the core problem is not others but you. Maybe your attitude this time is wrong.

Not every leader I worked for was exceptional. A few had the unfortunate habit of saying "I" way too often and in the process took credit for things the rest of us accomplished--a most effective way to drive a wedge between a leader and followers. Good leaders unselfishly give credit to those who deserve it. They also do not give credit to those who didn't earn it. One of the biggest flubs I made as a leader was calling my entire staff together and praising one of my workers for his excellent work. I was practicing Ma's "praise in public, criticize in private" philosophy. The only trouble was, as my Navy chief told me after the big announcement, I praised the wrong person. Somebody else did the work. That well-intentioned action made me look ridiculous and took several months to recover from, but I had no one to blame but myself. After that I double-checked before I handed out praise. Still, Ma's philosophy was on the money. If you embarrass a follower in front of his or her peers, your problems will escalate.

Another problem I have with some leaders is that they are clueless about how to motivate people. In fact, one of the people I worked for in academia was an accomplished de-motivator. He could snuff out people's passions like no other person I ever met. Actually, many people who claim to be leaders aren't really leaders at all. Instead they are managers, which means something different to me.

Leaders do the right thing regardless of the consequences to them personally. Managers do things right. The difference is subtle but significant. Managers make sure jobs are completed, every "i" is dotted, and every sentence has a period at the end. They tend to be good detail people and administrators. Leaders have much higher priorities particularly with respect to taking care of the interests of others, like employees, customers, even the outside public. Good leaders are the architects and visionaries that inspire others to move mountains. Good managers are remembered for things like efficiency, productivity, and cost savings. Good leaders change lives in positive ways, give us a greater sense of pride in ourselves and in our organization, and are sorely missed when they are gone.

Don't misunderstand me. Organizations need both good leaders and good managers. It is just that I believe leaders have the more crucial responsibility. Followers will do extraordinary things for great leaders because they do not want to be the person who lets their leader down, nor do they want to lose their leader's respect. I'm not saying that this is an either/or proposition. Some leaders are also great managers. My point is simply that organizations can suffer through managerial deficiencies. Without strong leadership, they are not going anywhere.

Characteristics of Good Leaders

Before closing this chapter, I must address a question a student once asked me. Was Hitler a good leader? Without question, he surely accomplished many of his objectives, but much of what he did was despicable resulting in his life ending in disgrace. Definitely, people can lead ruthlessly. History has proven that time and again. But is that good leadership? I don't think so. Looking at leadership from a follower's perspective, there is a big difference between following a leader because you have no choice, fear for your job or life, or as a result of intense indoctrination and the alternative of following another person on your own free will, with great enthusiasm, and simply because you want to do so. Consequently, Attila the Hun, Hitler, Stalin, and Saddam Hussein will never be on my list of leadership mentors. I identify more closely with leaders who have done, and continue to do, honorable things. To me it's not just what leaders accomplish but how they go about accomplishing it that counts. Personally, I have always wanted others to follow me because they trust my judgment and me and respect me.

Fred's Wish List of Outstanding Leadership Traits

What traits then do I believe distinguish outstanding leaders? Here's my personal list of desired characteristics.

Good leaders are forward-thinking visionaries. They see the big picture, recognize opportunities and threats before others, and seldom miss the little things.

They have high expectations and set high standards.

They have uncommon purpose and exceptional energy to see their work completed.

They are highly competent, and followers recognize this.

They listen to the people in the trenches, the ones closest to the action.

They clearly articulate their vision and needs.

They try to do the right things for the right reasons.

They are optimistic and have an uncommon knack for conveying hope even in the most trying of times.

They inspire and motivate people.

They are decisive and understand that they can't wait forever to make decisions. To lead, people need a degree of impatience.

They have courage to take risks and unpopular stands and stick to their principles and convictions.

They perform well under pressure.

They welcome constructive criticism and differences of opinion and have a thick enough skin to deal with the irritations of life.

They take good care of their followers.

They are reasonable people with good judgment and common sense.

They tell you the truth.

They don't ask followers to do what they themselves are unwilling to do.

They make followers feel proud to be a part of something special.

They are trustworthy and convey trust in their followers.

They surround themselves with good people, teach them well, give them the tools they need to succeed, help them grow with ever increasing levels of responsibility, and let them do their jobs.

They are fair and reward effort and achievement.

They are accessible.

They have excellent memories, particularly with regard to remembering people's names and faces.

They are not afraid to admit mistakes and apologize when they are in error.

They are generous.

They maintain a sense of humor.

They are human.

They set a great example through character and integrity.

Have I ever met a leader with every one of these traits? Not yet I haven't. Like the rest of us, leaders are human, not perfect. But I do know many individuals who have most of these characteristics, and I think that is why they have been so successful. Also, I have found that most of these desired leadership traits can be acquired if they are currently missing, which is encouraging to those trying to improve. Furthermore, it is comforting to know that most followers do not expect their leaders to know all the answers. In fact they prefer that leaders aren't perfect. What they want is for leaders to do the same thing most leaders expect their followers to do. Make a strong effort to live up to their potential.

Great leadership is not about image making. You can act and look statesmanlike, but that is not enough if followers doubt your sincerity. It's not about being exceptionally bright. That is inadequate if you are morally bankrupt or lack common sense. You can dazzle people with your mastery of the English language, but what good does that do if you have no real vision or strong convictions and can't get others to buy into your plans? Good leadership is not about what degree you hold or that your diploma was awarded by a prestigious university. All of these might help you obtain leadership positions, but they are not the things that in the end will honor you. The reality of what you got done under the situations you had to work with and how you went about doing it will determine that outcome.

AMERICAN

One of the biggest breaks I received in life was being born in America. That one event over which I had no control resulted in a life filled with opportunity and countless blessings for which I am enormously grateful. Unlike so many people in this world, never have I gone to bed hungry, lacking shelter, in need of good medical care and unable to get it, or in fear of what a brutal leader might do to my family or me. Being an American has been a very special privilege.

Dinner with Our Russian Friends

While teaching at Wake Forest University in 1989, I was invited to share dinner one evening with a colleague and three visiting Russians who were studying business in the United States. Prior to that meeting, my image of Russians was rather poor. Remember, I lived during the entire Cold War with the Soviet Union, a time when Americans worried about a potential nuclear attack. Russians were our enemies. It was also difficult to forget Soviet President Nikita Kruschev's 1956 threat before the United Nations when in a fit of rage, he removed his shoe and banged it against the podium promising, "We will bury you!" The "you" he was threatening was the United States. It seemed like every time I saw a Russian in the news, I saw a scowling, menacing face. The movies didn't help either depicting Russians as our number one enemy and a dangerous people. And later, when I read books on Stalin and communist leadership atrocities, purges and gulags for instance, that depiction certainly had merit. Thus, it was a big cultural shock to meet our three guests, two men and a woman, all gracious and outgoing people, one very jovial with a fine sense of humor. In no way did they match the Hollywood-TV-Fourth Estate's image.

Dinner at my friend's condo in Winston Salem was an unforgettable experience. Each of our guests was a senior-level executive or government employee. The younger male managed 1,000 plants. I found that astonishing. Our female guest had equally high responsibility in the government. My favorite visitor, though, was the humorist, the second man with the contagious laugh, a person quite adept at carrying on a conversation. One of the things he quickly taught me was that he was as worried about his children successfully navigating the mine field of their teenage years as I was. Apparently some things know no borders.

Before dinner I noticed how curious the three were about our American lifestyles. Especially this was true of our female guest who kept wandering off to the kitchen. Soon we learned that she was examining and studying the kitchen appliances. Never previously had she seen an automatic dishwasher and didn't know what it did. Later she told us that she was overwhelmed by the variety of fresh fruits and vegetables routinely available in American supermarkets, explaining that in Russia she had never seen more than eight varieties of such items available in one store at the same time. For the record, she was nearly 50 years old and someone I would have thought, because of her high government standing, who would have had access to more products. Our jovial friend likewise couldn't believe our abundance and wastage of paper, which he said was constantly in short supply even in the executive offices in Russia. I think all of us had an equally difficult time grasping the other's situation, yet the evening was quite enjoyable and made me ever more grateful for what we so often take for granted in our country.

The Question That Got Me Thinking about America

After dinner, one of my Russian friends asked me a question that nearly froze me in my tracks. "Fred," he said, "I don't understand it. How did America, which is such a young country, become so successful in such a short time?" In my haste to respond, I offered thoughts that immediately came to mind--freedom, opportunity, the right to try most anything, the creativity and optimism of our people. But I must be honest with you. Before that question was asked, I hadn't really thought much at all about the American success story and what caused it. That is not the case, however, as I presently write this. So let me tell you what I learned about America from my research and 63-year life as an American citizen. I feel a need to clarify the answer not just for me but also because it is important that every American as well as the outside world understand the United States of America better.

What Can I Tell You about Being an American?

America is a story about people, their principles and values, their dreams and priorities. Actually it goes beyond that to a story of individuals and how they live their personal lives. It is less about the system and more about the type of people Americans are and what we believe and do to help others and ourselves.

My country is unique in so many ways. The United States is the world's leading democracy and its only super power. With 6 percent of the world's population, America generates an astounding third of the world's gross domestic product.[15] Our universities are the envy of the world. In medicine and chemistry, during the last 20 years U.S. based researchers have won or shared most of the Nobel Prizes. We have the world's largest economy and are considered the most competitive nation on earth. In terms of combined public and private sector giving, our country is the most generous nation in existence. During one recent year it was estimated that American private charities alone spent more than $200-billion and that more than half of U.S. adults worked on volunteer projects that contributed an estimated 20-billion hours in donated time. Former President Clinton recently said that the U.S. contributes 25-35% of disaster relief world wide. Twice we have played a vital role in saving Europe from German aggression, and we have regularly answered the call to aid our allies in various parts of the world. We are a religious nation by world standards with more churches, synagogues, temples and mosques per capita than any other

---

[15] Many of the statistics in this paragraph were derived from David R. Sands, "America Enjoys View from the Top," *The Washington Times National Weekly Edition*, January 3-9, 2005, pp. 1, 22, and 23. The article is an excellent summary of American contributions and changing world opinion of our society.

country on earth. More than 80% of Americans tell pollsters that they believe in God. And yes, many of us have a lot of pride in who we are and what we have been able to contribute and achieve.

Immigrant Nation

Our country is not only an immigrant nation but also a land built with an immigrant's mentality. The United States has succeeded on the passions of self-motivated people determined to improve their lives. With the exception of Native Americans, our nation was built by individuals who left their families and roots often with not much more than the clothes on their back and a suitcase in their hand and immigrated to the United States to build a better life for themselves and their children. Unlike some countries, Japan or South Korea for instance, America does not have a very well defined culture or much uniformity except in its principles and ideals. It is a melting pot of diversity, a broad array of ethnic and other subcultures. A huge majority of our immigrants were the poor and oppressed fleeing from tyranny, poverty, and religious persecution. And the new arrivals used their creative energies and talents to produce exceptional results.

As previously noted, I am two generations removed from immigrant status. My grandparents on my father's side came here as poor, relatively uneducated teenagers from England and Scotland. My mother's family likewise emigrated from Europe. Three Horne brothers on my grandfather's side were stone masons who came to America from Germany more than 200 years ago. Recently my Aunt Eve shared the remarkable story of her mother who came to America alone as a young woman with no job, any home or support group awaiting her, just optimism and hope. And if there are two words that have traditionally defined our people, they are optimism and hope. Another is courage. People came to this land without guarantees, just high expectations that their lives would improve. They wanted the right to try without others impeding their way. And that desire continued on through subsequent generations. I have always just wanted people to let me pursue my own dreams, to let me attempt to do something special that I could be proud of. And then I wanted them to let me reap the rewards of my endeavors.

In America there are few limits to what we feel we can do and what benefits that will bring us. We think the sky is our only limit.

When You Wish upon a Star

America's success story is one of many dreams that indeed came true, and this success was an inspiration to the rest of us. And if our immigrants were unable to realize all their aspirations, they worked hard with the conviction that their children would have greater success. American history is filled with the sacrifices parents made to improve the lives of their children and grandchildren.

I've heard people say the American dream is dead. I guess they never heard of Arnold Schwarzenegger or Hean Vu Angulo, a Cambodian widow and mother who recently came to America hoping to find a better life for her 4 young daughters and her. Hean Vu Angulo worked 12-hour days, 7 days a week, went to school for 3 years to learn English, and scrimped and saved until she was able to buy her own business. In a story written by Dennis McCarthy and published in the *Los Angeles Daily News* on July 30, 2004, Hean Vu Angulo is quoted as saying, "When I was a little girl growing up in Cambodia I always heard America was a good place, a place of dreams. McCarthy then wrote, "It is," and added, "What makes this country great has little to do with political conventions or what party owns the White House. It has to do with people, like Hean--chasing the American dream." I fully agree with him.

Pursuing an American Dream

A third example is Dave, our youngest child. A few years ago Dave graduated from the honors program at The University of Georgia with the highest GPA in family history and a major in mathematics. But math is not his primary passion. Music is. When Dave was a teenager, he informed his mother and me that he wanted to be a professional musician. That's not unusual in this country where many young men and women want to be rock stars. But like any good parent, I knew something about the degree of difficulty in achieving this goal and wanted to make sure our son fully understood the odds he would be facing. Thus I asked him, "Dave, do you know how hard it is for a band to make it?"

"Yes I do, Dad, and I also know that despite the odds, some bands do make it, and I plan to be in one of them." That's my boy. And that my friends is what makes America special. I loved his attitude. American kids think big, and I wouldn't want it any other way. Sharon and I are doing all we can to encourage him and back his band's efforts to achieve stardom.

During high school and college, Dave played in several bands in Athens. Following graduation he moved to Boston to create another band. Currently he is a member of the Los Angeles based band Also where he plays drums under the name Scotland Stephenson.[16] My point, though, is this. I will be forever grateful that my parents encouraged me to follow my dreams. Dave and our other children deserve that same understanding and support, and they have received it. Sharon and I have great confidence in each of them.

Our Founding Fathers

A great nation begins with outstanding leadership and the highest ideals, and in this regard, we were incredibly fortunate to have had visionary, brilliant founding fathers, men like Thomas Jefferson and Benjamin Franklin who helped forge the Declaration of Independence, the U.S. Constitution, and the Bill of Rights. All of these significant documents were instrumental accomplishments that have defined this nation and its purposes for more than 200 years. Our country's ability to withstand the great tests of time is evidence of their extraordinary quality.

Those early leaders created a democracy and a republic, actually a representative democracy, where the power to govern flows from the people upward to our elected officials whom we trust to use good judgment and lead us well. America belongs to the people. As Abraham Lincoln in his Gettysburg Address stated, we have a government "of the people, by the people, for the people." The United States is our country,

---

[16] For more about Also and a sample of the band's music, go to www.also-music.com.

our tax dollars, our presidency, even our White House. And I think of the latter exactly that way as my national home, a place that should always be honored, respected, and never debased.

Our founders established three branches of government, the legislative, executive, and judicial branches, each with defined specific duties and checks and balances to make sure our democracy fulfills its purposes. America is a nation of laws intended to provide justice to all and equality. One of its most important tenets is not putting anyone above the law. Fairness is a compelling value. Capitalism became our economic system advocating private ownership of property, using property and capital to provide income, the freedom to compete with others for economic gain, and profit as a motive compelling achievement and hard work. And it is hard to argue with its significant accomplishments.

Liberty

When I think of America, the one word that most symbolizes our country is "freedom." On March 20, 1775, when The Second Virginia Convention was discussing British tyranny and oppression, Patrick Henry stood against those favoring conciliatory measures and boldly declared seven of the most famous words in American history, "Give me liberty or give me death!" Equality, liberty, and justice are three of America's highest and most admirable ideals. In our society, power and privileges are not hoarded by a ruling class or nobility but are made available to those with ambition, determination, and a strong work ethic. Personally I know many people who rose to the top of business, medicine, science, academia, and other professions from the most humble of beginnings. These individuals, as well as several U. S. presidents who came from small towns and modest homes and income, knew how to play the hand that was dealt them.

Twelve U. S. Presidents

Twelve presidents, more than one-fourth of all the country's presidents, served their terms during my life (Franklin Delano Roosevelt, Harry S. Truman, Dwight D. Eisenhower, John F. Kennedy, Lyndon Baines Johnson, Richard M. Nixon, Gerald R. Ford, Jimmy Carter,

Ronald Reagan, George H. W. Bush, Bill Clinton, and George W. Bush). And it was very instructive. I am not equally enamored or proud of all of them, but I do understand that each occupied one of the toughest and most important jobs any person on earth could hold. Being the leader of the free world comes with awesome, and I am sure, sometimes personally very painful, decision-making responsibilities. For the most part, I think they did a fine job making good decisions for the right reasons.

Of all of these presidents, the one I admire the most so far is Ronald Reagan, and I reach this conclusion for several reasons. His accomplishments were numerous including restoring a lot of respect and pride in a nation depressed by the Vietnam War and embarrassed by Watergate, successfully calling on the Soviet Union to tear down the Berlin Wall, and centrally contributing to ending the Cold War and advancing the cause of freedom. I like Ronald Reagan because of his character, his humble attitude, his sense of humor, his love and dedication to his wife Nancy and America, and his great sense of optimism and purpose. He was a visionary and a rare leader able to disarm his worst critics and enemies with his charming demeanor, a well timed joke, the ability to laugh at himself, his resolve, his sincerity, and his power of persuasion.

President Reagan believed America was a shining city on the hill, a bright light in a very troubled world. A man of strong religious and moral convictions, he had great courage to do what he thought was right in the name of liberty.

What I Love about America

While America is far from perfect, I love my country and am proud of what it stands for. Seldom has the United States ever shied away from a difficult challenge regardless of the cost. And that indeed is the price a world leader must be willing to pay for the survival and expansion of liberty and to remain respected. America has a history of standing up for great and noble causes like freedom of religion and freedom of speech. One thing I especially value is freedom of choice. No one dictated to me whom I must marry, what career and jobs I must take, when I had to stop going to school or which colleges I could attend, where I had to live, what my individual priorities must be, the limits to my ambitions, or even that I could not quit a job I found unsatisfactory. America gave me unalienable rights to life, liberty, and the pursuit of happiness. It gave me the right to disagree and challenge my leaders and conventional wisdom. And because it believed in equal opportunity, I had plenty of chances to succeed and prove myself. It did not, however, guarantee me equal outcome and success, nor should it.

Pillars and Symbols of American Society

Among the leading pillars of American society are religion; family; strong marriages; access to free, excellent K-12 public education; character; personal responsibility; faith in ourselves, in each other, in our leaders, and in our nation; and private property. Our national symbols are our flag (solidarity and inclusiveness), the bald eagle (strength and the ability to soar to great heights), a church steeple (the importance of faith and religious freedom), the Statue of Liberty (our beacon of freedom to the world), the American dollar (financial security), and a soldier in uniform (a commitment to defending our ideals and a willingness to come to the aid of others in need).

A Nation of Values

Americans greatly value the rights to privacy, to vote, and to be ourselves and different from others. We aren't very patient and don't take kindly to people telling us what to do. I like the fact that I have the right to espouse my individual views and you have the right to disagree with them. My parents taught me to tolerate and try to understand different perspectives even when I initially strongly disagree with them. Always we have been a nation of thinkers, debaters, and proponents of change. Flexibility--the ability of individuals to react and respond swiftly--allows us to solve unexpected problems quickly.

My parents and grandparents taught me many traditional American values: achievement; hard work; honor; truthfulness; honesty; rewards based on merit; freedom; fairness; loyalty; trust; self-sufficiency; self-discipline; responsibility; empathy; independence; respect; dignity; decency; courtesy; manners; gratitude; morality; modesty; civility; faith in God; a meaningful job that would support my family; patriotism;

service to others; love of country and each other; ethical behavior; individual and group rights; good health; financial security; safety; happiness; education; tolerance; the absolute value of each life; making our families proud of us; generosity; humility; privacy; good judgment; reasonableness; moderation; patience; common sense; courage; boldness; pride in self, family, heritage, and nation; a sense of humor; and confidence. It was easy to learn and practice them because they were simultaneously taught to me by my relatives, friends' parents, teachers at school, and my clergy and Sunday school teachers. Everybody seemed to be on the same page, or at least near it. There was virtually no inconsistency in what adults taught me. For many people of my youth, the American dream was marriage, 2 kids (a boy and a girl), a home of one's own, good health, a new car, some money in the bank, a good job, and some time to enjoy life.

Living by traditional American values, I was able to fulfill many of my dreams and even add to my list. For instance, I dream of the day when other countries assume more responsibility and take care of more of their own business so American military men and women can stay home with their families where they want to be in the first place. I dream of peace throughout the world. I want corruption and abuse to cease. I want the world to see and appreciate the goodness of the American people and stop misinterpreting our intentions. It is not my goal to whitewash our deficiencies and flaws, for like all nations and people, we most certainly have them. I just want people to seek the truth about America instead of simply swallowing hook, line, and sinker the highly biased, distorted images fed to them daily by the media, ours being one of the primary sources. Unfortunately, getting any of this to change won't be easy because regardless of citizenship, people tend believe what they want to believe.

Does Money Drive America?

I do think, however, that America has become a much too materialistically-oriented society. Has money driven us in this direction? To a great extent, yes. I think many citizens spend foolishly to keep up with the Joneses. But it does take money to support a family and even a moderate lifestyle. As a parent I felt compelled to increase our money supply to self-finance our children's college educations, own our own home, know we had some money in the bank for emergencies, and obtain a few luxuries, like being able to take the kids to Disney World at least once. I never wanted to be dependent on the government or anyone else to help support me.

During our 40-year marriage, our lifestyle has never been extravagant. Sharon and I invested our money in our children and paying off our mortgage. Rarely did we buy new cars, travel to exotic places, or fill our closets with costly fashions, nor did we ever own a vacation home, buy a membership in a country club, or rack up a portfolio of extensive securities. When you support yourself largely on one salary, pay all your taxes (at one time estimated at roughly 46% of our gross pay), keep your credit-card debt to a minimum, and purchase adequate insurance, there aren't many dollars left. I'm not complaining. I feel fortunate that we have been able to do what we did and am grateful that we live in a country where this was possible.

With Freedom Come Responsibilities

Our founding fathers wisely concluded that there could be no real freedom without individual responsibility, which meant both following reasonable guidelines for behavior based largely on religious principles and doing one's duty to serve the nation and community. In other words, it means giving something back to a society that gives much to the individual. Our nation gambled its future on its citizens using good judgment and making good individual decisions and then holding them accountable for their choices and actions. Some of the key assumptions were that men would be loyal to their wives, respect and follow the law, be good fathers, be good mentors, be honest taxpayers, be generous souls, and do their duty.

Consequently, I have always believed it was important that I obey the law; pay my fair share of the costs to run government, our schools, and the military; conduct my personal behavior and life in an exemplary way; pay my bills; take care of my family and neighbors; and serve when called such as in the military and on jury duty.

Jury Duty

Speaking of jury duty, Sharon and I have been summoned to jury duty far too many times. Jury duty is one of those responsibilities that most Americans wish they never had to fulfill, but they do it anyway. In truth, however, I have always dreaded receiving that envelope from the clerk of the court ordering me to report to a court room as a member of a jury pool, for each time that happened, my life and everything I had planned were put on hold. Moreover, the judges I worked with had little regard for any excuses including my responsibilities to the 350 students I would not be teaching in my absence. I guess they just thought fully capable substitutes were a dime a dozen.

Regardless, I took my jury duties very seriously and did my conscientious best to help the juries I served on reach the right verdict. The reason was simple. If by some great misfortune I am ever charged falsely with a crime and brought before a jury, or a member of my family is the victim of a crime where justice is needed, I want the best jury possible. Jury duty may be an irritation to law-abiding people and a great inconvenience, but it is crucial to this nation of laws and fairness.

Murder

Once I served on a murder-trial jury in a case involving a 23-year-old male accused of killing another man of similar age, former childhood friends, both of whom grew up in two-parent homes in the same middle class single-family-home neighborhood. I'll never forget that week in the courtroom. What an American tragedy.

There was no victor in this murder trial, just great sadness. Daily from the jury box I looked out at a crushed middle-aged couple, the parents of the deceased, their child and dreams gone forever. I don't know how you can be a parent and not feel sympathy about this life-changing loss. Present, too, in the courtroom were the defendant's parents. It was obvious to me that they loved their son, and they, too, were having a very difficult time. I could only imagine the questions and thoughts that must have been going though their minds. Some of the most emotional testimony came from a neighbor, a good woman who with tears in her eyes told the jury how from her kitchen window she used to watch two happy young boys playing together in her front yard. One of those boys sat before her charged with the murder of the other. One set of parents lost their son forever. The other saw their son go to jail for life. Families and lives and a neighborhood shattered by a senseless bullet.

When you participate in a murder trial like this, you don't easily get over it. Actually, I don't ever want to forget it because as long as I remember that trial I will continue to seek answers for helping our troubled youth.

From reading this, one might conclude that some Americans don't set a high value on each individual's life. That's true in a minority of cases. Most Americans, to the contrary, place a tremendously high value on saving one life. That is why American Marines regularly put their lives on the line not to leave anyone behind in battle. And time and again I have seen families in this country sacrifice all their net worth to save one of their sick children. Sharon and I would not hesitate to do this. But that week in court I saw two sets of parents who loved their sons and tried to do their best to raise them into fine men just unable to save them from violence. And all we twelve jurors could do was listen, watch, and make a decision based on the law and the evidence presented. That is, do our duty. I wish I could have done more in that courtroom to save those young men, but it was too late. Never have I felt a more compelling need to go home, hug each of my kids, and tell them I loved them.

The Day Americans Will Never Forget

On November 22, 1963, I was taking a math exam at Elon College when my professor appeared before us, noticeably shaken, and in as calm a voice as he could muster informed us that President John F. Kennedy had been shot. For hours that day, I, like most Americans, stayed glued to the TV praying for a miracle that never came. John Kennedy was dead, and my nation went into mourning. It was one of the saddest periods of my life. I hate violence, and the assassination of my president on a Dallas street in my country was totally incomprehensible to me. November 22, 1963, was a turning point in America, a day when America forever changed, a day that signified an escalation of violence and many other signs of distress in my nation.

Ideals Can't Just Be Words

My country is an ever evolving nation, constantly feeling pressure to change. Some of the demands for change are clearly justified. Two I immediately think of are the civil rights movement and the women's rights movement. Freedom, justice, and equality were not equally granted to everyone in the United States, and that was wrong.

Since I am neither a person of color nor a woman, I can never completely appreciate what both endured in their struggles for equality. But I have at times been treated unfairly, been threatened, and have known the pain and frustration that accompanies condescension and control by others who treated me as a lesser human being. And I detested it. Early on, I learned something very important about individuals and groups in superior positions of power. Seldom do they voluntarily give any of it up. Almost always, the pressure to change is externally generated. I think of my physics class that taught me the principle of inertia, that a body at rest tends to stay at rest until something moves it. And then when it moves, it tends to stay in motion until something stops it. America is like that. It took great initiative on the part of blacks, women, and other supporting activists to expand equality. And once that pendulum began its swing, it kept moving, perhaps even too far at times.

Civil Rights

I am proud to say that during my life America made great strides to end discrimination against blacks, steps that were long overdue. It was ridiculous that they were prohibited from going to many state supported public universities, couldn't eat in certain restaurants, were denied rooms in hotels, had to use separate rest rooms or drinking fountains, or were required to sit in the back of the bus. If America's ideals are to have real meaning, then life, liberty, and the pursuit of happiness must not be selectively applied to only certain citizens. Blacks deserved access to public accommodations, equal employment opportunities, equal pay for equal work, access to excellent public education, the elimination of unfair voting restrictions, equal access to housing, and equal justice under the law. They deserved to be treated as equal first class citizens and with dignity, not second class citizens as was the case.

Fortunately, all of this finally began to change in positive ways after WWII as more and more Americans finally began to grasp the pressing need for change. Certainly, though, I can understand why blacks thought change was such a painfully slow process, because that is exactly what it was. It shouldn't have taken so long to right so many wrongs. On the other hand, it is a testament to our democracy and people that significant positive change indeed has taken place. I'm not saying the job is complete. It isn't. There's a big difference between changing laws and changing respect. Too many people treat blacks with equality because they have to, not because they want to, and I look forward to the day when what we do is driven more by what is in our hearts. And that goes both ways. Perhaps what most needs to change in America are attitudes, something that both whites and blacks need to address more seriously.

Women's Rights Movement

The women's rights movement dates back to the 1800s, but most of the actual changes in women's rights came during my life. In truth, as a young man I had little appreciation of the level of discrimination against women. The subject was not discussed much by my mother or even among the high-school girls and young women I knew in college, at least in my presence. One exception was Granny Horne who remained to her death upset and quite vocal about her father's refusal to let her continue going to college. About the most obvious thing to me was that college-graduated women in the 1960s seemed very much limited to two careers: nursing and teaching. I just never heard any of them protesting or expressing a desire to become doctors or business executives or such. But this changed quickly about the time I graduated from Elon in 1965.

"Level the Playing Field!"

What rights and privileges did American women seek and/or gain during my lifetime? I made a list that includes equal access to jobs outside the home; equal pay for equal work; the end of glass ceilings that limited their access to top leadership positions; protection against sexual abuse, sexual harassment, and domestic violence; equal access to higher education; equal access to participation in athletics; marital property-ownership rights; equal access to bank loans and credit cards; control of reproductive rights; the end of housing discrimination; being able to join formerly all-male organizations; and access to military academies and combat service. Most of these things seem very reasonable to me, and if I had been a woman, I am very confident that I would have been on the front lines fighting for them. Many battles took place over freedom of choice. A woman does not have to seek a professional career in business, government, or other professions, but it should be her decision if she has a passion to choose that route. I would be one very selfish father and grandfather if I didn't support the rights of my daughter and granddaughters to pursue happiness in such directions. Clearly much of the women's-movement fight was over dignity, fairness, and respect. Again let me say that I am proud that America found the wisdom and courage to end so much of the discrimination against females. My country did what was right, and it was also long overdue.

Disturbing Trends

During my life I have witnessed a number of disturbing trends. One of the more significant has been a decline in respect for my country, and that really bothers me because I want people to admire America. Unfortunately, the demise has happened both abroad and within our own borders. On the international front I'm most troubled by strongly negative opinions expressed in polls in European and other countries, previously some of our best allies. I don't know all the causes of such harsh criticism, but I suspect I can identify several of the sources. Two are propaganda and bias. Others are jealousy and envy. Much of it is likely due to misinformation. I am also a realist. Some of America's disdain has been well earned. We have done this to ourselves. For example, our pop culture, so vividly displayed on television, in movies, in video games, and through our music permeates and influences societies worldwide often in ways that people find distasteful and unacceptable. This is particularly true when those negative images affect people's children and change their behavior in undesirable ways. And I empathize with such parents and share their distaste. It distresses me what media excesses have done to the children in my country.

America is a dichotomous state. Our liberties both bless and curse us, freedom of speech for example. Our press and advanced broadcasting capabilities, like CNN and satellite news, expose every American blemish, real as well as contrived, to the world and then repeat stories incessantly until people believe each problem is far worse than reality. Good news doesn't sell. We've all heard that statement, and it has a lot of truth in it. The damage, though, from constant bad news is very real. Steady self-criticism profoundly harms America's image and directly threatens our country's future. Of course foreigners are going to believe we are a troubled nation when our own people--the press and the blame America first crowd--continue to flame the biases. And worse, our own people begin to believe it. I'm frustrated that our media so rarely report America's good qualities and strengths, which are far more numerous than its flaws.

On the Domestic Front

Internally, it's not that most Americans are unhappy. To the contrary polling evidence indicates that the majority of U.S. citizens are generally happy and optimistic about the future. What troubles me is that sizeable minority. Too many Americans are visibly dismayed and agitated, not necessarily about the same things, just enough things like the environment, abortion, same-sex marriage, and public education. Open forums and civil discourse that used to mark our society seem to have been replaced with arbitrariness and close-mindedness. From politics to family squabbles, there seems to be so little compromise today. We used to debate issues. Now we draw battle lines in the sand and dare anyone to cross them.

The central issue in America today, I believe, remains "rights." Who most deserves rights? Whose rights need protection? And who must surrender rights so that others get theirs? Our people are struggling to determine the matter of whose rights take precedence. Is it the majority's, a minority's, or one individual person's? America came into existence emphasizing the rights of the majority of its citizens. Today it seems to be the rights of minorities or even one person. Increasingly, rights in America look like a zero-sum game.

What Do Americans Have to Be Angry About?

The premise of this book is that most Americans got a pretty good hand in life so what are we complaining about? What is the source of our growing animosity toward each other and our country? My conclusion is three basic things: frustration over not getting full rights and respect, a breakdown in trust, and a culture war. Regarding the first one, reality and experience taught me that no matter what our founding documents like the Constitution say, life will never be completely fair. Sometimes I have an edge over you, and sometimes you have an edge over me. Genetics and things like money determine that. Yet Americans will always continue fighting for as much fairness as they can receive. That's normal, and I support this effort until demands become unreasonable and start diminishing my rights or the rights of the vast majority of Americans. The drive to remove God from public places, holidays, businesses, and government, maybe even our society, is a prime example.

The Breakdown in Trust

America was built on honor, honesty, and loyalty, things a society requires to flourish. People need to believe what others tell them, and individuals need to do what they promised. Today, though, for many reasons, our citizens are far less trusting of each other than any time I remember during my life. Too often we doubt each other's word and question each other's motives. Our citizenry has become increasingly suspicious and cynical.

During my teaching days, I regularly asked my college classes if someone dear to them had ever lied to them. As I watched virtually all the students' heads bob up and down, I then asked them if they had been able to forgive the person who broke their trust. Again I saw the nods, just less of them. Finally I asked them if they ever fully trusted that person again. And I followed this by inquiring, "And if not, why?" Usually someone responded, "No, because I was never sure when they would tell me another lie. I don't know when they will let me down again." And that was exactly my point. When you can only trust someone 99% of the time, you have little faith in them at all.

I used to tell our children never to lie to their mother and me. "Some day you may be accused of something you didn't do or be in some other sort of trouble, and if that happens, you will want your mother and me totally to believe you. You don't ever want to give us any reason to doubt your word." I think they got that message very well, and of course, for it to work, Sharon and I made it a point not to lie to our sons and daughter. They needed to trust us as well.

Americans are quick to forgive but seldom ever forget, especially when they get burned. Lying has a steep price. Unfortunately, during my life I have witnessed an escalation of lying in my country.

One of the greatest gifts I ever received in life is a wife whom I totally trust. Sharon does what she says she will do. It may be as small as keeping something private that needs to stay secret between us or as critical as honoring her marriage vows. And it is just as important to me that I know she trusts me equally as much. I can't imagine what it would be like to be married to someone I didn't fully trust. If people want to find happiness, their odds will improve dramatically by always telling the truth.

Lying, though, is just one cause of the decline in trust. What has divorce and the breakdown in marriages and families done to trust? How about infidelity? Watergate? Have you ever been cheated by a businessman you trusted, like the auto repair man who ripped off our family? When we give people power and entrust them to lead organizations honorably, we expect them to live up to the highest possible standards. Too many people in high places have left us stunned and ashamed by their selfishness and excesses. Elected officials, for example. We also used to place unquestionable trust in our religious institutions and our clergy, but many Americans have lost much of that prior unquestionable faith. In particular I am thinking of the pedophilia scandal and subsequent cover up by the Roman Catholic Church. If parents can't have confidence in the clergy, shepherds we have always trusted to protect and look out for the welfare of our children, then, of course, they will become cynical of other institutions and people.

Charles Van Doren

One of the first times I realized that I couldn't always trust people was 1959. Although television was in its relative infancy, millions of Americans like I regularly watched a popular quiz program called *Twenty-One*. What captivated me was the brilliance of some of the contestants, people who answered very difficult questions time and again. None did this better than Charles Van Doran, a champion who mesmerized me with his intelligence. Therefore, try to imagine how astonished I was when Van Doren admitted under oath that the show was rigged by the producer. In advance, he was fed the questions and answers. Right then my trust in media accuracy, honesty, and intent became severely damaged.

That day the media taught me a painful lesson, one I only wish it had taught itself as well. The recent scandal at CBS over the running of the Dan Rather bogus story on President Bush's Texas Air National Guard service revealed that nothing much has changed. There is so much spin in the media today. What are we watching: news, entertainment, or agenda? Fact and fiction have become so blurred that it is hard to know what the truth really is.

My list continues with quick references to business scandals, our legal profession tainted by lawyers more interested in beating the law and getting rich and famous than following the law's good intentions, judges regularly usurping their authority to rewrite laws, politicians placing the interests of lobbyists ahead of the people's interests, and charitable foundations caught violating the trust of generous people. The list seems non-ending. Yet, by no means am I implying that you cannot trust most Americans. I truly believe I can. My point, though, is that when enough trust is abused, everyone suffers and none more so than the honest and innocent. The whole system begins to crumble.

The Culture War

America is deeply entrenched in a culture war, a most heated struggle that has raged on relentlessly during most of my life over what this country should be. At stake are many of America's ideals, values, principles, institutions, traditions, and customs. The culture war pits religious against secular interests, advocates for more government against those insisting on greater independence and personal responsibility, abortion advocates versus right-to-life proponents, capitalism versus socialism, morals versus sexual liberation, and equality of opportunity versus equality of outcome. Like many things, I think this war began with many good intentions but at some point started going out of control. With each year I have become increasingly frustrated as little by little, one small piece at a time, so many of the things I have always loved and admired about my country have been chipped away. As a result, my life and my children and grandchildren have been affected.

For instance, I have great problems with what seems to me to be an all-out assault on my Christian faith, efforts that have weakened marriage and families, a declining morality that has dramatically increased the number of abortions and children born out of wedlock, and growing crassness that fills our ears with vulgarity and degradation. I long for moderation and reasonableness. There can be no real freedom without some constraints. Society only works well when people assume individual responsibility and use common sense. During my life I have witnessed a decline in America's decency and manners, which I deeply regret because they make life so much more bearable and pleasant. In general, marriages and families are weaker. The lines between right and wrong have become blurred. Behavior is more extreme and arrogant. I long for a return to higher standards.

"Here's Johnny."

For many Americans, January 24, 2005, was a very sad day because one of our most beloved Americans, Johnny Carson, died. Johnny was a television legend, one I suspect who will never be matched in terms of admiration and respect, an icon to the best that television has ever provided. For thirty years he hosted NBC's *Tonight Show,* the late-night variety show that I watched hundreds of times. During those years not once can I remember going to bed not feeling better about the world or not having laughed very hard at Johnny's splendid humor. He had a special way of lightening all of us up, and I do think America needs to lighten up.

Johnny was the master at uplifting America's spirit. Not once in those 30 years did I ever hear Johnny Carson use profanity, abuse or humiliate one of his more than 22,000 guests who appeared on his show, or resort to offensive gestures in truly bad taste. Throughout his remarkable career Johnny was always a gentleman on the air, and I have no doubt that is why so many Americans loved him. Despite his great fame and fortune, he always remained humble. He just seemed like everyone's good next door neighbor.

In dozens of testimonials following his death, Johnny was repetitively described as a kind man, a marvelous listener, a person who sought to help others and bring out the best in his guests, a man who launched so many of his guests' careers. Johnny had class. He was also my mentor, the man I most tried to match with my humor-in-the-classroom efforts. The man had such incredible timing, wit, and body language.

So now let me ask you a question. If he and people like Red Skelton, Lucille Ball, and so many others of Johnny's day were so successful showing dignity and class and doubling us over in laughter, why have so many of today's media icons and far too many writers, producers, directors, and networks resorted to the path of profanity and crassness? Why do so many talking heads resort to finding the flaws in their guests and making the effort to humiliate them? Why can't news programs conduct civil discussions without becoming screaming matches and showing excessive rudeness? What has happened to America's manners and high ideals? I want to see America return to greater civility.

Decline of Civility in America

It's not just the media. For a long time I have been troubled by the steady decline of common courtesy in America. I'm not precisely sure when my people, at least what I believe are too many of them, stopped saying please and thank you and elected to be more disrespectful toward one another. As a result, our image has suffered, which happens when bad behavior replaces reasonable rules of conduct. At the start of my life, America set the bar very high and expected citizens to rise to the occasion. Today the trend is for decent folks to lower themselves and adopt the mannerisms of the most obnoxious among us. Nothing better exemplifies this than the proliferation of profanity in America, particularly the use of the f-word among our media stars and young. Why anyone would so foolishly cheapen themselves and gamble away their dignity and respect is beyond me. We are a far better people and nation than this.

From the Playtex Living Bra to Sex in the City

Far more consequential to America's health was the sexual revolution that took us from modesty to exhibitionism, imagination to explicitness, and high moral grounds to high promiscuity, all in the period of about 40 years. I'm not arguing about the joys of sex, for I understand how wonderful that is between people who love each other. My concern is over what the sexual revolution has done to our kids and the enormous societal problems that resulted from it, like kids having kids, children born out of wedlock, children growing up in homes without fathers, and all the inherent social ills like poverty, drugs, crime, and about 1.1 million abortions in the U.S. annually that accompany these things.

When I first started watching TV, censorship was so tight that Lucy and Desi Arnez, stars of the *I Love Lucy* show, were required to sleep in separate beds. The first time a TV ad for the Playtex Living Bra appeared on TV, it shocked many viewers who couldn't believe television was showing a woman actress in her underwear. Today you know what your children see on TV--just about everything but the final deed. And how far away is that?

The sexual revolution and the media's continued efforts to push the envelope scare the dickens out of me because I was a teenager once and have raised teenagers, and I understand the immense pressures that come simultaneously from peers and hormones. I also learned how little control even the most diligent and responsible parents have during some of their children's most dangerous life-changing moments. Everybody's doing it is one media theme. Nobody gets hurt is another. Older folks know neither is true. But it's obvious to me that many kids don't grasp these truths until it is too late. Well, people do get hurt, and adults are putting our children in great peril. It bothers me that Hollywood and Madison Avenue are pushing many of our children toward a lifetime of problems, missed opportunities, and regrets.

What Can We Do?

So, I ask people in every walk of life, and we all are responsible for the welfare of our children, to move back toward moderation and decency, to strengthen personal moral behavior, to exhibit more courtesy, all to teach our children better and lessen the heartache ahead for them. We need to help our children obtain a better shot at long-term happiness. And it is imperative that no matter what children think, they need to know that everyone is **not** doing it--having sex in middle school and high school, hooking up with total strangers for one-night stands in college, having affairs with married men or women, and being disloyal to wives and husbands. It's not true. I have done none of these things and neither have many others. But life has taught me that it is simply insufficient to know this and not share this important message with our children. We must tell them, teach them to have more patience, and explain why we believe these things are important, for if we fail to communicate such matters clearly, our children will be convinced that it is appropriate and necessary to be sexually active as a child. And many will endure tragic subsequent consequences. We need to teach our children to hold those aces until they can use them to win the game of life.

Three Good Americans

Despite these concerns about my country, I remain quite optimistic about America's future. The reason is simple. America has great heart. Its strength is the goodness in our people and their determination to do what is right. Already you have read about many of them, people like Fred and Willa Deane Birchmore, Renegade, Ron Simpson, Jeff and Judy Mason, and Frank Smyth, but they are just the tip of the iceberg. This nation is blessed with an abundance of extraordinarily fine individuals. So I think it is fitting to end this chapter with stories about my kind of people, Americans that represent the best in what my nation stands for, ones I so admire and respect. Two of them are men, one a woman. I want you to consider what they did and why to make this world, in their own special way, a better place. The first put his life on the line for us. The second dedicated his life to helping adolescents with alcohol and drug addictions. The third is one of the most generous and thoughtful people I have ever known.

Ray

Let me begin with Raymond Thomas Stephenson, Pop's brother, my unassuming, humble, 84-year-old uncle. At 19, Ray enlisted in the Army, which he did for two reasons. Primarily, he didn't want to see his brother Wilson, who was mentally slow, drafted, and he was led to believe that by enlisting, the draft board would leave Wilson alone.[17] Second, Ray wanted some control over his destiny and knew that being drafted, which was probable, would give him virtually none. As a result, he wound up serving with the Army's 295 Joint Assault Signal Company that participated in some of the most horrific battles in the Pacific during World War II, places like Eniwetok, Saipan, and the Philippines.

Ray, who rose to the rank of sergeant, was a member of the 6-man Signal Detachment Team #3 that consisted of an officer and five enlisted men: a field artillery scout, two radiomen, and two wiremen. Ray was one of the radiomen. His job was making sure he established ship-to-shore and air-to-shore radio contact that was used to direct naval and aerial gunfire and bombing support crucial to infantry success. Most of the time Ray landed on the beaches with the Marines in the first amphibious assault waves. Always his team stayed near the front lines. The work was extremely dangerous, sometimes positioning the team behind enemy lines.

Ray would never talk about his war experiences until recently. He said it just brought back too many painful memories. "Fred," he said, "there would be very few wars if politicians saw what I saw. The beach was covered with bodies." When I asked what weapons he carried, he responded, "I never used a weapon, and I am so grateful I never had to kill anyone. I'd have had a tough time with that." The reason Ray avoided using his weapon was that his job was making sure the radios were moved, readied, working properly, and then quickly moved for-

---

[17] Ray told me that his brother Bruce enlisted first in an effort to keep Wilson out of the service. Then Ray enlisted. Wilson was drafted anyway and later died in combat.

ward again. When I asked him what his proudest moment during WW II was, he simply replied, "I got out in one piece."

Who knows what America, my home, would be like today if people such as my Uncle Ray hadn't put their necks on the line. Yet I find it so admirable that Ray has never thought of himself as a hero. He never sought attention, thanks, or praise for his contributions and bravery. In his mind, he was simply doing his duty and his job to the best of his ability. He just wanted to come home as soon as possible. That is all most U.S. veterans have ever wanted. But whether Ray wants to hear it or not, I am proud of him. Like my father and his other brothers Bruce and Wilson, Ray was there when America needed him most. He gave his best for his country and for the rest of us.

Mike Spicer

In 1981, Mike Spicer, Dick Farrell, and Peg Baker, with $25 between them and considerable faith in God and each other began planning a treatment center for chemically dependent teens in Des Moines, Iowa. The catalyst was a teenage girl who got drunk and died in a high-speed car wreck. Dick had been trying to help her and became angry that Des Moines had no program that might have saved her life. He thought that was absolutely wrong and somebody needed to care more about the kids in his city. So he contacted his friend, Mike, and Mike listened to Dick's pleas. However, Mike didn't get really passionate about the idea until he tried to assist another adolescent who was seeking help and learned that it would cost $10,000 up front to enroll her in a private dependency treatment program. These kids didn't have money like that. Some were homeless people. So Mike, too, got mad and went to work.

Mike Spicer was my son-in-law's father, a man I didn't really know enough about until Dick Farrell gave his eulogy in 2004. What I learned that day was amazing.

Mike told Dick to find the most organized person he knew, and Dick then brought Peg into the picture. And the 3 of them--Mike, the CEO administrative type, the planner, the leader, the "how to do it" guy; Peg, the organizer, manager, detail person; and Dick, the passionate one with the deep emotion, personal touch, and talking skills to sell the program--took a collective leap of faith. Mike told the others, "If God wants a treatment center, there'll probably be one." And from this humble beginning three good Americans raised millions of dollars and developed the largest adolescent chemical dependency treatment program in the United States, a program that in its first 10 years treated nearly 1,200 adolescents ranging in age from 11 to 21 who completed 60-day in-patient stays at their center. Additionally, far more members of the adolescents' families were counseled. Mike, Peg, and Dick named their program Our Primary Purpose (OPP), a title chosen from the preamble of Alcoholics Anonymous.

Our Primary Purpose was an autonomously run program that could accommodate 50 in-house patients in two facilities located in Des Moines's Lutheran and Mercy Hospitals. Its main objective was to get kids sober from alcohol and drugs and keep them that way so that they could function successfully in society. Dick says they didn't try to save people but just gave them the opportunity and the tools to do these things themselves. It was Mike's, Dick's and Peg's intent that if they could establish a core group of successfully recovering people, the latter would provide the future and continue to help additional young people.

Dick says that what makes him most proud is that the three of them watched hundreds of young people who had such serious problems, many who in their weakest days could not go to high school, stabilize their lives, obtain good jobs, establish happy marriages, become good, responsible parents, and make fine contributions to society. Many graduated from college as well. "They are active in Alcoholics Anonymous, and some work in programs in Des Moines today and are helping hundreds of other young people. And it does take young people who went through chemical dependency to show others the way back."

For 10 years Mike was the CEO of Our Primary Purpose. He ran the center, made most of the decisions, and saw to it that the organization's mission and goals were accomplished. Early on, Dick said Mike told him to get ten people with different specialized skills on board. And when he got them Mike told the ten of them, "Now get ten more like you." Within 4 months, about 200 people were involved in Our Primary Purpose. Dick says that Mike had the reputation of being a tough guy; underneath, though, he was tenderhearted, especially for the kids for whom he would do most anything. No one was turned away from OPP because they lacked money.

Our Primary Purpose was a spiritual program, and Mike was a very spiritual guy. Dick recalls the day he was trying to write the OPP philosophy and couldn't manage to do so. Mike told him to pray about it, and he did, and the words flowed out--a philosophy statement that was never changed over the years. Another time a pessimistic hospital psychiatrist asked Mike how he knew Our Primary Purpose was going to work. Mike answered, "Cause God said so." Mike's strong faith, will, and leadership skills were instrumental in making a miracle fall into place.

The revealing thing about Mike is that he understood the downtrodden because he was a recovered alcoholic who was helped by Alcoholics Anonymous. He is living proof that America gives people who want to help themselves a second chance and that there is still time to make your mark on society regardless of your past. Perhaps this is Mike's greatest legacy. If you ever feel there is no hope, think of Mike and understand there is.

In my life, I helped quite a few people. But Mike taught me what it means to save people, and there is no greater gift than doing the latter. At his funeral I witnessed one of the toughest looking bikers I ever saw, a man covered head to toe with tattoos, kiss Mike on the forehead. Men and women in tears told the family how they loved Mike and that without him they believed they would have died. I was deeply touched. Mike was a tireless supporter of Alcoholics Anonymous and the Salvation Army, two other faith-based initiatives that have helped countless numbers of people. Yet what I most admire about Mike was that he was a kind, good man who with the help of a great team of passionate, caring people and God's guiding hand made a substantial difference in people's lives and society. Mike gives us all a much higher goal to shoot for in life.

Redefining Generosity

I know an amazing young woman and mother who has taught me so much about generosity. For years she has done things voluntarily that brought great joy and help to others, hundreds of people in fact. For five years, she has coordinated the Martha's Table efforts at her church that collects all the ingredients and one day each month makes between 3,500 to 4,000 egg salad sandwiches to feed the poor and homeless in Washington D.C. Like many mothers, for years she has actively led and supported youth sports teams and Girl Scouts organizations, but not just in typical ways. For instance, at one very cold soccer game she showed up with gallons of Starbucks coffee for every adult on both sides of the field. Another time she suggested that the Girl Scouts encourage patrons to buy and donate Girl Scout Cookies to our military personnel and then arranged to take the kids and 400 boxes to Norfolk to deliver them personally to the ship. She wanted the girls to experience the joy of giving, which they did. Never does she seem to be too busy or broke to help those in need and others who could use a morale boost.

What is especially inspiring is that for years she invited her young daughters to participate with her in a wide variety of endeavors that benefit others. The girls have helped her make cookies to send to military personnel overseas, assisted in making the sandwiches for Martha's Table, delivered books to a homebound woman, sent cards and made visits to the veterans hospitals, and shopped with their mom and annually joined her in delivering a Christmas basket to a needy family in the area. And they are still doing these and other things with their mom. On several occasions the oldest daughter has asked guests to her birthday parties not to give her anything but instead make donations to the animal shelter.

My role model has taught me to do unusual and unexpected acts of kindness. When her family moves and the movers arrive, and when painters and other repair men come to work in her home, she goes that extra mile to feed them lunch or a snack. Recently she took an extension cord, table, and 40-cup coffee pot out to her front lawn one sub-freezing day and told utility crews installing electrical wiring on her street to help themselves and warm up. This, I believe, is what makes her efforts so special. People can't believe she is so thoughtful and nice.

The most wonderful thing about this exemplary woman is that she is our daughter Katie. Once I asked her what gave her the idea to do the things she does that improve the days and lives of others. Her answer was, "Mom. She taught me. You remember all those things she did to help people like delivering books to the homebound? We did a lot of those things together."

Final Thought

So now you know more of the truth about America, about some of America's good people, and how truly fortunate I am that many of them are part of my personal family. Life, I know, has its frustrating moments. I've experienced my fair share of them. What I have learned, however, is that they won't stop you if you just remember to count your blessings and give thanks. And definitely, always try to be the type of American you want your kids to become. Teach them well.

HUSBAND, FATHER, AND GRANDFATHER

Sharon and I met in September 1962, during her freshman orientation week at Elon College. I was a sophomore at the time and a member of the freshman-orientation team responsible for helping the freshman feel more welcomed to campus. In other words, I wanted to meet women. That evening I spotted a very cute brown-haired girl talking with a distinctive Long-guy-land accent. I guess you could say fate brought Sharon and me together. For if both of us had gotten our high school wishes, she would have attended a university in New York and I would have gone to the United States Naval Academy, and none of a multitude of blessings that have happened in our lives together would have occurred. Since then we have been virtually inseparable.

There we were, two Yankees surrounded by a campus full of Southerners. Well, not entirely. Sharon, like I, had strong Southern roots. Her mother and father, Kay and Fred Smith, were raised in North Carolina, the former in Greensboro and the latter on a farm in nearby Monticello, and both our families had a long history with both Elon College and the area. My grandmother lived in Burlington 6 miles east of the campus; Sharon's grandparents, Turner and Ina Smith, lived on a wonderful old 600-acre dairy farm about 13 miles northwest of Elon; and her other grandmother, Macy Bostick, lived in Greensboro. Sharon grew up in New York as a result of her dad taking a job with Grumman Aviation, where Fred was an aeronautical engineer.

Merrick

My first trip to Merrick, New York, to visit Sharon and meet my future in-laws was certainly memorable. Fred sent me very detailed directions on how to travel from the Connecticut Turnpike to their home on Long Island and warned me to get in the far right lane on the Long Island Expressway immediately after seeing the first sign announcing my exit. "Do it right away or they may not let you in." I had no idea what he was so concerned about. But I found out.

The first 160 miles of that trip from Rhode Island to New York were simple. The last 40 were beyond my imagination, for I must have traveled on parts of a dozen roads, and not any roads, but interstates, bridges, expressways, parkways, you name it, on most for only a mile or two. The route took me north to south across Long Island, about 20 miles east of Manhattan. All I can say is that if you ever need to visit western Long Island, memorize the directions because you can't afford to take your eyes off the road to read the map. The exits come up very frequently, and traffic, even in the 1960s, was awful.

Actually, I found my way to the Long Island Expressway (known then for good reasons as America's biggest parking lot), saw my exit sign, and immediately tried to get into the right lane. Six miles later, four miles beyond my desired exit, I was still trying to do so as those nice New Yorkers never let me in. When I eventually made my escape, I had no idea where I was nor how to get to Merrick. A phone call and many stress-filled minutes later, I finally arrived.

Meeting your future in-laws for the first time is one of the things in life most people never forget and for good reasons. Today we joke about my first visit, but back then it wasn't humorous. I felt like I was under a high-powered microscope. Well, I was. Sharon and I searched long and hard to find some privacy for a little necking, and Kay worked even harder to make sure she knew what we were up to and stayed out of trouble. At one point the basement door crashed open and from the top of the stairs Kay yelled, "You two get up here!" We got her message.

And then there was Susan, Sharon's 5-year-old sister, who thought it was great fun to surprise us every chance she got, like jumping up from behind the couch at bad moments. A guy couldn't get a break edgewise in that home, and I most definitely thought I had earned at least one after taking that 200-mile drive through hell just to reach

Merrick. But, what goes around, comes around. When our daughter was dating, I wished I could have rented a Susan-type kid as a security guard. All Sharon's parents were doing was looking out for her interests, just like Sharon and I did for our Katie (and Jeff and Dave). One time my friend's mother told me she wished she had a fire hose to cool down some of the boys dating her daughter. Kay did a very effective job. I can appreciate this better now.

Milking Cows

One of the side benefits of dating a girl from a farming family was that I got to spend many enjoyable days on the farm. The place was, and still is, beautiful, and while in college, Sharon and I would go there and walk across the 600 acres of fields and rolling forested hills. What we loved the most was taking the old dirt road down to Reedy Fork, a small river that borders about one-half mile of the property. How marvelous it was to be able to wander for miles on her family's property. I loved it.

Her grandmother, Ina Smith, not her grandfather, Turner Smith, actually ran the dairy farm. Papa T preferred being a plumber, so Mother Smith became the boss farmer and got the work done with the help of Uncle Robert and hired hands. When I first laid eyes on the farm, Mother Smith and Uncle Robert were milking about 50 Holstein cows, those distinctly colored black and white bovine creatures made famous by Gateway computers and Chick-fil-A restaurants. You cannot imagine how much I quickly learned about cows, which I guess is quite understandable since I started with total ignorance.

One of my early startling revelations was that virtually every cow was pregnant almost all of the time. Did you know that about dairy cows? I didn't. The reason is that they need to have calves to become "fresh" to produce high quantities of milk. Another thing is that they needed to be milked twice daily, every day, no exceptions. Forget vacations. One day at the farm I read a story about a record-setting farmer whose cows produced an average of 20,000 pounds of milk per head per year. I had no idea they could do such. Mother Smith's cows averaged about 12,000 pounds. But what hit me between the eyes was that this record-setting farmer and his wife said that they had missed just 3 milkings in 20 years. If that doesn't define dedicated workers, nothing does. Incidentally, the best herds in America today are now producing more than 27,000 pounds. At the Turner Smith farm, cows were milked starting at 4 a.m. and 4 p.m. every day. It took about 3 hours per milking.

On cold winter nights, I slept under 6-inches of quilts in the unheated upstairs bedroom and needed every one of those blankets to avoid frostbite. We would be roused at about 3:30 a.m. to walk to the barn where Uncle Robert was usually lighting the kerosene heater. The great incentive for rising early was Mother Smith's country breakfast which always followed the milking. If you have never eaten homemade biscuits smothered in homemade (the key) sorghum molasses and butter, you haven't fully lived. Mush the molasses and butter together first. Tremendous.

After breakfast, we usually stuck close to the farmhouse. To occupy my time on cold days, I often read the dairy magazines trying to educate myself about farming. One story that interested me was about a farmer who played classical music to help his cows relax and produce more milk. I didn't know that either. And it made me curious because Uncle Robert always turned on the radio and played music in the milking parlor. So one day, thinking I would demonstrate my new knowledge, I asked him, "Robert, do you play music to increase the cows' milk output?"

"Shoot, no, Fred. I play music because I like it."

So much for dairy magazines and theory. But that's farming. Every day taught me something useful, funny, or both.

"Get out Here! The Hired Hand Is Drunk."

During Sharon's senior year, Mother Smith suddenly passed away leaving the farm in a difficult position. One evening Sharon got a call around 9 p.m. that went something like this. "You've got to come to the farm right away. The hired hand is drunk, and the cows need milking." We left immediately because that is another thing I learned about cows. If they don't get milked on time, it hurts. When we arrived at 10, the cows were in the barnyard, even lined up on the ramp, waiting for the door to the milking parlor to open. They knew the routine better than we did, but Sharon and I that night needed to do all the milking regardless. Just the two of us.

Sharon was no pro either, but she was far more experienced than I. So she told me, "Pull that lever and open the back gate to the milking stall. Then pull the other lever to open the barn entrance door. That will let a cow in. Shut the barn door as soon as the cow enters or another one will follow. Once the cow is in the stall, shut the stall's back gate. Pull that lever to drop feed into the bin. Wash the cow's udder. Attach the milking machine. When the cow is done milking, detach the milker and hit that lever to open the barn exit door. Then open the front stall gate to let the milked cow exit. Then shut both the exit door and the stall and start the process over again. Got it?"

"Okay," I said. Keep in mind that the farm had a 3-stall milking parlor.

For one hour things progressed rather smoothly. Then Sharon let a cow in, went to work on another cow, and I inadvertently let the same un-milked cow out into the barnyard. About a minute later, Sharon asked, "Where's the cow I just let in?" Right then I knew I was in deep (*bleep*)! Figuratively and absolutely. Then she gave me an order. "Get out there and find that cow!" Out "there" were 48 cows in a 140-foot-by-75-foot barnyard, practically every square foot covered in about 3 inches of cow manure, and lit by one hanging 100-watt light bulb. I was about to get initiated into real dairy farming.

Now you might think this task would be simple, but do you know that most Holsteins all look very much alike, particularly at 11 p.m. under the barn's overhang and 50 feet from the light bulb, plus I had no flashlight. Mother Smith knew every cow by appearance and name, but I didn't and somehow had to find "Bessie." I knew the herd was divided into those waiting to be milked and those that were smiling, but I figured that since cows are creatures of habit, Bessie would head for the group of already milked cows. So I tiptoed across the barn (for good reasons) toward the milked cows on a stealth mission to find the only still-full udder. Ten minutes later, I found it and her. All the time I'm trying not to get stepped on by a cow or step in something. Now I had to cut Bessie out, march her back to the entry door, get her on the entrance ramp, and the toughest part, beg Sharon's forgiveness for my male stupidity, which she previously had clarified to me. To make a short story long, it took me about an hour to do this with uncooperative Bessie. She'd get up there and then run back to the group of milked cows. That night we finished milking at 2 a.m. But at least we did it.

Trailer Life

After 4 years of dating, waiting to finish our college degrees, and longing for each other's full-time company and other important benefits, Sharon and I got married in Merrick on June 11, 1966. My wife was a beautiful bride, still is, and her husband, as I look at our wedding pictures, looked like a teeny-bopper. I look so young. Well, we were young. Pete Fisk, my best man, worried me. Among the things he was interested in doing was painting "HE" on the bottom of my left shoe and "LP" on the bottom of the right one so that when I kneeled to pray during the wedding the church would get the message. But Pete and all our wedding party and guests were great, and off Sharon and I went on our honeymoon to the Pocono Mountains of nearby Pennsylvania. I guess I was in a rush to be with my bride because when we got up the next morning to go to brunch, I found the room key still in the outside door lock. That was the first time in our married life Sharon forgave me--the first of hundreds.

Following our honeymoon, we returned to Burlington, North Carolina, to our first home, a rented 50-ft. X 10-ft. trailer that we would occupy during the summer before we left for Navy OCS. I used to tell my students that trailer life had its perks as well as its disadvantages. As newlyweds, having to squeeze by each other in the hall was not a problem. Personally, I thought it was a thrilling fringe benefit. One down side was that our trailer park got noisy at night, especially the people in the trailer on our right. One evening we heard a man screaming, "You've been unfaithful to me again!" The next night we'd hear the same frustration. Only the man's voice was different. She had two lovers. Actually, it was pretty funny, especially when we finally saw the woman both men were fighting over. She was no raging beauty. Trust me on this one.

Opposites

When I first started dating, Pop advised me that if I ever planned to get married to find a woman who was as compatible as possible to me. So I married a woman who is a night owl (I'm a morning person.), someone who is rarely cold (My feet and hands are cold most of the year.), someone who would live with a fan on 24-7 (I don't like the wind blowing on me.), someone who doesn't much like to eat fish (I love seafood.), and a woman who gets upset easily (Most of the time I stay pretty calm.). I love sports, playing or watching them. Sharon could care less except when her child or grandchild is participating. She would love to dance more. I don't share that passion because I'm awful at it and dislike totally embarrassing myself. I love to backpack and actually enjoy sweating. She'll hike if it's flat, like on a beach, or only from one Holiday Inn to another, and she abhors being dirty. The list could go on, but you get the point. Nevertheless, it is not that bad at all to have incompatibilities, and here are a few good reasons.

First, Sharon and I have always agreed 100% on the values we live by and what we wanted to teach our children, and definitely both of us wanted children. She was pretty funny about this though. She used to say when the kids were driving us nuts that she had the perfect birth control solution. She would loan one of them out for a week. Free. Also she used to say that we could never get divorced because neither of us would take the children. Of course, she was joking. Nothing meant more to us than our children. When we got married, I was number 1 in her book. When Katie was born, I became #2 on the list. Jeff? Now I was #3. David? #4. I lost count with the grandkids. The good news is that most of the time I remained in the top 10 on the good list and some days she bumps me to the top of the list. And anything is better than being on her other list. You don't want to get on that one.

Actually, my wife and I agree on most things from money to our love of cross-country road trips in our old Land Cruiser to enjoying quiet strolls on beaches together. But here is the added bonus. We complement each other in so many ways *because* of our different interests. For instance, I have some woodworking talent. She has all the technical and mechanical expertise between us. Sharon can fix most anything, and has, so I don't have to do it. Like what? She has repaired kitchen appliances, my table saw motor, even things in my car. She's a computer whiz, and she balances the check book. I write books on the former and make sure there is something in the latter to balance. So we look to each other for help and at the same time give each other breathing room to enjoy our particular, if unshared, interests. And definitely, two heads are better than one in solving a lot of life's unexpected problems.

One of the funniest things is that with her night owl and my very early-riser capabilities, we had the kids pretty much covered. No matter when they tried to sneak in or out, somebody was awake. And let me tell you my wife was an expert at getting right in our kids' faces and saying, "Breathe on me! Now!" She is a great mother, and we are a strong team. Both of us were determined to help the kids, and us, survive the teenage years, which we all did pretty well. Through our division of labor and mutual encouragement, we got a lot of good things accomplished.

In the Name of Love

We have had a wonderful, strong marriage, and let me tell you why. When we got married, Sharon and I made a deal. She would make all the small decisions and I would make the big ones. So why have we been so successful? There haven't been any big decisions. Actually, we really didn't make such an agreement. Several years ago I read a newspaper column about a man who told a similar story about his long-lasting, happy marriage, and I thought it was worth sharing that story with you. But we indeed have had a happy marriage, mainly because of four primary things: commitment, high respect for each other, mutual trust, and love. And in the name of love, I have done a lot of things for my bride, and she has done far more for me. For instance, I used to get dressed in the dark so my night owl could sleep in, which was fine until early one morning at work when a car's lights hit me. I had just consumed donuts and coffee at the student union and was walking up the hill to my office when I saw this strange glare coming off my pants. That happens when you wear your tuxedo pants to school.

On another occasion I realized only after getting to work that I was wearing different colored socks. A third time it was different loafers. This is another good reason for living close to work. In each case I had time to go home and fix the problem. After several of these potentially embarrassing events, I decided to assemble my clothes the night before. It was a pain in the neck, but I did it because I loved my wife. And if you think this is love, then consider another member in my family who brushed his teeth in the dark to avoid waking up his beloved and then announced, "That is the worst toothpaste I ever tasted. It's awful!" Diaper-rash ointment will do that for you.

A Real Man

Do you know what a real man is? I'll tell you. It's Sharon's definition. One day I heard her scream in the kitchen, and when I got there she shouted, "There's a cockroach over there. Step on it!"

"Sharon," I said, "I would but I'm barefooted."

"A real man would do it!"

On that day I became a real man.

How Do You Pick a Great Spouse?

My kids and I talked a lot about this because it's such an important issue. The first thing I told them is to pay very close attention to the people they're considering and answer one simple, yet very important, question. When the other person is doing things, who is that person typically most interested in making happy? Is it you or them? If it's you, that's a good sign. If not, beware. Next I told them to choose carefully because life taught me that people don't change much. If you expect otherwise, you haven't been talking enough to your parents. Yes, you might get your husband or wife to make some concessions and loosen up around the edges, but make your spouse mad and the earlier version will magically reappear. This is one of the best reasons not to jump too quickly into marriage. You need to give people time to show their true colors. My advice to my kids was take potential spouses as they are or don't say "I do."

Next I suggested they ask their suitors if they did or did not want children, because if one of them does and the other doesn't, I guarantee you that a lot of heartache is forthcoming. Children are a huge marital issue. And then I would get into such matters as how important money or possessions are. A lot of marriages have gone down the tubes over those priorities and the lack of adequate income. Others fail because one spouse spends far more than the household makes, even when substantial. Often I told them to make a list of everything important to them, not just now but long into the future. "Write your priorities and dreams down and then do a side-by-side comparison with your potential spouse's priorities." And it is surely better to do this ahead of time instead of after the wedding.

I also got into issues like honesty, character, and so forth to make sure my children considered values central to their happiness. And if that other person was incompatible, I asked my kids if they could just accept the recognized differences, which is what you need to do in many cases. You have to be flexible for a marriage to work. Lastly, I asked them to question how that person would fit into our family. Was this going to be someone everyone naturally loved or someone who was just not a good match? And they knew what I meant because we all have a lot of love for each other.

Katie came to us at age 20 and told us she wanted to marry John Spicer. Honestly, I didn't understand why a 28-year-old Navy lieutenant would want to marry a 20-year-old female even if she was my daughter. There can be a world of difference in the maturity levels. So I asked John that very question. His answer was, "Because she carries on the best conversation of anyone I ever met." I wasn't expecting that curve ball and had no answer for it. But he was right about that. Katie was very well read and advanced beyond her years maturity-wise.

When Katie and I talked, I asked her many of the questions outlined above and was satisfied that John was a very fine man and that he indeed did love her and she him. My first concern was my daughter's happiness. A secondary issue was my fear that she would not finish college, which her mother and I really wanted her to do. She had two years left at the time. Katie promised me that night that she would finish that degree, and she did, although it wasn't easy. The last quarter she took 21 hours, a combination of UGA classes, correspondence courses, and one other course. I was so proud of her. And John has been a great addition to the family. Katie says people tell her she married her father. I consider that a great compliment.

When Jeff was thinking of marriage, I talked with him, and I believe he paid a lot of attention to me and, as well, considered what a good selection his sister, father, and maybe even his mother made in finding the right spouse. Then he set his bar high trying to find a terrific lady and definitely succeeded, marrying a gem named Kendra, a true Georgia peach. Interestingly, a lot of parents worry when the genders of their babies don't match their desires. Here's what I learned. If you set good examples and the kids choose spouses carefully, you can't lose. They will bring you more of those sons or daughters you always wanted through marriage. And the good news is that you get to skip the teenage years with the sons-in law and daughters-in-law. Life has a way of answering your dreams and evening things out.

Lucky in Love

I have to tell you that I was very lucky in love. When you are young, I think people tend to gravitate naturally toward good looks and sex appeal, and indeed these are important for good reasons, but I doubt many young people fully appreciate some of the other benefits a strong marriage brings to the table. I love Sharon because she is my best friend, my most trusted confidant, my buddy, my partner in mischief, and the woman who dedicated her life to taking loving care of our children, grandchildren, and me. I like spending time with her and having her by my side as we explore the back roads of America. She has never tried to change me into someone she wished she had married and helps me every way she can.

I so greatly value Sharon's advice and have enormous faith in her judgment of people's character. Not once in my life do I recall her misjudging a threat to my family or me. Sometimes all she would say was, "Watch out for that one. I don't fully trust him." Sharon does the big things that make a marriage work. And she does thousands of little things that have made me happy. Yet sometimes I have still found my way into her doghouse, because that, too, happens in a long marriage. Survivors just learn to deal with it and with each other until the frustration and tears pass. And that happened in our case because of our great faith in each other and forgiveness. But it also helped tremendously that she and I both came from families with traditions of very strong, long lasting marriages. Our parents taught us by example not to give up on each other.

It's the Man's Fault

One of the first lessons of marriage is that if things go wrong, it's the husband's fault. And an apology is expected, even if you didn't do it or if like most problems, both sides contributed to the madness. I always knew when Sharon was angry with me because one of two things generally happened. Either I heard, "Fred Stephenson. . ." or things just got real quiet. I don't mean the silent treatment. I just mean she limited discussion noticeably. And I would eventually ask, "What's wrong?" To which the ultimate response was, "You should know!" If I had known, I wouldn't have asked. And when I told her so and repeated my question, she replied, "I don't want to talk about it." That used to drive me crazy. Well, it still does. I just never liked to see her upset and unhappy--especially with me.

I definitely made her mad a few times. Once it happened over pledging a pretty good chunk of money to a charity without clearing it with her first. I was wrong. It was her money, too, and she deserved the right to give me her opinion. Sharon is a very private person. Some things were just not public information, and I shouldn't have talked about them. And then she got mad at me for some things that happened with our children.

Sue's Wedding

When her sister Sue grew up and had her own wedding, they booked me to sing the solos. My father-in-law and I were also drafted to take care of 15-month-old David while the women went ahead of us to the church. As the women departed, they said, "Look, all we want you to do is take care of David and when the time comes, bring him to the church." We told them, "No problem." And we did our jobs well until just before leaving the farm when David accidentally fell out of the car seat and cut his head open on the gravel driveway. And what a crisis and verbal assault that created. My gosh, that boy was quick. I was sitting right next to him when he made the unanticipated lunge.

We two Freds decided we had no choice but to rush David to the hospital emergency room where they began stitching him up. Meanwhile, we could imagine the mounting anxiety at the church. A call was made letting Kay and Sharon know what happened, that David was going to be fine, and that we were now on our way. Part of the response from my wife and Kay is unprintable. The section I can quote is, "I can't believe two men didn't have the brains to take care of one small boy." They still don't believe it.

Listen up men. There are three things that I guarantee will get you in deep trouble: (1) hurting a woman's child or even not doing everything to prevent it, (2) hurting a woman's grandchild, and (3) messing up a woman's daughter's marriage ceremony. Fred and I must be gifted because we managed to do all three in about 1 second. It took a long time to recover from that one.

David's First Haircut

David, our youngest child, had the prettiest strawberry blond curls as an infant. Thus, when it came time for his first haircut, Sharon told me to have the barber cut them off carefully and bring them home to her. She planned to save some. I loved those curls, too. Thus Jeff (about 9) and I escorted David to the barber where I passed on the instructions and the barber in turn passed every curl to me. And I handed them to Jeff to put in a plastic bag. Only after the barber finished and I had passed about 50 curls to Jeff did I comprehend that between curls, Jeff had been squeezing that plastic sandwich bag unintentionally in his hand and now it was one big knotted mess. I tried taking a curl or two out of the bag with absolutely no success. Now we had to go home to face the music.

There seems to be a pattern forming, doesn't there? Sharon was so upset, and nothing worked to salvage even one curl. I can assure you the blame fell on one person's shoulders. Back in the doghouse I went. After a while I actually built a huge doghouse for Katie's German shepherd, and it does come in handy when I need it. That thing is big enough for three people. It's a real condo.

Parenting

Nothing was a higher priority in our home than raising our kids right so that in life they had the greatest chance for happiness and success. Our concerns for them were relatively simple. Foremost was their good health. We wanted them to be safe and unharmed. Next we wanted them to be kind, caring, considerate, generous, honorable people. It was also important that they love and care for each other and that they develop and nurture a tight bond between them as well as with us. Furthermore, we taught them to value education and wanted all of them to graduate from college. Additionally, we prayed that those choosing to get married would find good, loving, unselfish spouses, someone like we wanted them to be. And by the grace of God, some good luck, and we think a lot of hard work on our part and theirs, they have accomplished these things. We have been blessed with three fine children who every day convey their love for us and other people. This does not, however, mean they were saints.

Parenting has been the most challenging yet rewarding part of our lives. The other day I read a cute saying from an unknown author that went like this, "Advice for the day: If you have a lot of tension and you get a headache, do what it says on the aspirin bottle. 'Take two aspirins' and 'Keep away from children.'" Sounds right on the money to me. Like running a dairy farm, we have been on this wonderful job without taking a day off for four decades and loving every minute of it--well, almost every minute of it. On a few occasions we were really tested, often pushed to the point of sheer frustration, often confused about how to deal with rebellious children and the generation gap. In the process, what we learned is how important it is that parents stick together and be consistent in their parental teachings. No book is going to provide you with all the magical answers for raising children. Every child is unique, and each child's friends and environment are distinctive. No parenting blue print fits them all. Just decide what you are trying to do and don't ever give up on your children.

Consequently, we tried to deal with things one day and one issue at a time, listen to our kids better, treat them as responsible people, keep our expectations high yet reasonable, be fair to them, allow them to grow into adulthood their own way, and be consistent yet firm in what we tried to teach and tell them. And it did help to present a unified front with clearly defined house rules that we expected them to follow. Katie, Jeff, and David needed to know that we meant what we said and that we always told them the truth.

I find it so interesting that each of our children has a unique disposition and personality, different passions and natural talents, and different skills and attributes. Some of this they learned, but far more seems to have been cast from a very deep gene pool. I used to take considerable credit for the outstanding things our children did that made us so proud. Simultaneously, I felt guilt and regret for the things that they did that I wished they had not done. Eventually I smartened up enough to realize that many factors contribute to the deeds of our children, and I needed to accept less of the credit for both the good and the bad. Some of those genes they inherited go back generations--way past the parents. And definitely, each child's environment, friends, and experiences do indeed influence all types of behavior.

What truly pleases me is that all of our children turned out well as adults and have rock-solid, we think admirable, values. If any of them tells you they will do something, you can take it to the bank. Mostly, though, what Sharon and I appreciate are their love for us and each other and the memories, hundreds of fond ones that so enriched our lives. Our children have given us so much happiness. And you know what I learned that they valued most highly? They really appreciated our love and sharing our time and interests with them--the same things my parents did that meant so much to me. These things meant more to them than money.

One of the Best Jobs (I Didn't Say Easiest) on Earth

I love being a father, and what I always loved even more was hearing my children call me Dad. Once I read in Webster's dictionary the definition of a dad. It read "the man in the house who is responsible for eating the mushy bananas, old apples, and burnt toast." I'm kidding. Webster's didn't say that. But in my home that is precisely what my kids believed. I was also the person who got to walk at the front of the line on early morning hiking trips. Sounds strange, doesn't it, in light of my backpacking chapter and telling you how slowly I walked, but I didn't raise dumb children. They put me up there early in the morning to clear out all the spider webs.

Changing Diapers

Never will I forget the first time I changed one of Katie's diapers. I wasn't even sure how you could quickly tell they were wet, so I asked Judy Mason, our good friend and registered nurse. This was back before disposable diapers. She said, "Are they drooping?"

"No."

"Do they smell?"

"No."

"Well, I just slip my finger under the edge then."

"I dooooon't think so."

One of my trips to the doghouse involved diaper changing. In theory it should have been so easy, but my kids were vigorous squirmers. That is another point missed in those parenting books. My babies had more moves than Michael Jackson dancing on a fire-ant mound. Perhaps they thought diaper changing was aerobics class. Who knows? All I can tell you is that I had to use one hand to hold the thrashing little rascals on the table and the other to do the diaper drill, and one day during the excitement I accidentally stuck Katie with a safety pin. And brother did she let me know she didn't appreciate it. And her cry brought Sharon to her rescue and sent me to oblivion for a couple of days. Let me tell you, folks. I am empathetic to the landfill problems caused by disposable diapers, but in my opinion the latter are one of the greatest products every invented by mankind. For sure, they saved my marriage.

I used to tell my students that if they ever doubted their parents loved them, then figure out who changed their diapers thousands of times. If that isn't love, nothing is.

Six Flags

In my family I was the designated Six Flags over Georgia parent. Sharon would approach me subtly acting like she was going to give me a peck on the cheek and instead say in a most quiet voice, "I think (Katie, Jeff, or David, pick one) wants to go to Six Flags. When can you take her/him?" Note that she didn't say, "When can we take her/him?" I had that singular responsibility, but that was OK because I liked to go to theme parks with my children and ride most of the rides. But not all. It always baffled me why people like to spend money scaring their pants off. Who needs this when it comes free with parenting?

Anyway, when David was 9 or 10, I took him to Six Flags. Just the two of us.

"When do you want to get there, David?"

"When the park opens."

"When do you want to leave?"

"When the park closes."

I figured as much. So one day from 10 a.m. until 9 p.m. we rode every ride he wanted to go on and multiple times on some of them. We took 39 rides, which not only set a 10-year record for the thousands of students in my classes (I asked every class, and no student ever did more rides in one day) but also included every scary ride in the place. I'm talking roller coasters, parachute drops, free falls, whatever David wanted to do.

Let me tell you about one of those rides, something called Free Fall. It's a contraption that hauls people up a tower about 100 feet and then drops them straight down like a free-falling elevator. David said, "Follow me." I did.

First we got strapped into our seats, four abreast facing outward, knees bent at 90-degree angles. Next I felt a jolt and then heard "click, click, click. . .click" as our row of seats was raised to the top of that tower. Now we're sitting there with our feet hanging over space. Lovely.

At this point, David said, "Dad, give me a quarter?"

"Huh?"

"Please. I want to put it on my leg."

"Why?"

"I want to see what happens to the quarter when we fall."

I'm thinking. "So use your own quarter, son. I'm already broke." But I gave him one anyway. Then I asked David, "What happens next?"

"You'll see."

About this time there was another jolt followed by more "click, click, clicking" as we moved horizontally out over space.

Quickly David put the quarter on his knee just before I felt the last jolt that will stay in my memory indefinitely. After that I think I uttered one of my four-letter farm words as my stomach relocated to my throat. Sorry. I was beside myself. It took mere seconds to reach the bottom.

Theme parks are amazing. I spent many dollars that day and more the next at the chiropractor. During those 11 hours I figured we actually spent about 2 hours on the rides, 7 hours standing in line, and 2 hours walking between rides and eating. However, we had a ball together. And this, too, despite my neck strain and bruised knees, is what love and parenting are all about. And David never forgot it either. Memories like Free Fall never fade. But what happened to my quarter?

Coaching

When my children were quite young, I decided to try my hand at coaching their soccer and baseball teams. There were two reasons for this decision. Coaching was a great opportunity to spend a lot of good hours with my children as well as other boys and girls, and I knew that if I coached, I would have a lot more control over what my children and others learned. Experience taught me that not all coaches did the right things or for the right reasons. Additionally, I loved sports, especially baseball, and thought it would be fun to enjoy the game again.

The child I coached the longest was David whom I worked with for about 10 years from ages 5 through 15. What I quickly observed is that coaching was really not much different from teaching, which meant that it was relatively easy for me to make the transition from classroom to field. Both involve preparation, instruction, and a high level of motivation. Teachers can't take math tests for their students, and coaches, no matter how tempted, can't put themselves onto the playing field to win the game. All you can do is prepare your kids the best way you know how so they can achieve success. I just had no idea how much of a commitment coaching, even at the youth-sports level, was. For several years, I spent as many as 30 hours per week for 5 months at a time. Still it was definitely worth it--a great investment of my time and energy, for I worked with many great kids and some fine adults.

Shortly after Dave began playing Little League baseball, he made up his mind that he wanted to be the team's catcher. His goal was to be in the thick of things all game long not out in the field waiting for the occasional fly ball. And like his dad, he liked to lead. All of this suited me fine, for I loved coaching him and seeing the intensity and pride he took in playing and hitting well. What made me the happiest was his attitude. David was an easy kid to coach, a positive influence on the team, and a quick learner.

Catching is one of the most underappreciated yet important parts of baseball. Pitchers get the headlines for their wins. Hitters wow the fans with their home runs. But catchers are the quiet leaders in baseball who not only call the pitches but also often direct plays and position players in the field. On every pitch thrown, a catcher is involved.

How much I taught Dave and his teammates is questionable, but I can assure you of the following. The other players and he taught me a great deal. Together we won many league championships and had far more good days than bad. And Dave and I bonded very closely and developed a lot of mutual respect for each other from our hours on the field together and talking baseball strategy. I know of occasions where parent coaches and their children develop rocky relationships in such settings, but in our case, fortunately, we worked very well together and had fun.

Reflecting on my experience, I believe a person should give a lot of thought before deciding to coach youth sports, particularly in terms of estimating how much time and commitment are necessary. I say this because the last thing that needs to happen is a coach not giving the kids the time needed, developing a bad attitude toward a team, or quitting in mid season. On more than one occasion during my coaching years, sometimes when the boys and I were struggling with attitudes or results, I thought about opportunity costs. I knew that if I had been spending the same extra hours at my university job that I was investing on the field, I would be much farther along toward promotion and a higher salary. Definitely, there are tradeoffs to accepting service commitments like these. Still, I would do it all over again under the same circumstances because coaching was one of the most rewarding experiences in my life. And I highly recommend others join the coaching ranks as a means of giving back something to the community and kids. Hopefully, some of them will be the former boys and girls I once coached, for I know they would teach other kids how to play to the best of their ability and win or lose with class.

Bands

In middle school David developed an interest in drumming. I'm not totally sure why drums attracted him more than any other instrument, but it was obvious from the beginning that he had considerable passion for drumming. To give you a better perspective on this, let's just say that there were times when I had to encourage him to go to baseball practice, but with drumming, I had to encourage him to stop. If left to his own discretion, David would have played the drums 5 hours a day. Sharon and I thought 3 hours and a 9 p.m. drumming curfew seemed reasonable, at least if we wanted to have any neighborhood friends left. Drums are not dainty.

By the time Dave was 16, he was good enough to be invited to play with college students in bands performing in the clubs in Athens, a world-famous band town, home of REM and the B-52's. Great successes like these two bands achieved stimulated many aspiring musicians like our son to strive for equal greatness. Athens just might be the hottest small-city band town in America. On any given night, there might be 50 bands performing across the city.

Thus Dave introduced his parents to this band culture, and it was a rare day when we missed one of Dave's shows. Now that probably sounds like normal parental behavior until you consider one very important fact. Seldom did any of his bands ever begin playing before 11 p.m., and on occasions when his band was the headliner, it often finished playing about 2:30 a.m. Furthermore, many shows were scheduled on weeknights, meaning that Sharon and I didn't get to sleep until 4 a.m. and then were up by 7 to go to work. Nevertheless, we loved seeing the bands, and especially Dave, play, but it was no wonder why we stayed tired, especially me. As previously noted, this morning person usually went to bed by 9:30 p.m. Our presence, though, meant a great deal to Dave, and notwithstanding the damage to our ears, we thoroughly enjoyed all of the bands he played with over the years. The kid, and the bands, were good. Very good.

Kids' Questions

One of the toughest questions my children asked me was "What should I major in?" Another was what career to pursue. Honestly, I couldn't tell them what to do. My wife and I struggled with these questions throughout our lives. With so many options available, it isn't easy to figure this out. So I simply told them what I knew and began asking them a series of questions, trying to get them to think it through to draw their own good conclusions. This was my advice.

"I can't tell you what to major in or do for a living. So get a pad and pen and go alone to that special place where you can really think. Then start writing down all of your priorities in life, not just the current ones, but way out into the future, things like money, status, having children, time off, etc." Sound familiar? Well it works as well for career choices as for choosing a spouse. "Just write down everything that comes to your mind. Then repeat this process again a few days later seeing if you need to expand the list. Next prioritize the list. What you want is something that closely matches your hobbies and natural interests. Ask yourself what you do because you want to, not have to. Doing these things should help you pick your major and career as well as anything I know."

What I understood was that people need to find jobs and careers they enjoy because that is a key to happiness and success. Both take great passion. And while my advice didn't really answer their questions directly, my goal was to get them thinking and planning.

Car Trips with Kids

Car trips with kids are something else. One thing I quickly learned was that I was crazy to run the car like a democracy. Whenever I asked, "What would you like to eat for lunch?" it seemed like all I got were disagreements and unhappy people in our car. Another thing I discovered was that vehicles are totally designed wrong. Somebody could make a fortune if they built compartmentalized back seats, you know, the ones with Plexiglas dividers and individual sound systems. That's because car trips quite often turn into free-for-alls.

Jeff and Dave still razz us about our Griswald summer vacation. In 1993, the boys and Sharon and I packed the car, strapped two mountain bikes on the trunk, and took a 6,000-mile trip to visit Katie and John in San Diego and explore Utah, Colorado, and other gorgeous locations along the way. I thought it was pretty nice that Jeff, our adult

21-year-old college son, went on the trip to keep his younger brother Dave, who was 14, company, and they did have a lot of fun together in the fabulous Southwest. For about three weeks we spent nearly 24 hours a day in each other's presence including staying in the same motel room nightly to save money.

Think about this: a night owl (Sharon) who wants absolute quiet in the early hours of the day, a morning person (I) who likes to go to bed early, a college kid, and a nocturnal 14-year-old boy who likes to watch TV or play video games beginning about 11:00 p.m. To say the least, it was interesting. In the car, everyone wanted to listen to music, just different types. Game Boy noises drove me nuts. Petula Clark drove the boys insane (I think they eventually hid our tape because it mysteriously disappeared). And yet, through it all, we had a great time and truly bonded together more tightly. It might just have been the most instructive give-and-take experience our family ever had. What an adventure.

When Your Kids Take Your College Classes

One of the more unusual things that happened to me occurred when Jeff, and later, Dave, took classes from me when they were attending The University of Georgia. That took guts on their part, but both wanted to do it. Yes, we all had some concerns about other students' reactions, things like believing I was favoring my children; however, I assured our kids that they would be treated identically to other students. Their mother told me that if I didn't treat them well to forget coming home. So there I was again walking that fence. Nevertheless, I was excited that now I would no longer be hearsay to my family, none of whom had a real clue how I taught students except from what others told them. I'll always be grateful to Jeff for being the ice breaker.

Should parents teach their children in their classes? Is that really a conflict of interest and unfair? I didn't think so and decided, why not? I spent my whole career trying to teach every child of every parent the very best I could. Why should I not do this for my own children, especially when they wanted to take my classes and I believed I could help them more than most of the other teachers offering the same course? Second, I knew I would treat them fairly, and I think they knew that as well. And they did indeed work hard and do well in my courses, honestly earning the grades they received. Both are smart people, certainly brighter than their dad.

Jeff took two courses from me. In the first, a class of 300 principles of marketing students, that rascal chose a seat dead center in the room--the hardest place for me to get to him. Yet, I did get to him like everyone else with that cordless mic, and he did answer his share of questions in class. I remember the first time I passed him the mic. I said my standard thing to all students, "Tell us your name."

He looked at me so puzzled and finally said, "Jeff."

And then I asked him the question, and he answered it. I was waiting for the class reaction because Jeff and I truly are look-alikes. I saw none. Guess most students were still asleep.

It got more interesting when Jeff took my logistics class because it was much smaller. Furthermore, by this time, many of the other kids knew we were related. But Jeff worked hard and earned an "A," which made his dad happy, too. He got no special breaks, but that didn't stop a couple of classmates from writing on their course evaluations that it was unfair that my son was in my class. They were wrong, but it's hard to eliminate conspiracy theories. Interestingly, Jeff became a marketing major and has had a most successful career as a marketing executive. Maybe that first class with his dad was a positive influence.

When Dave came along, I wanted him to take my principles of marketing class, and he wanted to do so. In part, I think Jeff influenced him because we both enjoyed our time together in the two classes I taught him. One day I asked Dave's class a question about the European Union, and Dave asked for the mic and gave a fine answer. For days thereafter people came up to him and told him what a great answer he gave in class. He told them thanks but said all he did was read the text. The whole answer was in there, but so few of them read the book.

During the quarter that Dave was in my class, he became good friends with Jim Holden, another sharp kid who sat next to him. Both were serious students who never cut class. One day Jim innocently said to Dave, "You sure seem to know a lot about Dr. Stephenson."

"I should. He's my dad."

So you can imagine my surprise when Dave failed to show for his 3rd exam. I'm looking at Jim, whispering, "Where's Dave?" And Jim was motioning back, "I don't know? I was about ready to ask you that question." As soon as the exam was passed out, I went back to my office and called him. It woke him up. My son had slept through my exam.

So I invoked the Jeff rule. One day several years earlier I got a panicked phone call from my older boy who told me he had inadvertently slept thorough his alarm and had missed his science exam. And he was sure he was going to get a zero. I just told him to calm down, go see the teacher, and I suspected he would be a decent guy, understand it wasn't intentional, and let him take a make-up. And Jeff did these things, and the teacher gave him that break.

I always acted similarly unless I was convinced I was being lied to. But from that day forward, when a kid made a mistake many of us have made at some point in our lives, that is, sleeping inadvertently through an alarm, I invoked the "Jeff rule." A decent man gave my son a break, and I would do the same for others. And I did do this several times as a teacher. Dave was one of the recipients. If you teach, you need to be reasonable. It doesn't matter whose child you're teaching.

Interestingly, Dave decided after a few business classes that he wanted to major in something else. Katie, like Jeff, majored in marketing at UGA.

Ringers

When Jeff was a junior, he invited Dave and me to play on his intramural softball team in the annual all campus men's tournament. Both Katie and Jeff were always really good about inviting Dave to participate in many of their activities and teaching him as much as they could. In fact, Jeff and his buddy Chris Howard were the people who first taught David how to hit a baseball, which happened before kindergarten.

About 125 teams were involved in the softball tournament. I was eligible to play because I was a faculty member, and Jeff's team was a pick-up team of his UGA friends. Dave was eligible because he was a faculty dependent. And did our team play surprisingly well finishing in the top eight. Personally, I never hit the ball better at any level of competition. Maybe it was because I practiced baseball so much with my Little League team. But I am telling you this story for another reason. One of the fraternities we crushed protested the game, and do you know why? Because of Dave and me, two guys they thought were ringers. I heard the whole thing between the coach and the ump and butted in.

"Let me get this straight," I said. "You are protesting the game because you claim you were beaten by a 50-year old 5-foot 8-inch man and his 15-year-old son? Do you really want the world to know this?"

At this point he withdrew the protest.

I really savored beating that obnoxious bunch. And it was a lot of fun teaming up with my boys in the tournament or anywhere else I got the opportunity.

Katie

I've already introduced you to our daughter Katie, but now let me reminisce a little bit about her younger years. Early on it was apparent that we had one very quick thinking, far more mature than her age, daughter. It was all Sharon and I could do to keep up with her. When she was four, I asked Katie what she wanted to do when she grew up. "Help you finish your dissertation" was her answer. Those gears were always working full blast.

Katie was the most independent of our three children, the one who didn't take "no" for an answer very easily, the kid who always had to have the last word and tended to argue like an attorney. Her stubbornness and quick thinking, though, used to drive me crazy, mainly because she generally stayed one step ahead of both Sharon and me and often wore me out. Even as a little girl she had tremendous spunk. We've still got the letter she wrote us that was addressed "To the Other People in This House." She was about seven then. When Sharon and I talk about our regrets, one that always comes up is that we should have kept her in the swimming program. We didn't because money was short. Today, we would borrow the money if necessary to keep her more occupied and tired out. The kid had a motor that wouldn't quit, and there were occasions when she maybe didn't need to quit, but her parents certainly needed a rest.

Road Trip

Shortly after her marriage, John went to sea on the USS Independence, and Katie and I took a 6,800-mile road trip from Georgia to the Southwest and back. Just the two of us. Originally I had planned to accompany her to San Diego to join John, but the Navy sent him elsewhere. But since we had already planned the trip and were looking forward to it, we decided to go anyway.

I must be honest with you. Katie and I used to get on each other's nerves. Both of us talk a lot, and we each like to run the show. So my wise wife remarked, "If you two are still talking to each other after being together in a car for 18 days, that will tell me a lot." Smart woman.

Katie did most of the driving. I served mainly as navigator. And we visited outstanding places like the Grand Canyon, Arches National Park, Monument Valley, Bryce Canyon, and Zion, all so beautiful. And we talked and took photos and hiked and almost got the car stuck in the desert. One day she said, "I can't stand it anymore. I need to be by myself. You're driving me crazy." And I understood, because we had somewhat overdosed on each other. But I can assure you of one thing. When we got home we were still talking, loved each other more than ever, and pictures of that great trip are all over the walls of both our homes to this day.

The most amusing anecdote from that trip happened in Bright Angel Lodge at the Grand Canyon. At dinner, we noticed a lot of people really looking us over and finally realized they thought I had robbed the cradle. It's enlightening, isn't it, that most women gave me the evil eye, and most men smiled. Both thought my daughter was a trophy wife or girlfriend. You would have thought they would have noticed the resemblance. We have the same nose.

Vince Dooley

It is instructive how something that used to annoy me was truly a blessing in disguise. We wanted our children to be mild-mannered and respectful, but that very thing, her independence, and a second thing, her resourcefulness, have become tremendous assets in Katie's adult life. For their own protection, I want my women to have strong backbones and courage, and Katie certainly does. She is about as well suited for being a naval officer's wife as they come and manages their home, their kids, and their business just fine while John is at sea. And like her mother, Katie is a doer. One day I came home and found my bathroom sink in the hall and Katie installing new plumbing fixtures. Another time I mentioned my Land Cruiser was leaking, and two hours later parts of it were on the driveway, Katie had driven off to find the repair materials, and she finished the job unassisted. It hasn't leaked since.

When Katie started working full time early in her marriage, she took a job with the Marriott hotel chain in San Diego. She thought the hotel business would be a great career and profession for a person who would be moving regularly with her Navy husband. Hotels are everywhere. One of her first assignments was reservations.

One day a colleague asked her, "Have you ever heard of a guy named Vince Dooley?'

Every Bulldog knows Vince Dooley, the legendary former head football coach at The University of Georgia. Thus, Katie answered, "Yes. What about him?"

"Well, he's planning to stay at our hotel, and somebody booked him one of our least desirable rooms."

"Let me see his file." And in short order Katie had booked him in a really nice room and notified Coach Dooley's office of the changes. She also passed on a message that she was a UGA graduate.

Soon she got a call from Vince Dooley expressing his appreciation and that when he got to San Diego, he would be honored to take Katie and John to see the Padres play as his guest. And it killed John because he had the duty and couldn't go. So Katie and her girl friend went one night to the ballpark with Coach Dooley and had a great evening. But it doesn't surprise me because that's my girl. One of her church friends told me once that if Katie had been running the war in Iraq, it would have been over in a week.

Jeff

Of our three children, Jeff's my closest clone. His looks, personality, and sense of humor are similar to mine, it's just that he's the younger, better looking version. And thank goodness he has a far superior memory to the one I have. He's also far cooler under pressure.

Jeff is my chief hiking buddy. As noted in the backpacking chapter, we enjoy each other's company and share interests in many things like the outdoors, fishing, and football, and like me, he is full of mischief. Always has been. When we first moved to Boston, our first stop was a dead-end street of duplexes occupied mainly by young families starting out on their careers. Jeff has always had a great ability to tell a convincing tale. Between his vivid imagination and strong writing abilities, he should write a novel someday. He certainly has what it takes to be a book writer.

But I've digressed from my dead-end street story. One of the fathers who lived there was a practical joke artist who constantly practiced his talent on unsuspecting people. Everyone was fair game. One day he and his family invited our young children, Jeff and Katie, to have dinner with them, and we told the kids to go have fun, which Jeff apparently did. During dinner, Jeff convinced them that it was Sharon's birthday. This couple then felt so badly about having invited our children to dinner on their mother's birthday that they made Sharon a cake, and all of them brought it down the street to us to help celebrate her birthday, which incidentally, was actually many months away. The practical joke artist was had by our three-year-old son.

Later in life, Jeff used to call me at work and imitate different dialects. This faked me out just about every time. The kid was good, and he enjoyed fooling me. So he did this a lot. One day I got a call from a man with this deep, and I mean very deep, Southern drawl, and I said, because I was busy and sure it was my son, "Jeff, quit clowning around. I've got work to do."

And this indignant voice said, "What are you talking about?"

It wasn't Jeff.

One thing I especially appreciate about Jeff is that he is thoughtful and considerate, which makes me very happy because you remember what my mom told me about being nice. Among our three children, he was our hugger, the kid who invitingly extended his arms to us while another of our children extended a straight arm most of the time. When he was in college, it seemed like everybody wanted to hug him, particularly women about my age. And why not? He was cute. That's what the women told me. I think his warm inviting personality and smile got to them. Everybody seems to like Jeff. I believe that is because he treats people well and cares about them.

The Laundry Chute

Don't get me wrong. He was all boy, and if you have raised the male gender, you know they can be a thrill a minute. For instance, he liked wading in creeks catching critters including snakes. Shortly after we moved to Athens, I heard a loud crash and ran to the kitchen just in time to see Jeff burst out of the pantry looking quite disheveled. "Jeff, are you OK? What happened."

"I fell down the laundry chute."

That seemed impossible, but that 7-year-old had indeed accomplished this feat. Later I discovered that he had been sitting in the upstairs bathroom closet dangling his feet through the top of the laundry chute and just decided to go for it. It's a wonder he didn't tear his back up, or worse, get stuck. Nobody else ever did that. Four 2-inch screws and a sheet of plywood made sure.

Getting Some Help along the Way

Let's just say that Jeff's high school performance was less than stellar. During graduation, the associate principal got two of Jeff's buddies and him together and in a supportive way gave each a congratulatory hug, adding that he had had his doubts about whether the three of them were going to make it through high school. But he was pleased that they had succeeded. Well that was just the start. Jeff's future would introduce him to a professor whom Sharon and I will always be indebted to who recognized his potential and inspired him to excel, which he has done subsequently in all aspects of his life. All three of those high school boys graduated from UGA, one becoming a successful salesman, the second a parole officer and later a professional fireman, and Jeff who became a marketing executive. I think this says a lot about why adults shouldn't prejudge kids too severely and definitely not give up on the younger generation prematurely. Sometimes they just haven't found that spark yet to free their passions and talents. Like Katie, Jeff's traits that used to cause him problems in high school have turned out to be valued assets in adulthood. He's a good communicator. He is resourceful, funny, and a man of his word. People like him and trust him. And he is loaded with the technological skills I never had. And, yes, we are very proud of him. I am convinced one day he will lead his own company.

What Sharon and I most admire about our eldest son, however, is that he is truly one of the best husbands and fathers I have ever known, something we always believed he would become. Sometimes you can just tell. We feel so fortunate that Jeff's family lives close enough to us that we can be with them regularly. It is so obvious how much all of them love one another.

Dave

Which brings me back to our redhead, Dave, everybody's little brother, Opie, as Jeff's buddies used to call him, because as a kid he reminded them of Opie on the Andy Griffith show, my all-star catcher, our drummer, the kid who taught me all I needed to know about Free Fall and a lot of other things. Where do I begin? How about reading?

Practically every night when he was an infant I read 4-6 books to David, and that smart little fellow began to have favorites and make requests. And I would read to him, and he would fill in the words I failed to put in. For a while I thought he was an advanced reader. Then I figured out that he had memorized the books. Babies and infants need naps. David never took one, and he wasn't that thrilled about going to sleep at night either, so I read books to put him to sleep. And it worked so well that more often than not it put me to sleep first. Many an evening I awoke to David sitting on my chest, with his two little hands shaking my head, and my son saying, "Daddy, wake up and finish the story."

Better Check on David

David was both an adventurer and a professional escape artist. If he was doing something loudly, we went to check on him. If he was quiet, we wondered what he was up to and went to check on him. He had no fear and no real inhibitions. One day when David was 2, Sharon said,

"Where's David?" And from the porch we heard this small voice reply, "I'm on the porch having a beer." And when we opened the door, he was sitting in a chair trying to open a can of beer. Honestly, we do not drink much at all in our home, but apparently he saw me drink a beer and decided to imitate me.

David was a combination of Sir Edmund Hillary and Harry Houdini. Before he was 4, neighbors used to ask us if they could borrow him to test the security devices they installed to keep their infants in check. I'm serious. David could escape from anything. And I used to call him Curious George because he was indeed so curious. But if there was ever a clear need to keep medicines and poisons locked securely away from children, he was the poster boy for that. We were so concerned about David getting into dangerous stuff in our bedroom and bathroom that we rigged an eye hook high on the outside of the door beyond his reach so we could keep him safe. So what do you suppose he did? One day while our older kids were at the swimming pool and Sharon and I were in our bedroom, David came into our room, slammed the door, and the eyehook dropped in the lock. For two hours the three of us were trapped in that room until the older children came home and released us.

Before Dave was four, he figured out ways to pull out dresser drawers and walk up them like stairs, one time pulling the whole thing down and surviving when the dresser hit another piece of furniture. Another time he stood on his rocking horse and accidentally pulled a big TV over. The couch arm blocked it from crushing him. He climbed book cases, trees, ropes, ladders, you name it. Curious George was a monkey, right?

The Tree House

When David was 5, I built a super tree house in our back yard that had 500 board feet of lumber in it, a carpeted cabin with windows and a door, a huge front fenced-in deck--the works. The floor was 14 feet off the ground. I tell you, it was a kid's dream come true. And I'm talking about me. Sharon knew I primarily built the tree house because I had wanted one ever since I was a boy and visited the tree house that my Grace Church Boys Choir good friend Tommy Chace built on Narragansett Bay in Rhode Island. By far Tommy's was the greatest tree house I ever saw, and what really impressed me is that he built it practically all by himself as a kid. That thing was three stories high, its bottom floor was about 20 feet off the ground, and from that high perch I felt like I could see the whole world. Up there we were the kings of the mountain. So when we finally had a home and the right trees, I built ours in Athens, Georgia. And it was the envy of our neighborhood. To reach it you had to climb a rope ladder that swung in the breeze and made a lot of adults squeamish. David, though, went up that rope ladder the first time he tried it with absolutely no trouble.

Everyone but Sharon loved that tree house. She reminded me of that recently, and I said, "That's why we're so different."

"You're right, we're different. I wanted our kids to live to adulthood." Well, so did I, but I firmly believe kids need to take some "reasonable" risks as they grow. It conditions them to life's later challenges. And indeed, that tree house was quite a learning experience for all of us.

The tree house was a lot of fun until the day when as I watched from our home's back door, our 6-year-old fell backwards to the ground from the highest rung on the rope ladder. It scared me to death, and I couldn't do anything to stop it. But David bounced back up, wiped the dirt off his pants, and walked away. I couldn't believe it. What happened was that the more David climbed the ladder, the bolder he became. Unknown to us, he liked to let go with both hands before he reached for the next rung, and that time he missed. The dog house was beginning to look very familiar to me.

The next day David went right back up there. It didn't faze him a bit. But it definitely changed his climbing technique and gave me a different perspective on high tree houses.

The Rocking Chair

Our family's favorite David story involves an antique wooden rocking chair. T'was the night before Christmas when in about 3 hours we were expecting 60 guests to attend our annual family Christmas Eve party. As usual, David was restless and trying out new tricks. Suddenly

I heard him yelling, "I'm stuck. I'm stuck. Somebody help me." He must have been about 4.

When I got to the living room, David was stuck in the rocking chair, his feet, legs, and chest south of the wooden lower back support, his head north of it, and his neck under it. And he couldn't go forward or backwards because his head was too big and in his panic, his chest expanded preventing him from retracing his steps. He had slid in feet first. And it was both funny and not so humorous, if you know what I mean, particularly since we were supposed to leave for church in 30 minutes.

I wish you could have seen it. Here's this tiny redhead surrounded by four adults and 2 other kids all offering expert opinions on how to extract him and all the time David yelling, "Get me out of here!" But nothing worked.

Finally, one of the adults suggested we might need to get a saw and take the chair apart.

"Get the saw! Get me out of here!" came from below.

Then I heard Sharon retort, "We're NOT sawing that chair. It's a 100-year old antique!"

I finally told them maybe they should just all go into the den and let me try to relax David and get him out. And five minutes later we both walked into the room.

I found a new use for Mazola oil that day. I just took off Dave's shirt, greased him all over, and popped his chest and little butt right out of there. And that, too, defines fatherhood.

Wine Boy

David had a lot of nicknames. When he worked at Harris Teeter, a supermarket, jokingly we used to call him "Vegetable Boy." And when he moved to Boston after he graduated from college, he became "Wine Boy." First a little background information is in order.

Dave is bright and because of this gift he skipped his senior year of high school and enrolled in The University of Georgia's Honors Program. Then he graduated from UGA four years later with a math major and moved to Boston to start a band with his friend. But as any budding musician knows, you need to support yourself as you are developing your musical reputation. Thus, he answered an ad for a job in a wine/liquor store figuring he might as well tap into the knowledge he gained as a waiter in Athens during his college days. Unfortunately, the job had already been filled. Discouraged, he left and on a whim entered the next wine/liquor store to inquire about a job. And he got one, a one-week trial as the store's manager. And he succeeded. So at the age 21, Dave ran a retail establishment that did more business than the typical McDonald's restaurant.

It's funny how things work out. The kid who took my marketing course but who didn't want to get a business degree wound up very successfully managing a retail business and increased its sales and profits. As I said, Dave is smart and resourceful. We are very fortunate that all three of our kids are.

Anyway, there have never been many dull moments with Dave around. He, like Jeff, has been a wonderful son and the source of so many great memories.

Grandpa and Papa

Being a grandfather is special--truly one of the most fabulous jobs on the planet, something I wouldn't trade for all the money in existence. When our first child was born, I was overwhelmed by this incredible gift, this miracle of having our own baby to love. I couldn't believe how lucky we were that God had blessed Sharon and me with this precious little girl, and then He gave us two more miracles with our boys. The birth of our first grandchild, Katie and John's daughter, equally made Sharon and me happy, yet in a different way. The feeling was more a sense of calm and security. It dawned on me that some little part of Sharon and me would continue on into future generations, and that felt really good. It was like an added bonus to the tremendous joy we were experiencing.

I never told my grandkids what to call me. They determined that. Our first one called me Granddad and our second called me Grandpa until she won the former over. So now Katie's girls know me as Grandpa. Our grandson named me Papa, a name I loved because of Papa Horne, my beloved grandfather. But I like Grandpa just as well, almost as much as I love our four grandkids--three girls and one boy.

The Privileges of Retirement

One of the enormous privileges of retirement is the freedom to travel and spend time with our children and grandchildren, which we do as much as possible. Retirement also allowed us to really get to know our daughter-in-law Kendra and son-in-law John much better, two of the finest young adults I know. As previously noted, John is a career U.S. Navy Supply Corps officer who recently completed a tour as the head supply officer on the aircraft carrier USS Enterprise. If your son or daughter was ever to serve in the military, I hope they would serve under a man like John. Over the years I have met hundreds of leaders in all types of fields, and I am convinced John is one of the very best. He is thoughtful, considerate, and capable, and a far better leader and military officer than I ever was. I love and respect him like my third son.

Kendra is one of the hardest working, most loving mothers I have ever seen. It's a twenty-four-hour a day job taking care of two young children, but she loves it. And I love her like my second daughter. What a thrill it was for me to see our grandson's first step and our granddaughter's first time rolling over. Unfortunately I never witnessed either event with any of our three children because I was at work. Early retirement made this possible with our grandchildren.

Katie and John met at the Navy Supply Corps School in Athens. She was the lifeguard at the base pool. John was an instructor and avid swimmer. They used to joke that Katie rescued him.

Kendra and Jeff met at Lithonia Lighting where they both worked in marketing. Jeff used to tell me about this really attractive redhead he worked with, a woman who loved the outdoors as much as he did. According to Jeff, she had it all. He said that if Kendra wanted to, she could become a CEO. She was that talented. So I asked him why he didn't date her.

"She's dating someone else, and I don't think she'd go out with me."

At one of their wedding showers some time later, I inadvertently overheard several of Kendra's Mercer University sorority sisters talking about how Kendra was really attracted to Jeff but didn't think he would date her. For one year they stayed apart because each wasn't sure they were quite good enough for the other.

I think I had a part in their marriage. I told Jeff he'd never know unless he asked her out, so he did. The rest has been a wonderful marriage.

I owe so much to Kendra and Katie, the mothers of my four new buddies. By watching them work so hard doing all the things mothers do, I developed a fuller appreciation for Sharon's limitless efforts and contributions in our home. Both of our girls have made voluntary, conscientious decisions to stay home to raise our grandchildren, and they couldn't have given us any gift of greater significance. And they are doing a magnificent job. All 3 of our children and their spouses are people of impeccable character, and that, too, means more to me than you can imagine.

Playing with the Grandkids

Sharon and I have made it our mission to spend as much time as we can with each of our grandchildren doing things they love to do. We don't have the resources to give them all the material things they might want, nor would we do so if we had them, but we can give our grandchildren something far more important--our time, love, and undivided attention. My goal is to be there for them helping each one through as many of life's challenges as possible. I think they know that they can call me anytime to discuss anything on their minds. And I do believe that it helps to establish this bond and mutual trust early on when children are young.

Once I heard a saying that the reason children and grandparents get along so well is that they have a common enemy. Well, we don't have those enemies but instead just a superb opportunity to bring much joy to each other. And I intend to do my part to make that happen.

Also, I am trying to share with them my passions for things like hiking, backpacking, fishing, and woodworking. Both of Katie and John's girls have started climbing mountains with me. And my oldest granddaughter and her mom just finished their first backpacking trip with me, a 3-day, 2-night hike along the Appalachian Trail in Virginia. One of the favorite things my grandchildren and I do together is go to Athens Hodgson's Pharmacy for ice cream. For a buck, we get big double-scoop cones and sit on the back tailgate of the Land Cruiser dangling our feet and seeing who can win the ice-cream licking contest. Katie's girls also love horses and are becoming quite accomplished riders. And what a thrill it was to watch our oldest granddaughter catch a 5-pound bass. It was bigger than anything I ever caught.

One of our grandson's favorite things is watching the trains with his Papa. We've been doing this together since he was two. I take him to a nearby railroad crossing where we sit patiently sometimes for two hours talking and waiting for the irregularly spaced trains, and I love being with him. Interestingly, I didn't teach him to love trains. You know I have a Ph.D. in transportation, but I did not plant this seed. Perhaps it is genetic. My dad always loved trains as well. And what a sharp mind he has. He knows the names of different types of railroad cars, can operate a VCR, can name all the planets in order, pulls up his programs on the computer, and assembles and reconstructs his toy layouts with relative ease. He just turned four. I assure you he didn't inherit these abilities from me, but I am really glad he has them.

Last but not least, there is our baby granddaughter, someone I can already tell has a wonderful disposition. She has this unforgettable deep belly laugh, one that sounds like it starts in her toes and works itself up from there, exactly like her daddy laughed as a baby. And I do so enjoy hearing a child laugh. All babies are different, but I think our youngest is one of the sweetest babies around. Makes me think she is going to grow up to be a very nice person. And when she gives me one of her unsolicited hugs, she wraps me around her little finger.

Family

Well, that's the story of my ninth life. All of them have been very meaningful to me, but none more so than this last one, for it best defines who I am and what my highest priorities are. And they are simple. I wanted a family that deeply loved and respected each other and me, and I couldn't have asked for more than I received. How incredibly blessed and fortunate I have been.

It excites me to think about the possibility of additional grandchildren and hopefully, before I move on, great grandchildren and of course future marriages that will bring additional fine people into our family.

But I just want all my offspring to know, just in case we don't get to meet personally, that I was thinking about you when I wrote this book. It's for you. Always know I will be there in spirit loving you and trying to guide you toward a life of happiness and satisfaction.

Afterthoughts

It's been quite a journey, this trip through my 63 years and most of my distinctive lives, one I hope you have enjoyed as much as I have. One day while I was rereading the entire manuscript checking for repetition, I was surprised by the breadth of topics and advice provided. Honestly, that was not my original intent. My goal in writing the book was simply to lift people up from their doldrums, lessen the complaining, and encourage readers to count their blessings. I wanted them to recognize and use their abilities to make positive changes in their lives and fulfill more of their potential. Ultimately, I just wanted everyone to find more peace and be happier.

Two 8's has told you a whole lot about my family and me and what I've spent my life trying to teach our children and my college students. It's amusing to me that I have a Ph.D., that is, a doctor of philosophy degree, without ever having taken a course in philosophy, yet in reality I know that what I have mostly been teaching and writing about is indeed a philosophy of life. Where I learned it was not in any book or classroom but from experience--what I've absorbed from a wide variety of activities and situations, interactions with many types of people, my own successes and humbling mistakes, and numerous fine mentors. It's an education that comes free to everyone willing to pay attention to the world around them and who lives long enough to absorb what life can teach them.

My classroom teaching was filled with the use of analogies, stories, humorous or otherwise, tapping things younger people understood to try to convey my messages. My goal was to assist students over the inevitable speed bumps ahead in each of their lives. And I knew that to accomplish this, they first needed to trust me. I was convinced that if

I would just be myself and they accepted my sincerity, good intentions, and humanity, blemishes and all, they might pay a bit more attention to what I was trying to share with them. I'm hoping this book accomplished the same mission with you.

In any event, this has been the story about how I, a guy with a 1,070 SAT score, an easily distracted, generally slow at most things, forgetful human being but one with considerable determination and heart, played my hand, my two 8's and two 3's, to win what I think has been a challenging yet thrilling, fun-filled, big game called life. Well, most of it. I'm not done yet. Pop is 99, so who knows where the next thirty or forty years might take me and what new adventures and mischief I will get into. I'm excited to find out.

Retiring Young

Speaking of retirement, I get the feeling that a lot of my friends at UGA are worried about me because they haven't seen much of me in the years since I retired. I appreciate their concern, but the truth is I feel great and have never been happier. Actually, I've just been very busy doing many things I am very passionate about, such as writing this book, that I couldn't do while I was working because of a lack of time and constant interruptions. Do you know how great it is to be able to rise early in the morning and simply say, "Well, I feel like writing so I will"? It's fantastic.

Allow me to share a few things I have learned about retirement. My motivation is a number of people I've talked with who seem worried about retiring, all of whom could handle it financially. First, it's hard to decide when to hang it up. I did it when I began to see my passion ebbing for what I was doing. A good friend, one of the hardest working people I've ever known, a man who is older than I, once said, "Fred, I think about retirement, even slowing down, but I love what I'm doing so much." Then he shouldn't retire. What he is doing gives him great purpose and satisfaction. When that bulb starts to dim, I think he'll know it.

A neighbor told me that retirees fall into two categories. The first retires and then continues to do the same things they always did at work but now for very little pay. One professor I know continued to go to the university every day into his 80's. The second makes a clean break. Two of my friends chose this path starting new lives in retirement. I decided to be like the latter two individuals. Interestingly, one of the first questions I was asked right after I retired was whether I wanted to teach a college class in Gwinnett County, Georgia. My thought was that if I wanted to continue to teach, I wouldn't have retired early. Why drive 50 miles each way for very little money when all I had to do was not retire, teach 5 miles from home, and draw a full salary? And I haven't stopped teaching. I'm just trying a new medium in the form of this book and some talks I have been giving.

Anyway, I really favor the clean break approach but not a totally clean break. Let's call it a hairline fracture. It's not the best idea for people who have been incredibly involved in things and productive to stop cold turkey. One of the things that prevented that in my case was being asked by the Terry College of Business to continue to run our Trucking Profitability Strategies Conference in retirement. This kept me involved in business and transportation, which continue to fascinate me, maintained my contact with my great friends in trucking, and indeed, due to having more time to work on it, has helped improve the conference. So it has worked out very well for all of us. But I can assure you that one reason I am loving retirement so is that I have always had so many interests and hobbies. The people I see who don't tend to do well in retirement are individuals who are rather one dimensional. For example, their whole life was focused on their job. That certainly wasn't my situation.

My Retirement Life

How is retirement life different? For starters, I live in comfortable clothes. Only when it's essential do I button the top button on my shirts and wear a tie. It's time to relax and loosen that belt a notch when I want to. Also, I hardly ever wear a watch. In fact, sometimes I don't even know what day it is.

In retirement I have adapted to a somewhat regular routine. I like to write early. It's when I think most creatively. Then I exercise almost daily walking for an hour on our treadmill and working out on weights about three times a week. If I want to fully enjoy the rest of my life, I need I stay in good shape and am committed to making sure I do the things to make that happen. Plus, exercise greatly increases my energy level and actually lessens my need for sleep; although, I must tell you, I thoroughly enjoy taking naps in my leather retirement chair, one of the wisest purchases I ever made.

Three things I am enjoying immensely in retirement are spending more time with our children and grandchildren, spending more time with our parents, and spending more time together, just Sharon and I. Since I've already told you about our children, grandchildren, and Sharon, let me share some recent things about my dad and Kay and Fred Smith. Initially let me acknowledge how blessed we are that all are still living and in generally good health.

I love being with my dad. As you can imagine, he's not as mobile as he once was, and he deals with the pesky attributes of aging every day of his life, but that doesn't stop him from going to church every Sunday or going to town to eat breakfast six days a week where he spends time with his buddies--John, Ernie, Fairfax, Reverend Tommy, Buddy, James, the Chief, Dave, about 20 in total, members of the breakfast gang at Zack's restaurant in Burlington, North Carolina. Eleanor takes him to town and gives him a ride home after breakfast. And I take every opportunity available to go with him to Zack's because of the good times we have there together. The gang calls him "Pops," and from the time he arrives at Zack's until the moment he departs, they kid him and make him happy. For this, gentlemen, you have my deepest appreciation. The brotherly love I have witnessed each time I have joined the morning breakfast crowd is so very special. I just can't thank you enough for your kindness and encouragement to my dad. Every year on Pop's birthday the gang holds a breakfast birthday party with a cake or two for Pop. I've been there for some of these occasions. It was wonderful.

Farming

One thing I have really enjoyed in retirement is spending more time on the farm. When Fred retired from Grumman, he and Kay moved to the family farm in Monticello, North Carolina, where they built a new home and settled down to enjoy life. By then the farm was smaller, about 300 acres, after having been divided between the two children.

But it nonetheless is still a beautiful piece of property. Fred got the part with Reedy Creek bordering it--the land Sharon and I most love. The cows, though, are long gone, sold many years ago.

Kay is a morning person like I am, so one of us typically beats the other one to the kitchen, lets Inky out, and retrieves the newspaper. The latter starts our morning conversations, which we both seem to really enjoy. My mother-in-law is a very perceptive lady who has taught me a lot over the years, one of which is to respect and take care of your property and land. Another is to study and enjoy hummingbirds, those amazing creatures that flock to her porch every year. Sometimes we are treated to 5 or 6 of them at once in assorted brilliant colors. And we both love Inky. That black lab is the sweetest dog I've ever known.

There is plenty to do on the property, which is good because I thoroughly enjoy being farmer Fred in retirement. I'm sorry. There are three Fred's in my family, my dad, my father-in-law, and me. Right now I'm talking about me. I enjoy working on the farm, and Fred is patiently teaching me how to run and fix the equipment, things like tractors, riding lawn mowers, wood chippers, chainsaws, generators, and bushhogs. Fred has three tractors and considerable farming equipment, very little of which is remotely new. So I'm learning some things about maintenance.

Bushhogging, for you city slickers, means pulling a large rotary cutter behind a tractor and mowing the grass and weeds which try to take over a farm as quickly as possible. Every chance I get I try to bushhog all the fields and trails for Kay and Fred, and I find it relaxing. It is so different from anything I have ever done. One day while on the old John Deere bushhogging a field, the tractor engine began racing to very high RPM. So I immediately turned the engine off and hiked back to the house to find my mentor. Fred determined that the throttle was stuck. A part had fallen off. To make a long story short, we wound up trying to Rube Goldberg the thing, i.e., fix it ourselves, because we couldn't wait 6 days for a $6 part.

Fred told me to look through the barn for a piece of tubing about "yeah big," and I found a small piece of aluminum I thought would work. And Fred, as I had seen him do so many times before, bent and cut a piece of that tubing making a device that fixed the throttle. Then he asked me if I knew where the tubing I gave him came from. I didn't have a clue. "Well, it came off the LM. I am not sure if it was a spare part for the Lunar Module or some inventory from materials that were not used for the space craft, but it did come from the LM program."

I was stunned. The LM was the lunar module used in the Apollo space missions that landed men on the moon. It was also the power source that brought the astronauts from the aborted Apollo 13 mission, made famous by a movie with the same name, back to earth safely. Grumman made the LM and when the program was terminated by the federal government, Fred asked if he could have some of the spare parts they were preparing to discard, which he was granted. So we fixed the tractor with parts of the space craft inventory that sent the first Americans to the moon. Amazing. Among the aircraft my father-in-law helped design was the F14 Tomcat, made famous as the plane Tom Cruise flew in the movie *Top Gun*.

Fred can fix anything, and you have to be good at repairing equipment or you never get anything done on a farm. Things constantly break down, and you have neither the time nor the money to buy new ones. One of the more interesting projects we worked on together at the farm was the assembly, operation, and repair of a 900-pound wood chipper made in China and shipped unassembled to his farm. How he ever managed to make that thing work with its pathetic owner's manual is beyond me, but he did. And it is a good thing because that piece of equipment had serious safety flaws like bolts missing in key places to hold parts that could easily fly off and kill people. That chipper runs like a champ now and has made the farm beautiful.

Woodworking

I've additionally found the time to do the woodworking I've wanted to do for years. Like any hobby, there's a learning curve to develop a level of expertise that meets your objectives, but I'm getting there. You also need good tools and the right ones for particular jobs. So I have added a new table saw, drill press, band saw and several other pieces of machinery. My toys, Sharon calls them. At any rate, I've been doing some interesting things in my shop such as building a toy barn for my granddaughters, a stool for our grandson to help him reach the sink and his bed better, and a raised-panel cabinet for Katie my first attempt at intricate router work. That's my plan, to make things for the family. I'm not in it for the money. The toy barn with its 150 hours of effort and considerable love would have to sell for at least $2,500 for me to break even. And it gives me a big thrill to see the girls playing with it and even more satisfaction when they tell their friends with pride, "My grandpa made it." I do these woodworking projects because I enjoy them and love my family. It also feels great to make something nice that will be passed on to future generations in our family. I have always liked designing furniture and working with my hands. An added bonus is that Sharon is working on some of the projects with me, and I enjoy her company and help.

Mentoring

One of the things I really enjoyed during retirement was mentoring a promising young author while he wrote and published his first novel. His name is James Graham, his book is titled *Finding Life*, and I am sure you will be hearing about both. Such potential Jimmy has.

Jimmy was one of my sister Eleanor's favorite students, a young man she taught in the first grade, and it was through Eleanor that Jimmy, now a chiropractor in Beaufort, North Carolina, and I met. She told me Jimmy reminded her a lot of me and that he was writing his first novel. I sent him an email inquiring about his work, and that began our friendship and work together. He in turn reviewed this book's chapters and motivated me to work harder, so my student likewise inspired this old teacher. In one of our conversations, Jimmy told me that Eleanor was his most cherished teacher. But I was more than glad to help Jimmy with his book because I remembered how much I appreciated the help I received with our teaching book from Tom Stanley, author of such best sellers as *The Millionaire Next Door*. Tom encouraged me, and I wanted to help Jimmy. And what a wonderful, uplifting story Jimmy wound up writing, the first of many best sellers I predict.

What Else?

My future plans call for more hiking and backpacking, vacations with our children and grandchildren, fishing, reading for pleasure, photography, and road trips exploring America with my best friend, Sharon. Personally, I'd like to go on more picnics. Sharon, are you reading this? And I still very much enjoy watching the Georgia Bulldogs and other sporting events. Overall, though, I'm more of a doer than a spectator. I like being involved in the outcomes.

Sharon and I made a decision going into retirement that for one year we would not accept any non-family commitments that would restrict our freedom of movement to visit loved ones on short notice, and that was a good decision because immediately I was asked to serve on committees and boards, join choirs, give talks, and hold offices in civic clubs. I'm not trying to be selfish, but I was overscheduled most of my life and always running on someone else's terms. Sharon and I have previously done many of those things numerous times, and now we feel some others should step up to the plate. Mainly in retirement we desire scheduling freedom and are not planning to give it up just yet. The day may come when we want to do more of the other again, just not in the foreseeable future. For one thing, we are having too much fun. And we are indeed very busy. Not long ago I put in a 22-hour day woodworking, writing, and planning the trucking conference. Not all of your deadlines disappear in retirement. It's just that they are more self-inflicted.

Sharon kids me that once this book is finished I will have withdrawal pains. She may be right, but I'm not worried about it. Actually I'm quite anxious and looking forward to the future and its inevitable surprises. I would like to be more like my beloved mentor Fred Birchmore. After he turned 60, Fred hiked the entire Appalachian Trail, discovered Inca ruins and lost trails, rode bicycles hundreds of miles, built the Great Wall of Athens, wrote a book, and accomplished many more things. I'm committed to hiking more of the A.T., and wouldn't even mind learning more about cooking or cross-stitching. I'm not kidding. My sister does beautiful cross stitching and offered to teach me. And I still enjoy challenges and trying new things.

Thus

The way I figure it, I came into the world with some seriously good cards. How fortunate I was to have been born in America to loving, supportive parents and grandparents, all of whom were/are great role models. From the family gene pool I believe I derived my personality, good health, and fine sense of humor. Beyond that I benefited from some very good luck that introduced me to Sharon, many wonderful mentors, great friends, and a wide variety of opportunities and experiences, all of which helped me live a full life. And I do think it takes a lot of help and some good luck along the way to find happiness and success.

But I am also convinced that I did many things that contributed to the satisfying outcomes. Perhaps the most important was my attitude--a positive outlook on life that I seem to have had almost every step of the way. I do not spend a lot of time thinking about everything that might go wrong to stifle my dreams. Never have. And I also have known for a very long time that while I do not fully control my destiny, my efforts, actions, and decisions will largely determine what happens in my life's future.

I think it takes a lot of planning and thinking to do well in life. For a fact, I know my life improved because I was determined to get an education, live an honorable life, find and marry a wonderful woman and have a family, and seek jobs I would enjoy. It helped me greatly that I continued to have faith in myself even when no one else believed in what I was doing. I saw and took advantage of opportunities others missed or weren't motivated enough to make the necessary effort to seize. What I lived by was a set of principles, convictions, beliefs, and values that made great sense to me. And throughout it all, I tried to be honest with myself understanding my flaws and weaknesses and playing more to my strengths. Every day I tried to learn something new and improve. And this is still a high priority.

So what final advice can I leave with you about finding happiness and success in life?

- Take personal responsibility for as much of your life as you can.
- Go through life with a positive, optimistic attitude, one that should open many doors for you.
- Always try to do the right thing.
- Surround yourself with honorable, good people of the highest character.

- Make wise decisions and choices.
- Understand that no one has a right to expect you to be perfect because they certainly aren't.
- Laugh as often as you can.
- Focus on the present and the future because you can't change the past, just improve on it.
- Treat people well showing them the love, appreciation, and respect they crave and deserve.
- Maintain faith in yourself.
- Trust your God to guide and help you along the way.
- Be persistent, always placing one foot ahead of the other, for that is the secret to climbing life's highest mountains.
- And never forget that the most glorious days are the ones following storms, so battle your way through them.

I wish you the best.

Regards,

The baker, backpacker, professor, veteran, leader, teacher, son, grandson, husband, father, grandfather, and proud American.

LaVergne, TN USA
12 January 2011
212049LV00003B/22/A